SUBSTANCE ABUSE:
NEW RESEARCH

SUBSTANCE ABUSE: NEW RESEARCH

ETHAN J. KERR AND
OWEN E. GIBSON
EDITORS

Nova Science Publishers, Inc.
New York

For permission to use material from this book please contact us:
Telephone 631-231-7269; Fax 631-231-8175
Web Site: http://www.novapublishers.com

NOTICE TO THE READER

The Publisher has taken reasonable care in the preparation of this book, but makes no expressed or implied warranty of any kind and assumes no responsibility for any errors or omissions. No liability is assumed for incidental or consequential damages in connection with or arising out of information contained in this book. The Publisher shall not be liable for any special, consequential, or exemplary damages resulting, in whole or in part, from the readers' use of, or reliance upon, this material. Any parts of this book based on government reports are so indicated and copyright is claimed for those parts to the extent applicable to compilations of such works.

Independent verification should be sought for any data, advice or recommendations contained in this book. In addition, no responsibility is assumed by the publisher for any injury and/or damage to persons or property arising from any methods, products, instructions, ideas or otherwise contained in this publication.

This publication is designed to provide accurate and authoritative information with regard to the subject matter covered herein. It is sold with the clear understanding that the Publisher is not engaged in rendering legal or any other professional services. If legal or any other expert assistance is required, the services of a competent person should be sought. FROM A DECLARATION OF PARTICIPANTS JOINTLY ADOPTED BY A COMMITTEE OF THE AMERICAN BAR ASSOCIATION AND A COMMITTEE OF PUBLISHERS.

LIBRARY OF CONGRESS CATALOGING-IN-PUBLICATION DATA

Substance abuse : new research / Ethan J. Kerr and Owen E. Gibson, (editor).
   p. ; cm.
 Includes bibliographical references and index.
 ISBN 978-1-60456-834-9 (hardcover)
 1. Substance abuse. I. Kerr, Ethan J. II. Gibson, Owen E.
 [DNLM: 1. Substance-Related Disorders--psychology. WM 270 S94128 2008]
 RC564.S834 2008
 362.29--dc22
                2008023364

Published by Nova Science Publishers, Inc. ; New York

CONTENTS

PREFACE

Substance abuse is one of society's most serious problems. Drugs seem to be readily available in virtually every country in the world. Substance abuse is the overindulgence in and dependence of a drug or other chemical leading to effects that are detrimental to the individual's physical and mental health, or the welfare of others.

The disorder is characterized by a pattern of continued pathological use of a medication, non-medically indicated drug or toxin, that results in repeated adverse social consequences related to drug use, such as failure to meet work, family, or school obligations, interpersonal conflicts, or legal problems. There are on-going debates as to the exact distinctions between substance abuse and substance dependence, but current practice standard distinguishes between the two by defining substance dependence in terms of physiological and behavioral symptoms of substance use, and substance abuse in terms of the social consequences of substance use.

This book presents the latest research in the field.

Chapter 1 - At the dawn of the twenty-first century, global societies are experiencing a steep rise in the use of illicit drugs in general, and cocaine in particular. All available forms of cocaine, the adulterated as well as "crack", are potent drugs and highly addictive. These forms produce the highest pharmacological effects by acting directly on the central nervous system and could have serious health implications. Abusing cocaine is no longer limited to financially able individuals among the elite, rich and famous of the societies. Its widespread use that has plagued the poor neighborhoods within the inner city populations became alarming. A multitude of factors have contributed to this social problem. The most significant are: a). the ample supply of cocaine that makes this illegal drug relatively inexpensive to purchase on the street; b). the increased demand for cocaine by victims with insatiable appetites for the drug. c). the peer pressure exerted on vulnerable individuals among teenagers and the public at large.

The street form of cocaine is provided by highly determined, intensely organized suppliers, distributors, traffickers, and street pushers. These elements consistently exploit social weaknesses and system loopholes to benefit from their trade's highly lucrative financial rewards. These illegal organizations disregard the tremendous human suffering and sacrifice by the individual victims, their families, and the entire society. Fearless of the heavy penalties of breaking the law, these organizations ignore the law enforcement agencies, as they target both urban dwellers and suburbanites alike. Regardless of the tremendous efforts and resources that are allocated annually for the war against drugs, the use of cocaine throughout the world and particularly the United States continues to escalate to epidemic proportions. As the ratio of the one-time and the long term user of cocaine increases within the society, the probability that dental practitioners encounter cocaine abusers among their patients during the course of the daily practice is highly likely. This probability is increased especially where emergency dental services are provided, as this type of dental care is routinely required particularly among drug abusers.

Chapter 2 - This study compared the efficacy of two commonly used treatment approaches (cognitive–behavioral treatment and contingency management) for the treatment of cocaine dependence among methadone-maintained patients with and without antisocial personality disorder (ASPD). This disorder is strongly associated with substance abuse and recent study findings provide a strong argument against the perception that substance abusers with ASPD are unresponsive to drug treatment.

Method: Patients were randomly assigned to four study conditions including cognitive–behavioral treatment (CBT), contingency management (CM), CBT with CM, or methadone maintenance (also the control condition). The Structural Clinical Interview for Mental Disorders–IV was administered to 108 patients to assess ASPD.

Hypotheses: We hypothesized that ASPD patients in the three treatment conditions (CBT, CM, CBT + CM) would have better treatment responsivity over the 16-week course of treatment than would ASPD patients in the control condition (MM). Moreover, the authors hypothesized that there would be a cumulative treatment effect among ASPD patients over the course of treatment, with good performance in the CBT condition, better performance in the CM condition, and optimum performance in the CBT + CM condition. Conversely, the authors hypothesized that the positive treatment effect of CM would decline for the ASPD patients once the incentive was removed (i.e., during the post-treatment outcome period).

Results: A two-way analysis of variance showed that patients with ASPD were more likely to abstain from cocaine use during treatment than patients without ASPD. The strong treatment effect for ASPD patients was primarily due to the CM condition. A series of regression analyses showed that ASPD remained significantly related to CM treatment responsivity while controlling for other related factors.

Conclusion: Monetary incentives appear to reduce cocaine use among substance abusers with ASPD more than among those without ASPD. The results of the present study and other recent publications suggest that substance abusers with ASPD may be more responsive to treatment than previously believed.

Chapter 3 – In certain populations around the world, the HIV pandemic is driven by drug abuse. Mounting evidence suggests that these patient populations may have accelerated and more severe neurocognitive dysfunction as compared to non-drug abusing HIV infected populations. Many drugs of abuse are CNS stimulants, hence it stands to reason that these drugs may synergize with neurotoxic substances released during the course of HIV infection. Clinical and laboratory evidence suggest that the dopaminergic systems are most vulnerable to such combined neurotoxicity although multiple regions of the brain may be involved. Identifying common mechanisms of neuronal injury is critical to developing therapeutic strategies for drug abusing HIV-infected populations. This chapter reviews 1) the current evidence for neurodegeneration in the setting of combined HIV infection and use of methamphetamine, cocaine, heroin or alcohol, 2) the proposed underlying mechanisms involved in this combined neurotoxicity, and 3) future directions for research. This manuscript also suggests therapeutic approaches based on our current understanding of the neuropathogenesis of dementia due to HIV infection and drugs of abuse.

Chapter 4 - Drug dependence, or addiction, is a relapsing disorder characterized by the loss of control of drug intake, or compulsion to take the drug, associated with the appearance of a withdrawal syndrome after a discontinuation of its long-term use. Several authors have pointed out the need to define the phenomenon of addiction in behavioral terms establishing that, in a general way, addiction is a relapsing disorder that leads to a compulsive drug use, despite the harmful effects in some aspects of the person's functioning. Actually, with the progress in basic and clinical research, evidenced by the rapid advances at the molecular, cellular, neural and behavioral levels, the study of drug dependence has raised important conceptual issues that have helped the neurobiological research to better understand the changes in the neural mechanisms underlying the development of addiction, and the expression of the withdrawal symptoms.

Drugs of abuse produce, initially, a state of pleasure characterized by its positive reinforcing properties, and that is the reason they are taken. However, its repetitive administration leads to a natural adaptation of the central nervous system, including long-lasting changes. As the user's body adjusts to the drug, a bigger amount of it needs to be taken each time to get to the same first results. This can quickly lead to the use of more and more of the drug and, consequently, to addiction or dependence, characterized by the appearance of a behavioral repertoire toward an excessive drug intake, whenever the drug ingestion is interrupted. This means that, in addicts, drug-seeking behavior becomes compulsive. If a user stops taking the drug withdrawal symptoms appears, as the nervous system needs to adjust functioning without the drug. It may take weeks before the nervous system is back to normal, and during this time there is great temptation to use the drug again and then, discontinue the withdrawal symptoms. In fact, relapse is possible even after long periods of abstinence, even years after cessation of drug use. In this chapter, the authors will briefly discuss some basic neurobiological, motivational and behavioral processes that drive an individual from an impulsive to a compulsive disorder and, the importance of affective symptoms, such as fear and anxiety, as the promoting factors of relapsing.

Chapter 5 - Adolescence is an important development time when there is a significant restructuring in youth's social networks and support systems. A number of studies emphasize the negative role that peer groups play in determining youth's substance use, while still other studies find that youth substance use can be mediated by parental attitudes, family connectedness and monitoring. The main goal of the present study is to explore some of these associations in two different cultural settings. Data were collected among middle and high school students (ages 11-20 years) in Southern Hungary (N = 1240) and students (ages 10-19) living in a mid-sized urban area in Central Alabama, U.S. (N = 1525). The self-administered questionnaires were identical in both places and contained items that asked youth about their substance use (smoking, drinking, illicit drug use), and the parental/family influences in their life such as parental monitoring and parental attitudes towards substance use. Using multiple regression analyses in both samples, results suggest that parental monitoring (e.g., when parents know where their children are) is an important protective factor regardless of culture. Likewise, being beaten by a parent is an important universal risk factor. However, some differences may also be detected, e.g., parental attitudes towards substance use is an important influence only among Hungarian youth, while family structure is a significant predictor of substance use among US adolescents.

Chapter 6 - Evidence for the association between childhood sexual abuse (CSA) and later misuse of substances covers a wide range of licit and illicit drugs and spans multiple stages of involvement, including increased likelihood of use, higher probability of early initiation, and elevated risk for onset of substance use disorders (SUDs). Contributions to this literature represent a variety of approaches to addressing the association of CSA to alcohol and drug-related problems, which is complicated by the fact that many of the same factors that elevate risk for CSA exposure also increase risk for substance use problems. Methods for disentangling direct effects of CSA events on substance use outcomes from the effects of risk factors that are frequently present in families in which CSA exposures occurs (e.g., parental drug or alcohol problems) include measurement and adjustment for potentially confounding factors and the use of co-twin designs. Findings across methodological approaches provide support for CSA-specific risk for substance use outcomes, despite the significant contribution of family background factors to overall risk. In combination with the critical information about treatment presentation and response provided by clinical population-based studies, these investigations represent important steps for modeling the pathways from CSA to substance use outcomes and for informing intervention efforts with this high-risk population.

Chapter 7 - This article represents an overview of the literature on substance abuse among older adults. It begins with a review of the literature on alcohol use and abuse among older adults, which represents the greater bulk of available information, followed by a review of the literature regarding prescription and illicit drug abuse within this population. Additionally, this article details demographic variations in older adult substance abusers. Recommendations for future research are offered.

Chapter 8 - Substance abuse is one of the greatest challenges of our society. According to the Central Registry of Drug Abuse (Hong Kong Government, 2005) 9,734 heroin abusers were reported in Hong Kong. Heroin addiction remains the most common type of substance abused. Currently, heroin encompasses about 85.4% of all common types of substance abuse in Hong Kong. Heroin dependence is inevitably a chronic drug abuse behavior. Cheung et al. (2003) found that 73% of patients who sought treatments relapsed to heroin within 12 months after completion of various drug treatments in Hong Kong. In the study, patients had undergone treatments 8 times or more on average. Hence, heroin dependence has been identified as a recurrent relapsing behavior.

Substance dependence becomes a complex social problem when it is associated with homelessness. A local comprehensive research by Wang (2001) showed problems of substance abuse and homelessness, were indeed, causally constructed in a vicious cycle. The research revealed that a quarter of homeless people had a problem of substance abuse in Hong Kong. There was also an increasing trend in young age street sleepers (under age 40) in 2001. For those street sleepers who were under 40, 40% of them indeed desired an allocation of a public housing apartment. Failing to pay initial rent and deposit, however, has been an overwhelming burden for 75% of the homeless population. Since 1999, the Social Welfare Department of Hong Kong has refused to give homeless people advanced payment for renting houses, unless they could provide a down-payment rental receipt.

The enhancement of self-efficacy is recognized as an important role in helping people to avoid a relapse episode. In frontline practice, an emphasis on working with clients' strengths in social work is receiving increasing attention in this decade. Encouragingly, the Strengths Perspective is implemented with substance abuse. The strengths perspective is recognized as a new humanistic trend in substance abuse counseling. In this paper, by means of a case illustration, the writer will integrate the concepts of self-efficacy and the strengths perspective to illustrate how a homeless adult male will build his self-efficacy in recovery from substance abuse.

Chapter 9 - ubstance use/abuse/dependence is often comorbid with schizophrenia; psychosis and substance use were found to increase suicide risk. However, the interaction of factors involved in increased suicide risk in patients with comorbid schizophrenia and substance use disorder are quite complex and not explained by simple potentiation between psychosis and substance use. The factor that is almost always present is depression; it gives way to hopelessness, which was found to be the most powerful predictor of suicide in this comorbid population. Insight unto one's own illness may both increase and decrease suicide risk; increased awareness of having e debilitating disease may lead to depression and suicide, whereas realizing the need to comply with treatment to stay well may decrease it. Genetic, ethnic and social factors seem also to play a role. Western culture favors isolation of the mentally ill, thus paving the way to illicit drug use, hence loneliness and depression; homelessness and unemployment may also play a role, although new social bonds are likely to be established among the homeless and be protective to a certain extent, while unemployment may be worse for men than women and has a culture-dependent effect. Treatment should aim to manage both schizophrenic symptoms and substance use simultaneously, as improvement in one aspect may help the other. Integrated treatment approaches, such as treating the symptoms of the disease and the effects of the abused substance while rebuilding the patient's social network, are likely to yield the best results.

In: Substance Abuse: New Research   ISBN 978-1-60456-834-9
Editors: Ethan J. Kerr and Owen E. Gibson   © 2009 Nova Science Publishers, Inc.

Chapter 1

COCAINE ABUSE AND TODAY'S PRACTICE OF DENTISTRY

Mohamed A. Bassiouny[1]

Restorative Dentistry Department
Temple University School of Dentistry,
Philadelphia, PA

INTRODUCTION

At the dawn of the twenty-first century, global societies are experiencing a steep rise in the use of illicit drugs in general, and cocaine in particular.[1-4] All available forms of cocaine, the adulterated as well as "crack", are potent drugs and highly addictive. These forms produce the highest pharmacological effects by acting directly on the central nervous system and could have serious health implications. Abusing cocaine is no longer limited to financially able individuals among the elite, rich and famous of the societies. Its widespread use that has plagued the poor neighborhoods within the inner city populations became alarming.[5] A multitude of factors have contributed to this social problem. The most significant are: a). the ample supply of cocaine that makes this illegal drug relatively inexpensive to purchase on the street; b). the increased demand for cocaine by victims with insatiable appetites for the drug. c). the peer pressure exerted on vulnerable individuals among teenagers and the public at large.

The street form of cocaine is provided by highly determined, intensely organized suppliers, distributors, traffickers, and street pushers. These elements consistently exploit social weaknesses and system loopholes to benefit from their trade's highly lucrative financial rewards. These illegal organizations disregard the tremendous human suffering and sacrifice by the individual victims, their families, and the entire society. Fearless of the heavy penalties of breaking the law, these organizations ignore the law enforcement agencies, as they target

---

[1] Mailing Address: Mohamed A. Bassiouny, DMD, MSc, PhD., Professor of Restorative Dentistry, Temple University School of Dentistry, 3223 N. Broad St., Philadelphia, PA, 19140, E-mail mbassiouny@dental.temple.edu

both urban dwellers and suburbanites alike. Regardless of the tremendous efforts and resources that are allocated annually for the war against drugs, the use of cocaine throughout the world and particularly the United States continues to escalate to epidemic proportions.[6-14] As the ratio of the one-time and the long term user of cocaine increases within the society, the probability that dental practitioners encounter cocaine abusers among their patients during the course of the daily practice is highly likely. This probability is increased especially where emergency dental services are provided, as this type of dental care is routinely required particularly among drug abusers.

Table 1: Common Street Terms Associated with Crack-Cocaine [14]

Definition	Terms	Definition	Terms
Cocaine	Blow	Crack	Tornado
	Nose candy		Rooster
	Flake		Jelly Beans
	Lady		
	Rock	Crack and Heroin	Moon Rock
	Star Spangled Powder	Marijuana and Crack	Oolies
	Gift of Sun God	PCP, Marijuana, Crack	Wicky Stick
	Dama Blanca		
	(White Lady)	Crack User	Geeker
		Crack Addicts	Bingers
Coca-leaf	Heaven-leaf	Cheap Beer Used by	Liquid Candy
	Leaf	Crack/Cocaine addicts	
To inhale cocaine	Horn	Cocaine and Heroin	Snowball-Speedball

The consequences of the systemic effect of cocaine lie in its capability to potentiate dangerous adverse reactions to certain medications used in routine dental procedures. Therefore, identification of cocaine abusers among patients in the dental office can be a lifesaver. This is particularly relevant when determining the type of local anesthetic to be used and the proper time for its administration. Adopting specific precautionary measures could avert the possibility of a cardiovascular, respiratory, or cerebral incident in individuals with a drug abuse habit. This is particularly the case when these individuals are exposed to the stressful situation of a dental visit. It could also protect dental professionals from the possible danger of being contaminated with infectious diseases that are prevalent among abusers, although universal infection control precautions are routinely adhered to when treating any patient.

Due to the fast rate of dental health regression associated with chronic cocaine abuse, regardless of professional care, special management precautions must be undertaken. These could guard against the likelihood of a serious relapse of the dental health condition following comprehensive dental care. Thus, it could exonerate the dental team from potential medico-legal conflicts. It is paramount to understand the implications of cocaine abuse and the physiological and pathological processes that are induced by this drug. This can serve as an effective means to achieve important gains. Among these are determining the appropriate treatment plan and management, averting post-surgical complications, preventing recurrence of the disease process by executing effective follow-up protocol and providing guidance for those who are willing to seek professional help.

The foremost of these precautionary measures begins with identification of the cocaine dependent individual. Such a rewarding achievement does not come easy due to the elusive nature of manifestations associated with cocaine abuse, particularly without a statement by the patient during the early stages. The process of identification might therefore prove to be a challenging task. This is particularly so in the event of the conscious effort by the cocaine user to guard against exposure of their secretive habit, and the lack of reliability of self-response questionnaires due to the social stigma. This predicament brings into focus the crucial role of a dental team properly informed of all aspects of cocaine as an illicit drug and its relevance to the practice of dentistry.

Literature is replete with information related to epidemiology, pharmacology, and systemic disorders associated with cocaine abuse. Although the information pertinent to the oral and para-oral conditions is limited, it will be reviewed and discussed. The dental and para-oral manifestations commonly observed among cocaine-dependants will therefore serve as a welcomed addition to the armamentaria of the dental care provider practicing in today's societies.

COMPLICATIONS OF COCAINE ABUSE

Concurrent with the systemic health problems attributed to cocaine abuse, a range of localized oral health complications may be observed. These complications could be unveiled as immediate reaction, delayed response, or symptoms of long term effects. Regardless of the onset of these complications, they are either due to the primary action of the drug or secondary to its untoward effect on systemic and psychologic health. The side effects of the medications used for treatment further compound an already complex health problem by constituting a third factor. For diagnostic purposes, classification of the complications associated with cocaine abuse according to their onset as manifested by the changes in the systemic and local health will be employed. The array of medical complications associated with cocaine use that encompasses the effects of the cocaine abuse, whether immediate or long term, on systemic and psychological health have been reviewed. The immediate systemic complications are commonly manifested in association with all routes of cocaine administration. Quicker adverse systemic reactions are manifested following intravenous and smoking routes than other routes due to the speed of drug introduction into the circulatory system. Trans-mucosal routes, either orally or nasally, may give rise to the same response but with delayed onset because of the slow rate of absorption.

IMMEDIATE SYSTEMIC COMPLICATIONS

Some of the immediate systemic reactions that may occur in the dental office that have significant implications pertinent to the dental practice will be briefly mentioned. This is to

Table 2: Oral and Maxillofacial Complications of Cocaine Abuse

Signs and symptoms	Causes	Immediate Effects	Long term effects
Edema	Localized irritation of oral or nasal mucous membranes	Swelling, discomfort, bleeding, ulceration	Sinus involvement, sub-structure involvement
Oral Mucositis	Vascular changes, ischemia, mucosal trauma/infection, salivary disturbance	Pain, dysphagia, soft cariogenic diet, insufficient nutrition, infection	Gingival recession, alveolar bone necrosis and loss, perforations
Nasal Mucositis	Vascular changes, ischemia, mucosal trauma/infection	Pain, discomfort, infection, hyperemia	Ischemia, necrosis, perforation of naso/palatal/septal/cranial/antral bones
Oral Infections	Salivary disturbance, mucositis	Pain, septicemia	Infection sequellae
Hemorrhage	Direct trauma, reflex vasodilatation	Epistaxis or bleeding	Delayed clotting, hemostasis
Dry Mouth (Xerostomia)	Salivary disturbance	Dry mucous membrane, infection, pain, difficult mastication and deglutition, inflammation, insufficient nutrition	Discomfort, loss of weight, caries, erosion, loss of teeth
Dysphagia	Dry mouth, mucositis, infection, decreased GI function.	Discomfort, pain, insufficient nutrition	Malnutrition, weight loss
Dental Caries	Salivary disturbance, poor oral hygiene, cariogenic diet, cariogenic microbial flora	Decalcification of enamel and dentin, caries process, pain	Pulp involvement, loss of tissues, loss of teeth
Dental Erosion	Salivary disturbance, acidic diet	Decalcification of enamel and dentin, erosion process, loss of tooth structure, dentin browning	Pulp involvement, loss of coronal tissues, remaining roots, loss of teeth
Bruxism	Neurologic effect on masticatory muscles	Discomfort, pain, attrition	Discomfort, pain, attrition, loss of vertical height, Masseter muscle hypertrophy
Periodontal Disease	Salivary disturbance, infection, poor oral hygiene	Inflammation	Gingival recession, alveolar bone loss, loose and lost teeth
Hyperthermia	Central effect on CNS, peripheral vasoconstriction, reducing skin-heat radiation	Sudden onset of increased body temperature	Decreased body temperature after episode elapsed
Hyperpyrexia	Sympathomimetic effect on sweat glands	Increased sweating even in cold weather	Decreased sweating after episode elapsed

reinforce their magnitude, while avoiding redundancy. Systemic, oral and para-oral complications of cocaine abuse may occur immediately following administration of the drug. The stressful effect of the dental visit and procedures involved enhance the drug effect. The reaction to medications used for dental therapy due to immune system sensitization by cocaine, or the drug interaction with cocaine represents significant etiologic factors.

Immediate systemic complications during the dental visit include but are not limited to: immediate hypertension, myocardial ischemia and infarction, cardiac arrhythmia, allergic reactions to local anesthetics, drug interactions with analgesics and narcotic prescription medications, drug overdose upon induction of anesthesia following self medication, anaphylactic effect of cocaine adulterants, and infectious endocarditis. Some of these immediate manifestations could be experienced by the cocaine abuser even after a one time administration of the drug. The occurrence of systemic clinical manifestations after cocaine use was reported to be more common than expected.[15]

Acute Hypertension

Acute, not chronic, hypertension is commonly linked with cocaine use.[16] Self-premedication with cocaine prior to a dental visit induces a sudden rise in blood pressure. If administered a few hours prior to the dental visit, the psychological stress of the visit, the procedure, the associated pain, in addition to the incidental occurrence of unforeseeable complications could give rise to acute hypertension. If the increase in blood pressure level is elevated beyond the critical threshold of the individual's vascular resilience, it may predispose to vascular or neurological accident.

Myocardial Ischemia and Infarction

As a physiological consequence of generalized vasoconstriction of blood vessels, including those of the respiratory system and coronary arteries, hypoxia may occur. Hence, cocaine abuse may lead to serious acute cardiac complications including myocardial ischemia, infarction, and arrhythmias.[17] Cocaine-induced myocardial infarction associated with severe reversible systolic dysfunction and pulmonary edema was reported to resolve spontaneously with supportive therapy.[18] Cocaine produces a sympathomimetic action, thus inducing vasoconstriction, an acute rise in arterial pressure, tachycardia, and a predisposition to ventricular arrhythmias and seizures. This sympathetic-like action may result in mydriasis, hyperglycemia and hyperthermia. Cocaine is also known to produce hyperpyrexia, which could be secondary to the hyperthermia or it may be due to the direct action of cocaine on the neurotransmitters to the sweat glands.[19] Hyperpyrexia may contribute to the development of seizures that can be induced after a single dose of cocaine.[20]

Cardiac Arrhythmias

Cocaine has a direct toxic action on the heart and also sensitizes the cardiac tissue to the action of catecholamine. In a small dose, cocaine can slow the heart rate. A dose-related increase in blood pressure and heart rate was seen.[21] As a direct consequence of toxicity to the heart muscle, it results initially in asystole that is converted into ventricular fibrillation and eventually cardiac arrest.[22] Two reasons were offered for the occurrence of asystole and ventricular arrhythmias. These are the direct toxic effect of cocaine on the heart and the indirect permissive role of cocaine in accentuating the influence of epinephrine and norepinephrine on cardiac tissue.[23] Therefore, it was emphasized that healthcare providers must consider these unusual features of cocaine overdose as possible factors in a patient with ventricular arrhythmia and/or cardiac arrest. Life threatening cardiac arrhythmia requires prompt treatment with anti-arrhythmic drugs. Propranolol and amitriptyline have been recommended for the treatment of ventricular arrhythmias.[24,25]

Allergic Reaction to Local Anesthetics

Since the introduction of cocaine as a local anesthetic agent by Koller in 1884, this drug was used for ophthalmic surgical procedures. Being the first local anesthetic agent with a vasoconstrictor capability, cocaine's use in ophthalmic, otolaryngeal, nasal surgery, and dentistry has rapidly gained popularity since the beginning of the twentieth century. In this function, cocaine was found to block the initiation and conduction of electrical impulses within nerve cells by preventing the rapid increase in cell membrane permeability to sodium ions during depolarization.[26] The duration of action of the local anesthetic effect of cocaine is from 20 to 40 minutes when used for corneal procedures or as naso-oro-pharyngeal sprays.[27, 28]

Due to its recognized toxicity factor and addiction potential, synthetic products were developed to provide similar effects but with a much greater margin of safety. Procaine (para-aminobenzoic acid), an amino-ester derivative, was developed by Einhorn in 1905. Forty years later, in 1943, Lofgren synthesized lidocaine, the prototype amino-amide derivative of diethylamino acetic acid. The ester compounds are hydrolized in plasma by pseudocholinesterase, producing para-amino benzoic acid that causes allergic reactions in some patients. This first synthetic amino-ester local anesthetic agent has a weak potency, slow onset and short duration. The amides undergo enzymatic degradation in the liver. Allergy to amide agents is extremely rare, except for reactions to their preservative constituent, methyl paraben, whose chemical structure is similar to para-aminobenzoic acid. The metabolite compound of ester agents is attributed with the allergic potential of this anesthetic class. Lidocaine, the first of the amide group, has a high potency (twice that of Procaine), fast onset, and moderate duration of action. These characteristics make it versatile for use as a topical anesthetic, for infiltration and peripheral nerve block. The amide group is composed of extremely stable compounds compared with the ester agents. Since cocaine is a benzoic acid ester, there is the potential risk among cocaine-dependent individuals for an allergic reaction to the ester class of local anesthetics. These patients are most safely treated with the amide class of local anesthetics.[29, 30]

The use of these synthetic anesthetic agents without vasoconstrictor ability requires the addition of epinephrine to prolong the effective duration of the drug. Epinephrine is used to induce vasoconstriction of local blood vessels, thus decreasing the absorption of the anesthetic agent injected for local infiltration or nerve block, and reducing dissipation of the drug. Extra caution is needed when using an anesthetic solution containing epinephrine for cocaine-dependent patients. Induction of anesthesia must be at least 6-10 hours from the last intake of cocaine depending on the route of administration. When injecting the anesthetic solution, aspiration prior to administration is necessary to insure avoidance of injecting into blood vessels and slow injection is recommended. Monitoring the patient's vital signs is paramount. These precautions are necessary in order to avoid a severe hypertensive crisis, or cardiovascular or neurovascular accidents resulting from exacerbation of the cocaine action by epinephrine.[29]

Safety Factors for Management

The timing for the administration of anesthesia is an important safety factor. If the administration of cocaine is confirmed, the dental treatment procedure must be postponed for a minimum of six hours, even though the patient is asymptomatic. This is to ensure that most of the drug and its metabolites were excreted from the circulatory system. For cocaine users, it is recommended that outpatient general anesthesia be avoided, if possible, and a medical consultation should be sought. If a necessary procedure has to be conducted, an informed consent must be secured after warning the patient of possible serious morbidity or mortality, and always monitor pulse and blood pressure.[31] The peak blood level of cocaine is usually felt immediately following intravenous injection and smoking routes, while it takes about 30 minutes for other routes.[29] Therefore a much longer waiting period is necessary for individuals using the intranasal route of administration of cocaine. This route causes mucosal vasoconstriction resulting in a slower release of the drug into the circulation. Accordingly, slower onset, prolonged peak time and duration of effectiveness and slower excretion of the cocaine and metabolites take place. The latter may come to pass within 4 to 6 hours compared with 2 hours for most of the cocaine and metabolites to disappear from circulation following IV or smoking routes.

Chronic cocaine users with evidence of debilitation and psycho-systemic complications often manifest hyperactivity, dilated pupils, tremors, euphoria or aggressiveness, and hypertension. The individual may be undergoing a state of hyperthermia or tachycardia. These patients are accidents waiting to happen since they are prime candidates for cerebrovascular accidents or cardiac arrhythmias that ultimately trigger a fatal heart attack. For such a patient, standard precautions must be followed, but all scheduled procedures must be cancelled and medical consultation and/or hospitalization must be considered subject to the severity of the condition. This approach can prevent supra-addictive pharmacologic effects and toxicity that can result in seizures, respiratory distress or cardiac arrest.[31] A frequent clinical phenomenon is seen in patients on "crack" binges for several days before seeking dental treatment. These individuals who are "high" on cocaine exhibit distorted perception and may manifest violent behavior and could be homicidal. These patients should be handled in a gentle manner by a professional who seems to be a concerned friend rather than the traditional authoritative role played by dentist.[32] The treatment of patients who are chronic cocaine users with severe cocaine toxicity manifested by twitching, irregular breathing, occasional convulsions, tachycardia, arrhythmia or possibly cardio-respiratory collapse, must be restricted to hospital emergency rooms under medical supervision.[31]

Drug Interactions (Analgesics and Narcotic Prescription Limitation)

Mood disorders and depression are associated with cocaine addiction. Therefore, sedative medications may have to be given in reduced dosage to avoid excessive CNS depression. These conditions are treated with tricyclic or heterocyclic antidepressants. Hence, it is advisable to use small amounts of epinephrine (1:100,000) in patients using these drugs in order to avoid potentiation of the drug effect. Aspiration before injecting the local anesthetic (2 cartridges maximum) and injecting the solution slowly is recommended to avoid an exaggerated hypertensive response. Patients on heterocyclic antidepressant drugs may be prone to orthostatic hypotension; therefore, a gradual change from supine operating position to upright position should be implemented with caution. Furthermore, when analgesics, such as acetaminophen, are used, caution should be exercised to avoid its side effects in decreasing the metabolic rate of the heterocyclic, which would lead to a toxic level of the tricyclic antidepressant. When necessary, narcotic analgesics should be prescribed cautiously in limited quantities because of their potential for abuse.[33]

Anaphylactic Reaction to Adulterants

The street form of cocaine is commonly adulterated to increase the volume, thus reducing the price for marketing purposes. According to the office of National Drug Control Policy, Pulse Check Trends in Drug Abuse, July-December 2001 – April 2002 reporting period, several adulterants were often found in powdered cocaine. These included chalk, laundry detergent, talcum or baby powder, meat tenderizer, baby laxatives, caffeine, and rat poison. Inclusions of lidocaine, procaine, quinine, amphetamines, phencyclidine, heroin, caffeine, lactose, and antihistamines may also be added to street cocaine to dilute (cut) the drug. One or more of these adulterants are added to the street form of cocaine depending on the region or the city within the United States or abroad. The addition of adulterants, although essentially for commercial benefit, compounds the danger of cocaine's cumulative potentially adverse effects on the recipient's health. Some of these adulterants have their own cardiac toxicity effects.[34] Allergic thrombocytopenia due to the quinine in adulterated heroin has been manifested as ecchymosis of the oral mucosal membranes.[35] Similar findings might be possible among chronic cocaine abusers due to substances used to adulterate the pure powder.

Cross Contamination with Infectious Diseases

The intravenous administration of cocaine has been associated with cross contamination among the users who share needles used to introduce the drug into their blood stream. The risk for infectious hepatitis (HC) and HIV, the Acquired Immunodeficiency Syndrome (AIDS) virus among IV drug users is very high. This is compounded by unsafe sexual practices and multiple partners that lead to the spread of these diseases. It was also reported that increased incidence of Hepatitis C could be due to communication through open wounds in the oral cavity while sharing contaminated cigarettes with sex partners.[36] It is, therefore, essential to identify these patients by closely questioning any signs or symptoms related to Hepatitis, HIV and AIDS related complex. Screening tests for suspected cases must be requested including HBsAG Hepatitis B surface antigen. Those who give a history consistent with either Hepatitis or HIV should be referred to a physician for evaluation prior to the institution of any dental care. The physician's instructions must be instituted and closely monitored, and universal infection control protocol must be carefully implemented in order to avoid the risk of cross contamination between the affected patient, the dental team or other patients. Any direct contact with the patient's body fluids, blood, and saliva must be avoided by all professional personnel at all times.[37]

Intravenous drug abusers may run the risk of infectious bacterial endocarditis. This is particularly the case when the individual suffers from organic cardiac-valvular disease. Introduction of infectious contaminants or microorganisms into the blood stream through contaminated needles may inoculate the right side of their heart leading to endocarditis that could eventually damage the tricuspid valve. Precautions and antibiotic pre-medication that are recommended by the American Heart Association Guidelines to prevent endocarditis must be implemented for these patients. [38, 39]

IMMEDIATE LOCAL COMPLICATIONS

Acute localized oral and maxillofacial adverse reactions that are manifested primarily as a result of direct action of cocaine or secondary to its systemic reactions include epistaxis, post surgical bleeding, and delayed acute effects such as cellulitis, gingival ulceration, and cross contamination with infectious diseases previously mentioned.

Epistaxis

Inhaling cocaine directly through the nose is a method of administration known as snorting, horning, or insufflation. Snorting is the practice of inhaling a line of cocaine powder into the nostril by snorters, sniffers or snarfers. The line of drug powder is sniffed through a rolled paper, and in some cases a dollar denomination bill, that was used in the past. Following the administration of cocaine powder through this method, the initial effect on the nasal mucous membranes is vasoconstriction of blood vessels leading to ischemia. This could eventually render the affected tissues necrotic. Continuation of this process may lead in the long term to perforation of bone in the affected region. As the vasoconstriction wears off, a reactive hyperemia often results in engorged blood vessels of the mucous membranes, thus clogging the nasal airways, and may be accompanied by epistaxis.

Post-Surgical Bleeding

Recurrence of bleeding immediately after cessation, post surgically, may signal, among various other factors, a cocaine dependency undertone in a young individual with no history of hypertension, yet the blood pressure is persistently elevated. This is particularly so in the event that all precautionary measures and proper protocol procedures with no complications have been adopted and the surgery was uneventful. An interesting case was reported depicting this scenario.[40] A young healthy patient in the early teens was presented complaining of toothache with no history of hypertension or other contributory systemic disorders. The initially registered high blood pressure (systolic value above 160mmHg and diastolic fluctuating above 95 mmHg) in the presence of hyperthermia (body temperature above 100 degrees F) was thought to be related to the stress-imposed pain. After completing the course of a prescribed therapeutic dose of antibiotics and sedatives, the hyperthermia and blood pressure level that should have been significantly decreased to normal levels, persisted at higher levels. This should have signaled systemic undertones and a medical consult should have been sought. Meanwhile, the possibility of drug (cocaine) abuse should have been considered and questioned. This patient's history should be questioned and revisited with the patient placed under close observation following any surgical procedure. Following the uneventful surgical extraction of the third molar with suturing and packing procedures implemented with no complications, the bleeding had stopped. Within ten-fifteen minutes, the bleeding recurred three more times after it had been controlled repeatedly. This had occurred following the patient's intake of cocaine by snorting through the nose while in the recovery room. This incidence has confirmed the high addictive potential of cocaine, its sympathomimetic effect, and resultant immediate increase in blood pressure. It was suggested that the negative pressure used to inhale cocaine may be another factor limiting hemostasis after the surgical procedure. Once the patient followed instructions by refraining from snorting and the wound repacked with gauze, hemostasis occurred satisfactorily within normal time. Drug counseling was strongly suggested.[40]

Acute Gingival Inflammation

Some cocaine addicts claim that "snorting" cocaine can cause nasal congestion and epistaxis. These individuals, therefore, prefer the oral trans-mucosal method of administration by rubbing cocaine powder topically onto the gingival tissues.[41] This method can cause acute local irritation of the gingival tissues as well as abrasion to the hard dental tissues. The gingival irritation could result from the intense vasoconstrictor action of the cocaine creating localized tissue necrosis combined with mechanical irritation of the powder and its adulterants. Localized acute gingival inflammation may occur on the opposite side of the individual's dominant hand. This unilaterally formed lesion predominantly involves one arch and is manifested by soreness of the gingival mucosa and intense pain that forces the individual to seek emergency dental service.

Acute gingival inflammation was documented in a case of cocaine-associated rapid gingival recession and dental "erosion".[41] This condition was claimed to be secondary to topical cocaine powder application that was rubbed onto the gingival tissue of the facial vestibule, particularly in the molar-premolar region. The surface epithelium became desquamated and subsequent inflammation of the mucosa ensued. A gentle touch of this area resulted in spontaneous bleeding. This clinical condition was claimed to have mimicked that of necrotizing ulcerative gingivitis or the gingivo-stomatitis associated with erosive lichen planus.[42] Accordingly, when diagnosing such lesions, it is imperative to consider topical application of cocaine onto the gingival mucosa as a factor for differential diagnosis. On the histopathological level, a biopsy of superficial vasculitis and necrosis of the gingiva that was formed by rubbing cocaine powder was examined.[43] This lesion was manifested as necrotic superficial squamous cells with either absent or enlarged nuclei, sub-corneal abscesses and acute vasculitis resulting in superficial necrosis of the epithelium and underlying lamina propria. Continuation of this inflammatory process into the underlying structures of the muco-periosteum and supporting bony plate explained the process of bone resorption.

Gingival recession, ulceration and severe alveolar bone loss were noted in association with trans-gingival (rubbing) administration of cocaine.[44] The clinical appearance of the affected area of the gingiva often displays signs of acute inflammation and severe recession accompanied by severe alveolar bone loss at a later stage. Ulceration may be present depending on the stage of tissue destruction. If present, the clinical appearance of the red granulation tissues can often be mistaken for necrotizing ulcerative gingivo-stomatitis (NUG). The clinical features, odor, accurate health history, and microbiologic testing could differentiate between the two lesions. In persons subjected to acute psychological distress, necrotizing ulcerative gingivo-stomatitis (NUG, trench mouth) is commonly noted. This disease may likewise appear in individuals experiencing drug withdrawal.[45]

Cellulitis

The most commonly used methods of cocaine administration today in the U.S. are snorting, IV injection, or smoking. The former is the most preferable, though it is infrequently substituted with trans-mucosal route.[46] Recently, the sublingual route of administration that was adopted in the past, seemed to have resurfaced two years ago.[47] Two cases that have actively administered cocaine exclusively through sublingual route were reported. The individuals described in these cases were attempting to conceal their addiction habit to evade detection by medical or dental personnel. Employing the sublingual method of cocaine administration caused concerns of attending clinicians regarding the possible consequences. This concern was expressed due to the formation of potentially unique medical symptoms whose cause may easily escape detection.[47]

In view of the nature of the sublingual tissues and the presence of important structures, the localized application of cocaine could potentiate serious damaging effects to this region. The highly vascular sublingual tissues and the mucosa of the floor of the mouth are delicate lining mucosa. They line important structures including sub-mandibular and sublingual salivary glands, ducts, and duct orifices. Irritation of these tissues by the topically applied cocaine powder may lead to an inflammatory response. Inflammation of the floor of the mouth and the reactive hyperemia of the sublingual region could rapidly result in cellulitis. This, in turn, may lead to blockage of the airway with its fatal consequences.

LONG TERM LOCAL MANIFESTATIONS

Long term manifestations associated with chronic abuse of cocaine are multiple. These manifestations include: cross contamination with infectious diseases (HC and HIV), thrombocytopenia, stomatitis, periodontal disease, xerostomia, dental caries, dental erosion, temporomandibular joint dysfunction, bruxism, tooth wear, and mid-facial deformities. The reported case illustrated in figures 1-9 depicts the essence of long term manifestations associated with chronic abuse of cocaine.

Dental Manifestations Cited in Anthropological Studies

Several effects of coca-leaf chewing on the dental hard tissues were used as identifiers in anthropological studies. Among these were heavy calculus formation that was used as evidence for coca leaf chewing among an early coastal Ecuadorian culture.[48] Prior to this investigation, the formation of brown or green-colored accretions were noted.[49] Calcareous accretions on teeth were subsequently reported.[50] More than forty years later the change of tooth crown color to dark brown has been reported.[51] The loss of buccal alveolar bone[52] and the loss of posterior teeth[53] were among the latest identifiers used as dental evidence of coca-leaf chewing by ancient cultures. Indriati et al 2001 suggested that the cervical segment of teeth is more susceptible to caries formation than other areas in the oral cavity of the coca-leaf chewing population.[3] He explained that the reason for this phenomenon was the lowered density of the cementum compared with enamel. Therefore, the root cementum is more prone to caries. These lesions were evident and were clearly demonstrated. Their limited location to the facial cervical sections of the posterior dentition augmented their relationship with the "cocada" chewing. This deduction while serving as the basis for Indriati and co-workers' investigation, also cast suspicion on the possibility of conventional caries and suggests a chemically induced lesion.

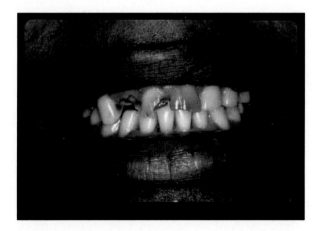

Figure 1. An extra-oral frontal view of a 36-year-old female, cocaine dependant for 14 years. This patient complained of a bad taste and odor of the mouth, and presented with a decayed and broken down dentition that frequently elicited severe pain and swelling of the face. This patient overdosed on an analgesic to alleviate pain and was seen at the emergency room.

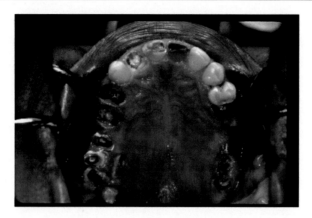

Figure 2. An occlusal view of the maxillary arch showing total loss of coronal segments of the posterior dentition and also a few of the anterior segment leaving decayed remaining roots destroyed to levels at or below the gingival margin. The associated gingiva shows signs of chronic inflammation.

Periodontal Complications

The tradition of coca-leaf chewing is continued in some communities that practiced this habit in the past. For example, in Bolivia alone, the national consumption of coca leaves accounts for several millions of pounds annually. The individual average daily consumption amounts to 30 grams of coca-leaf. The user places the wad of leaves often mixed with lime (used to liberate cocaine alkaloids) against the cheek mucosa, chews the bolus for 2-3 hours, two to three times daily, swallows about 50 –70% of the masticated leaves and throws the residue away. In a clinical and histopathological evaluation of coca-leaf chewers among the Aymara and Ouechua Indians in Bolivia, it was reported that half of the studied population sustained a form of glossitis. This was described as dry, smooth, red, beefy-looking or desquamated, resembling geographic tongue.[54] The results of this study indicated the presence of variations in the clinical appearance of the buccal mucosa of the 46 coca-leaf chewers examined. These variations ranged from normal to edematous mucosa. The edematous mucosa was thickened, soft, and spongy with gray-white opacity. These features were limited to one side where the subject deposited the coca/lime chew. There were no differences either in the clinical appearance of the mucosa between the two Indian groups studied or between males and females. Histological specimens showed several changes but none displayed any sign of malignancy. The histopathologic findings demonstrated a hyperparakeratotic surface in the majority of cases studied, while seven showed a normal amount of parakeratin on the lining mucosal surface. More than 75% of the total cases had some degree of abnormal retained, spongy-appearing epithelial cells in the superficial layer, characteristic of leukoedema.[54]

Excessive plaque and calculus deposits are frequently encountered among chronic cocaine-users. These, in the presence of retention factors such as carious lesions and broken down dentition, constitute etiologic factors that cause gingivitis. Aggravating these conditions in chronic cocaine users are the combination of neglected oral hygiene and the intake of soft foods high in carbohydrates. Progression of the resultant gingival inflammation leads to breakdown of epithelial attachments and destruction of the supporting apparatus causing pocket formation. Deepening of the gingival pockets is often associated with horizontal alveolar bone loss that may be manifested to varying degrees. This in turn leads to the condition of generalized chronic periodontitis commonly observed among cocaine-dependants.

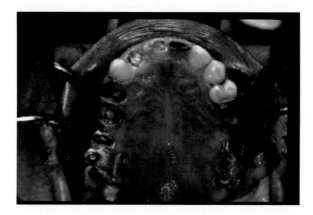

Figure 3. An occlusal view of the mandibular arch displays periodontal involvement. Rampant decay involving posterior teeth is evident. These manifestations are similar to that of the maxillary arch, but to a lesser extent.

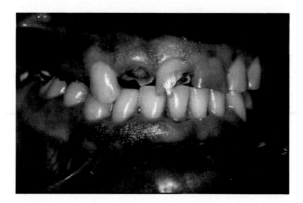

Figure 4. Right lateral view of the maxillary and mandibular dentitions in occlusion showing a collapsed posterior bite, extruded lower posterior teeth, and absence of vertical occlusal space. A combination of carious lesions, traumatic fracture, and periodontal disease is evident.

Oral Health Complications

Up to almost two decades ago, the dentally related information that was available on the deleterious systemic effects of drug abuse in general and the oral tissues in particular were rather limited. A high incidence of cervical dental caries was reported in 1949 among opiate addicts. This type of caries accounted for 9.3% of all caries in (opiate) dependent persons versus 0.16 percent for the controls.[55] When this type of atypical cervical caries was used as a parameter to detect opiate dependence in a double-blind analysis, many false negatives but no false positives were produced.[56] Some of the dental caries found in opiate drug dependent individuals was characterized as being atypical. This type of carious lesion was predominantly located on the gingival third of the labial and buccal (vestibular) surfaces of the teeth, rather than interproximal or occlusal aspects as found in the traditional carious lesions. These atypical caries were described by Lowenthal in 1967 as being larger in area, darker in color, harder in consistency and less painful than routine smooth-surface caries.[56] Literature reports at that time on adverse effects of marijuana and cocaine were scarce. Documented studies on the adverse effects of cocaine abuse on oral and dental health in those days did not exist.

Toward the end of the eighties, dentally related reports on cocaine were limited to observation-based information. Incidence and prevalence of dental caries, periodontal disease, and missing teeth were reported to be higher in drug dependent and abuse-prone individuals compared with the normal population.[29, 57] These two reports[29, 57] emphasized the possible reason for the apparent destruction of the oral and dental tissues. The first cited the probability of these pathologic oral conditions to be more related to personal and health neglect associated with drug-seeking behavior than the actual effect of the drug.[57] The second report suggested the reason for the high incidence of missing and decayed teeth of "long-term" severely addicted patients was attributed to their tendency to spend most or all of their money to obtain cocaine. Therefore, they are rarely able to afford timely appropriate dental care.[29] This report went further to state that concomitant systemic and oral manifestations occur as a result of cocaine-induced anorexia and disturbance in electrolyte balance. Among these manifestations are angular cheilitis, candidiasis, signs of vitamin deficiency, and glossodynia.[29] Accordingly, negligence of systemic and oral hygiene, improper budgetary allocation by drug addicts that led to lack of dental care, and associated anorexia and electrolyte imbalance were considered etiologic factors of oral diseases of this population. Recent medical, physiological, microbiological, psychiatric research findings and epidemiological data shed light on newer information that contributed to understanding the oro-dental disease process associated with chronic cocaine-addiction.

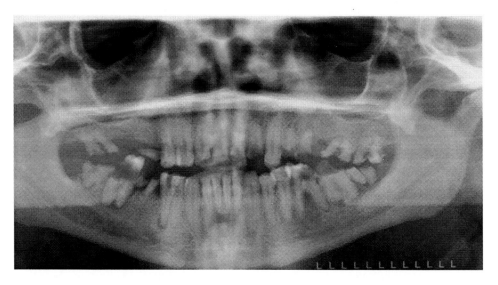

Figure 5. An oral pantomograph revealing the typical image of the dental and maxillofacial manifestations associated with long term cocaine abuse that were compounded by neglected oral health. The entire dentition was devoid of any restorations despite the ravaging decay process that annihilated most of the remaining teeth. Alveolar bone loss and remodeling are evident. The maxillary sinuses appeared enlarged and draped over the roots of the posterior dentition. Signs of turbidity of the maxillary sinuses and defective median nasal septum were observed.

Multiple Drug Abuse

The use of cocaine may be limited to a one-time experience and could be repeated once or twice in a life time. The frequency of use may increase these sporadic events to a monthly or a weekly use. Due to the addictive nature of the drug, increased frequency of intake may exceed once-a-week administration to a cocaine binge. In such an occurrence, the user continues to administer the drug for the extended duration over a limited time of one night or a weekend. The duration of cocaine abuse varies among chronic dependant individuals according to individual circumstances. The range of the duration of cocaine use was extended from one year to three decades, while the average duration amounts to ~10 years among chronic users.[58] Cocaine dependants are frequently addicted to one or more drugs in addition to their indulgence in the consumption of beverages. The common drugs used by this population are alcohol, heroin, marijuana, and tobacco.[16]

The most prevalently used drug in combination with cocaine is tobacco followed by cheap alcoholic beverages (beer), heroin and finally marijuana. Carbonated acidulated types of soft drinks are predominantly used as a substitute or in combination with the alcoholic beverages drinks. The excessive consumption of the combination of these drugs and beverages can only add and compound the destructive potential of cocaine abuse that is manifested as systemic and oral health complications.

Xerostomia

Dryness of the mouth (xerostomia) is a condition commonly detected among cocaine-abuse patients. It is considered to be one of the most critical local complications of cocaine abuse and is manifested by decreased salivary secretion and flow. The occurrence of dry mouth can be a consequence of psychological complications caused by cocaine abuse or a side effect of the medications used for their therapy. Withdrawal from cocaine or the medications used for the treatment of withdrawal symptoms can also be contributing factors. Xerostomia leads to deprivation of the oral tissues from the benefits of the redundant functions of salivary components. The multiple functions of saliva in the oral cavity are related to its fluid and solutes phases. Among the various functions of the fluid phase are cleansing of the oral cavity by clearing food debris and bacteria, dilution of detritus and washing away both solids and solubilized matter. Prolonged clearance of oral sugar during the unstimulated resting flow rate stage confirms the salivary clearance role.[59] By solublizing food substances, salivary fluid facilitates mediation of taste and perception, while lubricating the oral mucosa, thus aiding the speech process. The salivary digestive function has three tiers. These are: a). formation of a bolus; b). initiation of the digestive process of the starches by the alpha-amylase enzyme as the food is being masticated in the oral cavity; and c). lubrication of the oral mucosa by the viscous mucous secretion that is high in glycoproteins to ease deglutition.[60]

The protective role of the various solutes of saliva stems from their physical properties, chemical action, antimicrobial defense and enzymatic activities. The mucins are hydrophilic molecules, hence their high water retention lubricates and moistens the mucosal surfaces, aggregates microorganisms and thus protects the oral mucosa from infections.[61] The same action protects the dental hard tissues from bacterial plaque and their by-products as well as from erosive potential of acids. Mucosal protection is also achieved by the epidermal growth factor that plays a role in ulcer and wound healing. The last, yet critical protective role of the solutes pivots on the Stathrins and Proline-rich protein. Both proteins interacting with dental hard tissue surfaces by their calcium-bonding properties contribute to safeguarding the dentition.

The salivary antimicrobial agents maintain the oral flora in a stable balance. Saliva contains Lactoferrin and Lysozyme enzymes and Thiocyanate ions. The Lactoferrin enzyme binds with iron, thus depriving bacteria of essential metabolic components. The Lysozyme enzyme hydrolyzes bacterial cell walls, permitting the entry of thiocyanate ions, which are bacteriocidal, into the bacterial cell. Secretory IgA agglutinates microorganisms, inhibits microbial adhesion, and facilitates the cleansing action of salivary serious fluid.[60] Saliva also contains a peroxidase system that has antimicrobial properties and decomposes hydrogen peroxide. Histatins, a salivary protein, has an antifungal activity.[62] Thus, decreased salivary production and concomitant reduction of the antimicrobial potential of salivary solutes may lead to increased pathogenic microorganisms such as Candida Albicans, Lactobacillus, and Streptococcus Mutans. This could predispose to candidiasis infection (mouth thrush) and caries formation.[63, 64]

The latter is a common occurrence in a cocaine-addicted individual's dentition. Mouth thrush may not be frequently encountered due to the variable timing of organisms' flare-up and the sporadic dental visits by the cocaine dependants. These visits are often limited by the emergency requirements of these patients.

The physiological pH of saliva ranges from 6.5 - 7.4, the highest value observed at a high salivary flow rate. Salivary pH, calcium, and phosphate concentrations are essential for keeping the saliva supersaturated with hydroxyapatite. Maintenance of a chemical balance of calcium and phosphate ion concentration at saturation levels stabilizes the equilibrium at the hydroxyapatite of the tooth surface interface and may assist in the remineralization process of enamel.[65] The amount of the calcium and phosphate ions secreted by the submandibular glands is twice that of the Parotid glands.[66,67] Proline-rich salivary proteins prevent spontaneous precipitation of calcium phosphate, thus limiting the amount and rate of calculus formation.[60]

The electrolyte, bicarbonate, phosphate, and protein contents such as urea and ammonia act as buffering systems in the physiological pH range (6.5 - 7.4) by neutralizing the acids. The redundant roles of these components in the buffering mechanism sustain the normal bio-equilibrium at the surface of the dentition by counteracting acidic challenges from various sources.[60, 67-72] Saliva performs more than a double function to counteract acids in the oral cavity. Primarily, it participates in the formation of the enamel pellicle that protects against the corrosive action of acidic food and beverages.[73] The second function is the buffering action of saliva to neutralize acids. The third function is to dilute acid concentration and clear the alien chemical from the oral cavity. Having performed these roles, it protects the hard dental tissues from the erosive potential of acids introduced to the oral environment, thus preventing the formation of erosion lesions.

The oldest means of cocaine consumption, coca-leaf chewing, was also found to suppress salivary glandular activity. By decreasing the secretion of saliva and salivary flow, dry mouth, and glossitis were observed.[54] Xerostomia was manifested in association with cocaine administration.[74] In a recent study it was determined that 87% of cocaine dependants complained of dry mouth compared to <5% of the non-user control group.[58] The participants in this study were known to administer the cocaine or its modified form "crack" through nasal insufflation, smoking, or IV injection.

Figure 6. A close up view of the nasal cavity and maxillary sinuses show the nasal septum slightly deviated towards the left side. A thinning at the lower half of the septum near the floor of the nose is evident from the progressive radiolucency. This is extended up to about the middle of the septum where a thin section is traversed by an oblique dark line of communication from the bottom of the right nostril to the top of the left nostril. This line is surrounded by a halo of optical translucency, a sign of the resorption pattern of the bony septum associated with nasal insufflation of cocaine for an extended period of time.

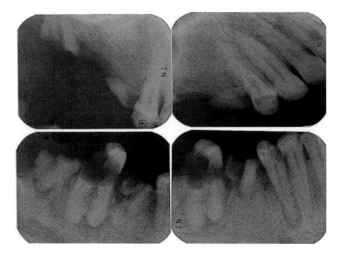

Figure 7. Periapical radiographs of the right maxillary and mandibular premolar/molar regions showing the remaining roots; some were still embedded in the supporting bone, while others were exfoliated and loosely attached to the gingiva. Extensive carious lesions ravaged this segment of the dentition and multiple areas of apical rarifying osteitis are present.

Caries

The decreased salivary flow creates an environment for the unchallenged acids from external, local and internal sources to dissolve the hydroxyapatite of hard tooth structures. This process leaves the dentin core vulnerable to both microbial organisms and/or more acid attacks. This sequence of events could explain the rapid, destructive process that affects the dentition of cocaine-dependants. A clear demonstration of these progressive disease processes of hard dental tissues was observed in the Philadelphia study of 78 cocaine addicts.[58] The results of this case-controlled study conclusively indicated a higher rate of destruction as manifested by extensive decay, number of remaining roots and lost teeth among cocaine users compared to non-users. It was pointed out that cocaine dependant individuals (mean age ~ 40 years) have lost, an average, about half of their dentition compared to only 6.0% of the non-user population in this study.[58]

The low salivary flow rate was reported to be associated with the high prevalence of caries among urban preschool Icelandic children.[75] These findings confirmed earlier suggestions that xerostomia predisposes to caries formation.[76] It was also concluded that xerostomia created by medications and irradiation treatments caused cervical caries, or more familiarly, rampant tooth decay. [76]

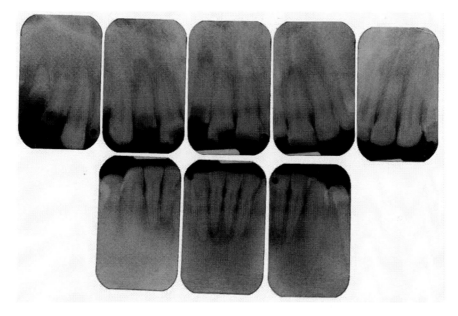

Figure 8. Periapical radiographs of anterior maxillary and mandibular regions show the extent of carious lesions and pulp involvement

Sequelae of Progression of the Carious Process

The carious process associated with cocaine users progressively invades both the coronal and root structures simultaneously, aiding in the rapid destruction of the dentition. The decayed teeth may reach a point of pulp involvement with possible formation of apical lesions; however, the intake of the abused drug frequently masks the pain. The destruction of the hard dental tissues continues until open communication with the pulp and the oral environment occurs. Such occurrences may lead to the release of pressurized infectious and gaseous products which decrease the intensity of toothaches experienced by the patient. Frequently, the affected tooth is maintained by the cocaine dependant in a semi-functioning condition while further loss of its tissues progress to a point that it is no longer visible above the gum line. As long as it is not painful, it could be left unmanaged. When it elicits pain, the patient often seeks extraction, supporting the observation that the cocaine addicted individual limits dental visits to an emergency basis only. The high incidence of carious lesions, the majority of which could be aggressive enough to damage most if not all of the coronal parts of the dentition, results in multiple remaining roots. Their radiographic features confirm the clinical findings, but show relatively fewer incidences of apical rarifying osteitis, than are expected from the clinical evidence.

One of the causes of this supervised neglect on behalf of the patient often stems from the deep self-belief that there is no hope to save one's teeth, as they will continue to decay as long as the habit of addiction exists. The lack of definitive dental treatment and dependence on analgesics and antibiotic medications sustain the status quo. The cocaine addicted individuals may also use the opportunity of using a decayed tooth that elicits pain or occasionally forms an abscess as a reason for a continuing source of prescriptions for scheduled drugs from unsuspecting dentists.

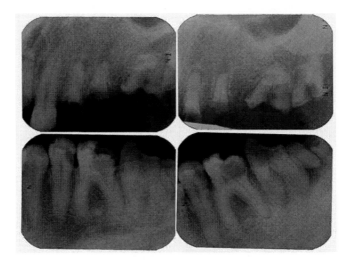

Figure 9. Periapical radiographs of the left maxillary and mandibular premolar/molar regions show remaining roots, furcation involvement, and alveolar bone loss. Extensive carious lesions resulted in loss of crowns, pulp involvement and multiple areas of apical rarifying osteitis.

Cervical Abrasion

Certain types of cervical abrasion lesions are associated with the transmucosal route of cocaine administration, [41] where cocaine powder is rubbed with the index finger against the gingival mucosa. This action often induces localized gingival inflammation and possible recession, and may inadvertently involve the cervical third of the adjacent teeth. Over an extended period of time, with repetition of this process, abrasion lesions may be manifested. These lesions are caused by the abrasiveness of the crystalline cocaine powder and its impurities and differ from the commonly noticeable cervical toothbrush abrasion lesion. The difference is manifested by the clinical appearance, location, extent, and mechanism of development of these lesions. These two types of lesions, however, have a few characteristics in common. In both cases, affected regions are mainly located on the contralateral side of the individual's dominant hand and the cervical third of the facial aspects of the affected teeth is primarily involved.

Where cocaine powder is being rubbed against the gingiva, the adjacent cervical third of the enamel (commonly premolar/molar region) could exhibit abrasion lesions that are characterized by being shallow, involve a large surface area, and have diffused margins. This lesion may be extended to the middle third of the crown or may possibly involve the root trunk where a localized area of dentin may be exposed due to associated gingival recession. The typical V-shaped cervical defect of toothbrush abrasion is generally absent. The color of these lesions rarely reflects normal appearance, and often demonstrates signs of enamel decalcification or browning of the dentin. The affected dentin may be tacky in consistency and signs of poor oral hygiene are often evident. The associated localized segment of the gingival tissue could exhibit signs of trauma and may have undergone abrasion of the epithelium, cellular desquamation, inflammation, swelling and/or ulceration. Bleeding may occur upon slight touch of the ulcerative gingival lesion. The periodontal condition of the individual is rarely favorable and the epithelial attachment could exhibit breakdown with localized marginal gingivitis or periodontitis and alveolar bone loss.

Toothbrush abrasion lesions, by comparison, often occur on the facial vestibular aspect of the dentition on the opposite side of the individual's dominant hand and to a lesser extent on the opposing side. The incidence of their occurrence is likely to be higher on the maxillary arch than the mandibular depending on the individual's oral hygiene habits. The predominantly affected segment of the dental arch is the canine/premolar area. The cervical third of the mesio-facial corner of the first molar is less frequently involved. Generally, the teeth affected by toothbrush abrasion are in concert with the confluence of their anatomic location, the dominant hand of the patient, the aggressiveness and force used, and the type and technique of tooth brushing (horizontal). The two or three body wear actions involved in tooth brushing may traumatize the free gingival margin leading to recession. It may also abrade the root surface with the resultant formation of a V-shaped defect (cervical notch).

This configuration of the toothbrush abrasion lesion is the result of the differential wear resistance of enamel and cement/dentin surfaces. The V-shaped groove may vary in depth. It may be too shallow to be detected or so deep that it could jeopardize the integrity and longevity of the affected tooth. The surface of the toothbrush abrasion lesion is usually hard on exploration and displays a natural dentin color. A dark line or area demarcating the location of the pulp chamber may be seen in deep lesions. Gingival recession may be observed, depending on the age of the individual, duration, and severity of the abrasion process. Nevertheless, the gingival margin often appears healthy, pink in color, firm in consistency, and displays normal texture and stippling contour. A gingival pocket often displays normal depth indicating the absence of attached epithelium breakdown or alveolar bone loss. Cervical toothbrush abrasion is encountered among the population at large. However, they are rarely seen among cocaine-dependants. Their occurrence among this population is due to the vigorous, wrongful horizontal brushing technique exercised by cocaine addicted individuals during the manic "high" episodes. The two abrasion lesions described may not require restorative intervention at the early stages, unless pain is elicited. Deepened lesions should be restored with bonding procedures to prevent further loss of tooth structure.

Oral Motor Para-Functions and Para-Oral Complications

Cocaine addiction was found to be associated with temporomandibular disturbance, myofacial pain and bruxism.[77] A comparison between individuals with a history of long term drug abuse and a similar number of a normal population of same age, gender, socio-economic status was undertaken. The objective of the study was to evaluate the long-term effect of cocaine addiction on the stomatognathic system. It was concluded that long-term drug addiction has a detrimental effect. This was expressed by the high prevalence of oral and behavioral signs and symptoms of temporomandibular disturbances. Individuals with a long history of addiction, who exhibit a problem with bruxism, frequently complained of myofacial pain dysfunction syndrome, rather than internal meniscus derangement.[77] These findings confirmed previous reports that indicated that persons who were frequently intoxicated with cocaine tend to display signs of severe bruxism.[29] These signs were manifested by flat cusps and abnormal wear facets on cuspal inclinations in the premolar/molar region. In a report on alcoholism and dental management, it was indicated that the combined use of cocaine and alcohol resulted in the most dental complications.[78] This was believed to be due to the culmination and enhancement of the adverse effects of the two dugs. These patients often suffer from severe xerostomia, advanced periodontal disease, high incidence of caries, missing teeth and severe attrition of the dentition. Furthermore, bilateral masseter muscle hypertrophy could develop either alone or in combination with alcohol-induced parotid gland enlargement producing a "chipmunk" appearance. The affected individual endures premature loss of teeth and disruption of the masticatory apparatus that leads to a vicious cycle of deficient nutrition.

The majority of cocaine addicted patients suffer constantly from both sinus pressure and pain, hence the increased demand for analgesics. These symptoms are clearly manifested by increased radiopacity of the maxillary and paranasal sinuses. The symptoms might mimic toothache or may occur in concurrence with pain from dental origin. Thus, for accurate diagnosis, these symptoms and patient health and social history have to be taken into consideration.

Incisal Attrition

Loss of several posterior dental units during a considerably short period of time is compounded by the process of severe attrition of the patient's incisors. This accelerated incisal wear is due to the uneven force distribution and concentration of the entire occlusal forces on a limited area of the affected teeth. Continuation of the wear pattern of the incisal edges leads to exposure of the underlying dentin layer that supports the enamel. Differential accelerated dentin wear undermines the enamel faster, leading to its further crumbling under occlusal forces continuing this vicious cycle. Eventual loss of vertical tooth height and vertical support of occlusion leads to collapsed bite.

It is clearly noticeable that loss of teeth from dentitions of chronic cocaine addicts is more associated with advanced caries process than advanced periodontal disease. This phenomenon is substantiated by the microbiologic evidence of selective elevation in the number of microorganisms causing caries associated with xerostomia.[63, 64] The result of this microbiologic investigation indicated that an increase in the number of filamentous organisms was noted in dry mouth conditions while organisms causing periodontal breakdown were not significantly affected.[63, 64] In short, the clinical images of a chronic cocaine addicted individual can be described as almost total devastation of the hard dental tissues and possible signs of multiple apical pathoses, in the presence of chronic generalized periodontitis.

The aforementioned sequence of events brings about the commonly experienced intra-oral manifestations of long-term cocaine abuse. The dental image of cocaine dependants that is distinctively different from the non-user population comprises the number of teeth lost, the extraordinary number of retained decayed roots, the extent of carious erosion lesions, the amount of hard dental tissue lost to abrasion and untimely attrition, the deteriorated condition of oral hygiene, and the status of the gingival health and level of the supporting bone.

PARA-ORAL MID-FACIAL COMPLICATIONS

Because of the uniqueness of cocaine's pharmacologic property being the only natural local anesthetic agent with a vasoconstrictive capability, it predisposes the subjected tissues to severe damage. When the powder is applied topically, the damaging effects occur as a result of a combination of the direct trauma to the tissue by the crystalline powder of cocaine and the superimposed ischemia of the tissue. These complications are readily manifested in association with local application of the powder on oral and nasal mucosa.

Pathogenesis

Intranasal inhalation or "snorting" is the most frequent route of cocaine administration in the United States. The vasoconstrictive property of cocaine leads to ischemia-induced necrosis of the nasal mucous membranes. This is combined with the irritating effect of impurities in the cocaine powder, such as talc, lactose, manitol, borax, amphetamines and plaster of Paris that lead to inflammation of the nasal mucosa. Nasal insufflation of cocaine powder produces multiple complications that range from rhinitis and epistaxis to inflammation of the muco-periosteum and osteitis leading to bone resorption. It may eventually predispose to perforation of the nasal septum and possibly other associated bony walls of the nasal cavity.[16] These events can occur within three weeks following the start of regular snorting, as reported by Kuriloff and Kimmelman, 1989.[79]

Reported Cases

Multiple complications have been linked to nasal insufflation of cocaine powder (snorting). These include chronic rhinitis, crusting, sinusitis, epistaxis, ossification or necrosis of the nasal septum, ulceration and alar deformities.[79-83] The first case of cocaine induced perforation of the palate was claimed to have been reported in 1912.[84]

A statement by Cottrell, Mehra, Malloy and Ghali 1999 indicated that septal perforation associated with cocaine abuse is a well-recognized condition, while palatal perforation is rare.[16] In 1999, these authors presented the sixth case of this category since that previously reported in 1966. Concurrently, in 1999, Villa presented a case of a 38-year-old man whose chronic snorting resulted in recurrent sinus infections and erosion of the mid-facial anatomy.[85] The author cited an additional 6 cases that developed palatal defects combined with a nasal septum perforation. Some of these cases presented signs that suggested cerebro-spinal fluid leakage. This particular case was reported to have occurred secondary to frequent and prolonged cocaine snorting. Consequently, osteocartilagenous necrosis of the sino-nasal tract was extended to involve the turbinates, maxillary and other nasal sinuses. It could have also led to naso-cranial communication and subsequent leakage of cerebrospinal fluid (CSF), as was suggested.[85]

During the following year, Lancaster et al 2000 reported what they believed to be the tenth case of palatal necrosis secondary to cocaine abuse in a 33-year-old female.[86] Another case was documented within 13 months, of a 56-year-old man who suffered progressive destruction of his hard palate, nasal septum cartilage, and soft palate that had been caused by chronic cocaine inhalation.[87] These cases were followed by six centro-facial destructive processes associated with nasal cocaine snorting. Five of these cases involved the nasal structures and the palate, while only one had no palatal involvement.[84, 88-90]

Health Care Provider's Role

Considering the number of cocaine abusers, whether they may be for a single lifetime experience or multiple uses, sixteen mid-facial defects were reported thus far. Although they may be considered a rare occurrence, they are significant findings that affect a sector of the cocaine-abusing population. The threat of the existence and repeated occurrence of this process among this group of cocaine abusers is eminent. In the absence of signs or symptoms at early stages, these lesions may go unnoticed. If nasal septum perforation occurs in conjunction with other mild manifestations such as stuffiness, discharge, epistaxis, sinus complication, headache, and earache that does not require medical assistance, this defect may pass undetected by the patient. If these symptoms are severe enough to compel the patient to seek the assistance of a health care provider, the defect may be detected through radiographic investigations.

Due to the rarity of palatal perforation, the probability of such finding may only be encountered in a considerably large patient pool. However, the likelihood of discovering such a case among patients in a large dental practice may not be impossible. The probability of these patients seeking the services of a dental health care provider for emergency services far exceeds seeking specialized medical care assistance. This brings into focus the crucial role of vigilant dentists in discovering mid-facial deformities at an early stage of the formation process during routine radiographic examination utilizing oral pantomograph. Unfortunately, the focus is often on repairing the damaged teeth and replacing the lost teeth, detracting from observing details in the para-dental region such as the sinuses, TMJ, and other maxillofacial structures unless a complaint is registered. These details are invaluable to the overall understanding of the patient's health condition and should not be overlooked.

Clinical Features

In the event of their occurrence, oro-nasal communications may be presented as a miniscule hole that can be hardly detected by the patient. The affected individual presents with a complaint of passage of ingested fluid through the nose and/or the experience of a nasal tone during speech. The clinical features of the extent of consequential oro-nasal communication (ONC) resulting from cocaine abuse varies. It may be manifested as small as a pinhole at the roof of the palate. On the opposite extreme, these defects can be so extensive as to involve the majority of nasal, ethmoid, and maxillary structures. An example of such an extremely extensive defect of oro-nasal communication (ONC) was reported by Seyer et al 2002. These authors described a 50-year-old woman with a history of cocaine abuse who complained of speech with a nasal tone and an ill-fitting palatal obturator. The patient was reportedly in good health. External examination revealed a rhinolalia and bilateral collapse of the nasal ala. Intraorally, the palatal process of the maxilla, walls of the maxillary and ethmoid sinuses, turbinate bones, and nasal septum were absent, leaving only a large defect lined with crusted, malodorous, necrotic debris. The maxillary alveolus was spared and the patient did not complain of pain nor was she apprehensive, despite the appearance of the lesion.[84]

Mari A. et al. 2003, reported three cases of oro-nasal communication (ONC) of individuals (1 man and 2 women in the third decade of life) residing in Barcelona, Spain, with a history of cocaine abuse.[89] The first suffered a defect of the labial philtrum, columella, vomer, septal cartilage, turbinates, and a 1.5 centimeter oro-nasal communication (ONC) was evident. Crusting and ulceration were seen in the destroyed nasal cavity. The second case presented with loss of vomer and nasal cartilage, accompanied by a saddle nose deformity. The third case was of particular significance to dental health professionals from the medico-legal aspect. This case was described as a 30-year-old woman presented in a private office with a complaint of ONC that was claimed to be due to the traumatic effect of a periodontal scaling and curettage procedure conducted by a periodontist a year before. Upon examination of the patient, a large ONC was evident with absence of the vomer and nasal cartilage. The diagnosis of naso-oral destructive process as a result of cocaine abuse was determined by revisiting the patient's social and health history. This patient admitted to have had a prior habit of snorting two grams of cocaine every weekend for 4 years and still continued her use throughout the duration of treatment with a prosthetic obturator appliance. The clinician in charge noted that the lesion, allegedly created by the periodontist, could not have been as severe as the presented ONC by the patient. It was determined that the incident of periodontal scaling and curettage was thought to be the coincidental occurrence that precipitated the attention of the patient to the symptoms of ONC.[89]

Differential Diagnosis of Mid-Facial Lesions

Differential diagnosis of cases with such destructive mid-facial lesions is essential to draw a conclusive diagnosis that could form the foundation that underlines and supports proposed treatment options. Differential diagnosis is pivoting on differentiation between varieties of etiologic factors involved. Of these, snorting cocaine must be considered an integral part. According to Ghali, GE, 1999, six categories of causative factors of ONC lesions should be initially considered for differential diagnosis.[16] These are traumatic, infectious, granulomatous, collagen vascular, neoplastic, and idiopathic. In order to narrow down the differential diagnosis among these etiologic factors, a detailed and thorough history, and a physical examination combined with laboratory studies, are invaluable. The traumatic process causing ONC may include post-surgical, post-injury, and factitial lesions. Infectious processes include bacterial, fungal, spirochetal and parasitic organisms. Constitutional symptoms and Venereal Disease Research Laboratory (VDRL) test can be used as armamentaria to exclude fungal and spirochetal infections, while culture and tissue identification of microorganisms can rule out tuberculosis (TB), syphilis, histoplasmosis, and blastomycosis. In full blown cases of AIDS, oral lesions such as ulceration and Kaposi's sarcoma may be present. These can be ruled out by the hematological test for the HIV virus and/or biopsy of the lesions.

Granulomatous processes with their rare occurrence can be ruled out with special histologic stains. The collagen vascular processes, such as Wegener's granulomatosis, the most common of this group, also include periarteritis nodosa and Churg-Strauss syndrome. Wegener's granulomatosis can be distinguished by a positive kidney, lung or nasopharyngeal biopsy for vasculitis and proteinurea, red cell casts, elevation of serum creatinine and presence of antineutrophil cytoplasmic antibodies in nearly 90% of the patients affected. Biopsy and histopathologic identification could also rule out neoplastic processes as in the case of lymphoma and squamous cell carcinoma. Idiopathic process that includes polymorphic reticulosis can be identified by typical histology that shows acute and chronic inflammation obscuring the atypical lymphocytic infiltrate, while granulomas are typically absent and giant cells may be seen but are uncommon.[79]

DENTAL MANAGEMENT OF COCAINE ABUSERS

Available literature highlighted the use of cocaine as today's non-prescription illicit drug of choice, among both one-time and long-term abusers. During the seventies and through the eighties, the average cocaine users were young, white males, well educated, middle class or above, and who usually had no regular drug abuse record. Enhancement of purification and potency of the drug during the eighties and into the nineties, coupled with the significant reduction in price and availability on the main streets, rendered its widespread use among all socio-economic groups. By crossing all barriers, whether by generation, gender, education, or socioeconomic background among the North American population, cocaine abuse has spread among those residing in both urban and suburban communities. At the dawn of the twenty first century, the classic socio-economic and educational profile for the cocaine abuser no longer exists.[91] Drug abuse victims may present as patients to any dental office or facility seeking dental care. Some of these patients may not display symptoms or signs that manifest the disorder, despite the possibility of the presence of underlying physiological, pathological, and/or psychological changes in their condition. It is unlikely and generally unexpected that most of these individuals' self-reported history would give clues to their addictive habits, due to the social stigma associated with crack-cocaine use.

The high prevalence of cocaine abuse within the global society increased the likelihood of drug-abusing individuals to be among the daily patient pool of the dental practice.[1,5,6,46] This urges the need for dental professionals to become aware of the changes that could be brought about by cocaine abuse. If these changes are noted, they should raise the concern of the dental professional to promptly implement special precautionary measures to be taken during the patient's dental management. Overlooking, not recognizing, or not suspecting cocaine abuse and consequent failure to adopt the necessary precautionary measures may result in a range of repercussions, some of which can be life threatening. It is the purpose of this section to discuss the clinical means for identification of cocaine abusers, and highlights some considerations applicable to their dental management. The information provided would be a welcome addition to the dental practitioner's armamentaria in today's societies.

Clinical Means of Identifying a Cocaine Abuser

Some individuals are frank enough to disclose information related to medications taken, drug abuse and allergic reactions. These individuals often offer a statement that "they quit the habit for a certain period of time". However, disclosure of details related to the duration of addiction, form and method of drug administration, frequency, and amount of drug intake, or a combination of this information are not freely offered. As for the majority of the drug dependant population, however, deliberate and concerted efforts are made to hide or deny the habit of addiction. This is not an unexpected occurrence and when it occurs, it presents a challenge for dental professionals, particularly in the absence of glaring signs or symptoms indicative of drug abuse. Thus, appropriate diagnosis may be inconclusive, especially of more recent users. Therefore, investigations conducted to disclose the etiology of any suspected signs or symptoms of suspected individuals that could have raised curiosity, could prove beneficial during the course of dental management.

For a determined dental professional, there are several common clues. If identified, they may collectively assist in drawing an explanation to the raised curiosity or suspicion. This brings into focus the crucial role of the properly informed and skilled dental team to delicately identify their patient's secretive recreational habit through thorough medical and dental health histories. Identification of most cocaine abusers might be possible when a well-structured, self–response questionnaire is followed by a well-patterned interview geared to obtain a comprehensive health and social history, medications taken, hospitalizations, dietary and individual habits. The information gained would be a crucial addition to the routine physical head and neck, dental examination, and radiographic investigation. Accordingly, the dental practitioner should therefore be versed in the art and science of interviewing. Knowing well the delicate nature of this issue, the sensitivity, and resistance to expose a well-kept secret by drug abusers who have a tendency not to divulge such confidential information, indirect questioning techniques should be applied to obtain much needed details. During such an interview, the dental professional must pay attention to the patient's general appearance, behavior, body language, and method of response to posed questions.

The interviewer's questions must be posed with compassion, a sense of understanding and care, and directed in a non-interrogative manner. The wording of the questions should be chosen carefully so that it reflects a non-threatening intent. This type of interview should be conducted with a non-authoritative, empathetic, compassionate, non-judgmental, and sincere manner. An impression of professional curiosity and the need to know the detailed health status of the patient in order to avoid possible untoward consequences of medication interaction and or allergy must be conveyed. A professional set-up in private surroundings could add reassurance to the patient and guard their confidentiality. The patient should be made aware of the crucial role of health and social history information given in arriving to a definitive diagnosis. The potential risk of possible chemical interactions with medications used for treatment should be explained and an informed consent should be secured prior to the start of any procedure.

Upon conducting the physical head and neck, intra-oral, and dental examinations, attention to detail must be given priority to gather beneficial information that may lead to the disclosure of a cocaine abuse habit. These clues should be differentially diagnosed and accurately discriminated from the traditionally known signs and symptoms of oral and dental pathology. To cite but a few, consistent rubbing of cocaine in its crystalline form against the gingival mucosa and lining mucosa could lead to inflammation and possible ulceration.[41] This gingival ulceration can be easily mistaken for the Necrotizing-Ulcerative-Gingivo-Stomatitis (NUG) that is characterized by a distinctive odor. Definitive diagnosis can be confirmed with microbiological testing. Ulceration of the mucus membranes could also be misdiagnosed for traumatic or peptic ulcers, known for their history and clinical features. Cocaine crystals consistently rubbed against a localized area of the dentition may lead to formation of cervical lesions that could be easily confused with either toothbrush abrasion or localized erosion lesions. Accurately diagnosing these cervical lesions by questioning their history, the patient's oral hygiene and dietary habits may prove fruitful. The amorphous topography of the palatal aspects of maxillary anterior teeth in a teenager may be either overlooked or misdiagnosed as perimolysis that is induced by voluntary purging of the stomach contents of patients suffering from bulimia nervosa.[91] However, a closer look at all affiliated information may lead to the disclosure of causative factors attributed to a pervasive developmental disorder that affects children born to "crack mothers".[92]

Chronic addiction to cocaine with the resultant neuromuscular disorders may lead to bruxism. This masticatory apparatus deficit is often manifested by wear facets of cusp tips and or slopes and subsequent loss of occlusal anatomic landmarks. It may also be associated with temporomandibular joint disorder or myofacial pain. These signs and symptoms may mimic those caused by other etiologies that must be excluded. Among these are erosion induced by acidulated beverages combined with normal occlusal wear in young individuals.[93] These erosion lesions are characterized by the feature of decalcification at the cervical third of the facial aspects of the dentition. Similarly, facets caused by attrition of the occlusal table over an extended duration are commonly manifested in senior citizens' dentitions due to the aging process.

Cocaine addicts neglect their hygiene practices in general and their oral hygiene in particular. This is attributed to indulgence in the street drugs, way of life, lack of self interest, and altered emphasis. Also playing a major role in this phenomenon are the mood fluctuations, the influence of the drug on the thought process, and unwillingness to take time necessary to execute such basic daily exercises. As a result, poor oral hygiene, excessive amount of plaque and calculus deposits predispose to gingivitis and periodontitis. The presence of these conditions combined with xerostomia (dry mouth) and increased incidence of carious lesions, remaining roots, and lost teeth are common features among cocaine addicts. The affiliation of these conditions could pass undetected unless the differences between the characteristics of clinical features of cocaine-addicted and non-users of similar age and background are clearly identified. The discovery of any of the aforementioned types of soft and hard dental tissue markers should be considered a warning sign. It should provoke suspicion by the dental professionals of possible drug abuse, thus urging the dental practitioners to revisit the dental and medical health histories, and the recreational habits of the patient.

Cocaine addiction often leads to loss of appetite and loss of weight. This is despite the increased consumption of carbohydrates such as hard candy, potato chips, and carbonated beverages that are less costly, ready to use, and highly caloric. These are often used as substitutes for proper nutrition and balanced meals due to the difficulty of allocating already limited money, after purchasing the illicit drug. For the same reason, and the continued need to satisfy one's desperate desire to acquire more cocaine, the individual is constantly in need of money which may form a strong motive to break the law.

Rarely do clinicians get an honest, straight answer from the suspected patient, due to the illegality of the drug used. In a young individual, the persistence of high blood pressure levels during the dental visit, in the absence of a history of hypertension, should alert the clinician to a possible cocaine abuse habit. This increases the need for physician consultation and laboratory investigations such as blood, urine, or saliva before embarking on surgical procedures in the oral cavity that necessitate local anesthetic administration.[40]

Cocaine intoxication often renders the individual manic, restless, hyper-alert, and irritable. If taken in a combination with a central nervous system depressant such as alcohol, it could alter the cocaine stimulant effect and induce depression. The health history of patients with mood swings and bipolar personality should be questioned and thoroughly investigated. Bilateral loss of eyebrows and eyelashes were reported in association of smoking freebase cocaine.[94] Initially, cocaine use and the resultant high might be considered an aphrodisiac, but after habitual intake and subsequent addiction, the individual experiences a decreased interest in the opposite sex. When desire is unevenly shared among sex partners, these personal differences often lead to social problems and can be an underlying factor for criminal actions.

A few specific physical signs, if noted, might also represent helpful clues for identifying cocaine addicts. These include a scar or multiple scars along the arm or the leg veins that are commonly observed among intravenous cocaine abusers who inject the substance directly into the blood stream. These individuals tend to hide the needle marks by covering their arms and legs, even during hot weather conditions, with long sleeve shirts and long pants. Individuals who habitually sniff cocaine powder develop intermittent nasal sniffing habit even though they may not display any signs, symptoms or present history of allergy or common cold. Dilatation of the pupils of an individual that is unrelated to change in light intensities may represent an obvious sign of current drug abuse.[94]

Cocaine inhalation may trigger pain in the maxillary premolar-molar zone that spreads to the orbital and pre-orbital region. The intensity of this one-sided pain (named cluster headache) could last 30-120 minutes. This type of pain is commonly manifested 1-2 hours after cocaine administration through the nostril on the side through which the drug was inhaled.[95] If it occurs, it should be differentially diagnosed and identified so that preventive measure could be implemented rather than resorting to the treatment of the symptoms. Cocaine induces hyperthermia, hence the profuse sweating observed even during the cold weather.[1] Due to severe physiologic and pathologic changes associated with cocaine abuse, dehydration due to polyurea, diarrhea, and excessive sweating is manifested in several forms. Dry mouth could be the most noticeable symptom. Rise in blood pressure without history of hypertension may also be detected.[40] According to a law enforcement officer, "chronic cocaine abusers tend to have the shakes, their pupils are dilated, they often display excessive sweating even in colder temperatures, and sometimes appear spaced and incoherent, and their speech is slurred".

Recognition by family, relatives, or friends of signs or symptoms related to the cocaine abuse problem could be very helpful in identifying such individuals. This, particularly, may be the case if special attention is given to various statements made by the accompanying individuals. As for underage patients, observation by parents or guardians of paraphernalia used to prepare cigarettes, syringes, presence or misuse of money, and conspicuous disappearance of articles from the family or friends may shed light on an underlying drug abuse problem. The discovery by the patient's family of an unidentified white crystalline powder provides substantial evidence for cocaine abuse involvement. Cocaine powder has a bitter taste and produces numbness when applied to the tip of the tongue.

Considerations for Treatment Planning

All treatment options must be considered and presented to patients regardless of socio-economic status, gender, age, race, social history habits or addiction. However, it is unreasonable to expect of a long term-cocaine addicted individual, who has not given up the habit and whose dentition is annihilated, to value highly specialized dental procedures. Setting aside the cost consideration, when an overt manifestation of poor personal health and dental hygiene are evident, delivery of extensive fixed prostheses or implant appliances with any reasonable prognosis would not be expected. Unless optimal oral health and home care conditions seem promising and the patient is in the recovery stage, dental treatment should be limited to a basic modality. Emergency treatment such as endodontic therapy for pain control and minor oral surgery must be undertaken. Investing efforts and funds for comprehensive treatment should be re-evaluated at a later stage when the patient's reliability and questionable compliance is in check. Permanent fixed restorations should be postponed until the addiction habit is under control and diligence in home care is exercised and successfully monitored. Under these favorable conditions, the basic principles of dental treatment protocol offered are still maintained the same for every patient regardless. The choice of treatment modality would be based on the dental history and conditions of the patient, the individual demands and financial considerations. Special consideration should be given to a patient's complaint, age, health and the ability to maintain proper oral home care.

Patients undergo a routine screening process after acknowledging the receipt of a notice of privacy practices and signing their consent for the accuracy of the self reported questionnaire. This agreement is to give permission for necessary examinations, conducting relevant investigations and undergoing comprehensive treatment under the conditions and policies of the treating dental health professional or organization. The patient should consent to understanding the explained inherent risk in all dental procedures commonly conducted in private dental offices and particularly those associated with cocaine abuse.

Cocaine addicted individuals with their life style, emphasis and priorities often miss their scheduled appointments and display erratic attendance records during routine dental care. Except for the emergency visits to alleviate pain due to acute inflammation of the soft tissues, deep cavities, failed restorations, sharp broken teeth, pulp involvement, or abscess formation, most of these individuals often do not show the necessary cooperation or compliance during delivery of routine dental treatment. It is therefore essential to consider simplification of the treatment plan that is customized to fulfill their general and dental health care needs without imposing constraints on the patient or care provider. Thus, treatment should basically be limited to alleviating pain, eradicating infection and restoring function with fundamental restorative and prosthetic techniques.

These limitations are amplified by the lack of funds and the imposed financial constraints on cocaine addicted individuals. These restrictions may alter the individual attitudes towards dental treatment. Comprehensive dental care may never be considered nor completed and a simple extraction or emergency therapy would be the preferred treatment of choice over an involved and complex plan.

Considerations for Routine Dental Care

Cocaine intoxication has been associated with a multitude of symptoms that may develop rapidly. Caution, therefore, should be exercised when treating cocaine dependent individuals in the dental office due to the possibility of self pre-medication by the drug. Acute hypertension and numerous resultant complications could occur following administration of cocaine. Vital signs and specifically blood pressure must be monitored at the beginning of every visit. If cocaine is taken in a dose high enough, it could develop intoxication during the delivery of dental treatment. Initial stages of intoxication are manifested by euphoria, alertness, sleep disorder, and feeling of enhanced energy. These may not present a danger to the individual or office staff. However, some patients, when intoxicated may exhibit assault behavior that could be disturbing and potentially dangerous to clinical personnel. This behavior, along with paranoid ideation, could have serious medico-legal consequences.

In the presence of loss of appetite and malnourishment, the consequent hypoglycemia could represent a danger to the patient. Moreover, sensitization to epinephrine that causes potentiation of cocaine's action could represent an inherent danger to the patient, particularly during a lengthy restorative procedure. This can compound the potential allergic reaction to ester types of anesthetic agents. Therefore, timing of induction of anesthesia, selection of the type of anesthetic agent, and refraining from the use of epinephrine are important safety factors to be implemented. Monitoring and insuring the use of a physician's prescribed pre-medications, particularly antibiotics could circumvent serious consequences.

The intermediate stage of cocaine intoxication could be manifested by delirium, syncope, nausea and vomiting, that should be keenly watched for during the normal dental procedure, particularly those requiring the application of a rubber dam. This means of isolation is regularly used during routine restorative and endodontic therapy that is commonly required for pain control in emergency dental management frequently associated with cocaine addicted individuals dental needs. The latent stage of intoxication including chest pain, tremors, seizures, hypertension, hyperthermia, respiratory paralysis, cardiac arrhythmia may also occur, necessitating urgent emergency medical management since the inevitable consequence could be fatal. Although a self-limited patho-physiology of the intoxication complication could take place and recovery may ensue within 24 hours, referral of the patients to the emergency department can be to the best interest of their well being.[96, 97]

The dental professional must be aware of the possibility that cocaine addicted individuals could use the drug as pre-medication which induces a sudden rise of blood pressure. This is particularly the case when the dental visit and expected treatment is perceived by the patient to be a stressful event. Therefore, vital signs must be closely monitored and physician's instructions must be strictly adhered to. Following any dental surgery procedure, these patients must be closely monitored to prevent self-medication which could result in possible post operative complications such as excessive bleeding. During the course of treatment of cocaine abusing individuals, the provider must be keenly vigilant to detect physiological changes that allude to allergic reactions, excessive bleeding, cardiovascular or neurovascular accidents.

Universal protocol of infection control, while it must be implemented for every patient, must be adhered to during the entire management duration for the drug dependant with strict caution. The fear of cross contamination with HC virus far exceeds the risk of HIV among cocaine dependant individuals. The risk ratios of contamination with these two infectious diseases are significantly higher from cocaine abusers than the non-user population.[58]

Consideration for Follow-Up Dental Care

Patients should be advised against the use of illicit drugs and when necessary should be referred to a physician for consultation or treatment of systemic complications. If possible, literature dealing with this problem may be given, indicating the health hazards, seeking assistance, and appropriate organizations. Lists of names of drug rehabilitation organizations, support groups, specialized child-care centers, and qualified specialists should be made available for use when sought. Subsequent referral for psychiatric care or other health and social welfare professional or groups is highly recommended.

Whenever possible, assessment of the progression of a patient's condition and the efficacy of the preventive protocol instructions should be undertaken. Oral home care instructions must be given, follow-up visits must be scheduled, and progress monitored. If receptive, they should be referred whenever possible to nutritional counseling. The objectives are the improvement of the dietary regimen and elimination of causative factors that adversely contribute to the deterioration of the oral health condition in particular and systemic health in general. These preventive measures could not and will not bear any fruitful results, and would not be followed or adhered to, unless the habit of addiction to cocaine is at least under control and the patient is in the recovery stage.

CONCLUDING REMARKS

Based on the available statistics related to the prevalence of cocaine use, it is no longer uncommon that dental health care providers encounter cocaine abusers in their busy daily practice. These patients may present with minor changes in their hard and/or soft dental tissues that represent slight departures from the norm. Such changes may be overlooked, ignored, misdiagnosed, or go undetected. The underlying causes may escape identification, which could have serious repercussions. However, with diligent pursuit of a thorough investigative process, the outcome can assist in the disclosure of the causative factor and understanding of the overall complexity of the patient's systemic, psychological, and dental health. Consequently, while avoiding possible untoward mishaps, the dental professional could successfully plan and safely implement the proper course of management.

REFERENCES

[1]   Gay GR, Inaba DS, Sheppard CW, Newmayer J. Cocaine: History, Epidemiology, Human Pharmacology, and Treatment. A Perspective on a New Debut for an Old Girl. *Clinical Toxicology*, 1975; 8(2): 149-178.

[2]   Zylke JW. Drug War Intelligence Gathering: Risky, but Useful to Physicians. Medical News and Perspectives. *JAMA*. Oct. 1988; 260(15): 2169-2170.

[3]   Indriati E, Buikstra, J. Coca Chewing in Prehistoric Coastal Peru; Dental Evidence. *Am J of Physical Anthropology* 2001; 114:242-257.

[4]   Drug Facts, Office of National Drug Control Policy, Cocaine-Crack. September 27, 2004.

[5]   Substance Abuse and Mental Health Services Administration. *Results from the 2003 National Survey on Drug Use and Health: National Findings,* September 2004.

[6]   National Institute on Drug Abuse and University of Michigan. *Monitoring the Future 2003 Data from In-School Surveys of 8th, 10th, and 12th Grade Students*, December 2003.

[7]   National Institute on Drug Abuse and University of Michigan. *Monitoring the Future National Survey Results on Drug Use,* 1975-2003, Volume II: College Students and Adults Ages 19-45 (PDF), 2004.

[8]   Centers for Disease Control and Prevention. *Youth Risk Behavior Surveillance-United States* 2003. May 2004.

[9]   National Institute of Justice. *Drug and Alcohol Use and Related Matters Among Arrestees*, 2003, (PDF), 2004.

[10] Substance Abuse and Mental Health Services Administration. *Emergency Department Trends from the Drug Abuse Warning Network, Final Estimates,* 1995-2002. July 2003.

[11] Office of National Drug Control Policy. *Pulse Check: Trends in Drug Abuse, Drug Markets and Chronic Users in 25 of America's Largest Cities*, January 2004.

[12] George S. Has the Cocaine Epidemic Arrived in the U.K.? *Forensic Sci Int.* 2004; 143 (2-3):187-190.

[13] Brugal MT, Domingo-Salvany A, Diaz de Quizano E, Torralba L. Prevalence of Problematic Cocaine Consumption in a City of Southern Europe, Using Capture-Recapture with a Single List. *J Urban Health*, 2004; 81(3):416-27.

[14] Office of National Drug Abuse, Drug Policy Information Clearing House, Street Terms: Drugs and the Drug Trade. September 2004.

[15] Arzona-Castaner D, Johnson C. Cocaine-Induced Myocardial Infarction Associated with Severe Reversible Systolic Dysfunction and Pulmonary Edema. *PR Health Sci J*, 2004; 23:319-322.

[16] Cottrell DA, Mehra P, Malloy JC, Ghali GE. Midline Palatal Perforation, *J Oral Maxillofac Surg*, 1999; 57:990-995.

[17] Brecklin CS, Gopaniuk-Folga A, Kravetz T, Sabah S, Singh A, Arruda JA, Dunea G. Prevalence of Hypertension in Chronic Cocaine Users. *Am J Hypertens*, 1998; 11(11 Pt 1): 1279-83.

[18] Bunn WH, Giannini AJ. Cardiovascular Complications of Cocaine Abuse. *Am Fam Physician*, 1992; 46(3):769-73.

[19] *PR Health Sci J*, 2004 Dec; 23(4):319-322.

[20] Roberts JR, Onattrocchi E, Howland MA. Severe Hyperthermic Secondary to Intravenous Drug Abuse. *Am J Emerg Med*, 1984; 2: 372.

[21] VanDyke C, Byck R. Cocaine. *Sci Am*, 1982; 246(3):128-41.

[22] Fischman MW, Schuster CR, Resmekov l. Cardiovascular and Subjective Effects of Intravenous Cocaine Administration in Humans. *Arch Gen Psychiatry*, 1976; 33:983-89.

[23] Kalsner S, Nickerson M., Mechanism of Cocaine Potentiation of Responses to Amides. *Br. J Pharmacology*, 1969:35:428-39.

[24] Antelman SM, Kocan D, Rowland N, deGiovanni L, Chiodo LA. Amitriptyline Provides Long-lasting Immunization Against Sudden Cardiac Death from Cocaine. *Eur J Pharmacol*, 1981; 69: 119-20.

[25] Rappolt RT, Gay GR, Inaba D. Propranolol: a Specific Antagonist to Cocaine. *Clin Toxicol*, 1977; 10:265-71.

[26] Ritchie JM, Greene NM. *Local Anesthetics*. In: Gilman AG, Goodman LS, Rall TW, Murad F, eds. The Pharmacological Basis of Therapeutics.7th ed. New York, McMillan, 1985:309-10.

[27] Wilson C, Fisvold O, Doerge R, *Textbook of Organic Medical and Pharmaceutical Chemistry*, Lippincott, Philadelphia, Pa. 1966, pp. 592-595.

[28] Wylie, WD, Churchill-Davidson HC. *A Practice of Anesthesia*, Yearbook Medical Pubs. Chicago, IL 1966.

[29] Friedlander AH, Gorelick D. Dental Management of Cocaine Addict O Surg O Med O Path, 1988; 65:45-48.

[30] Longnecker DE, Murphy FL. *Pharmacology of Local Anesthetics* in: Dripps, Eckenhoff, Vandam. Introduction to Anesthesia 8th ed. WB Saunders, 1992; 201- 215.

[31] Pallasch TJ, McCarthy FM, Jastak JT. Cocaine and Sudden Cardiac Death. *J Oral Maxillofac. Surg*, 1989; 47:1188-1191.

[32] Isaacs SO, Martin P, Willoughby JH. "Crack" (an extra potent form of cocaine) Abuse: A Problem of the Eighties. *Oral Surg Oral Med Oral Pathol*, 1987; 63:12-16.

[33] Little JW. *Dental Implications of Mood Disorders, General Dentistry*, Sept-Oct 2004; 52(5):442-50.

[34] Mathias DW: Cocaine-Associated Myocardial Ischemia-Review of Clinical and Angiographic Findings. Am J Med, 1986; 81:675.

[35] Kraut RA, Buhle JE. Heroin-Induced Thrombocytopenia Purpura. *O Surg O Med O Path,* 1978; 46(5):637-640.

[36] Ward H, Pallecaros A, Green A, Day S. Health Issue Associated with Increasing Use of "Crack" Cocaine Among Female Sex Workers in London. *Sex Transm Infect,* 2000 Aug; 76 (4):292-3.

[37] Council on Dental Therapeutics. American Dental Association. Sterilization, Infection Control Methods Offer Defense Against AIDS. *ADA News,* August 9, 1983.

[38] Cottone JA, Hepatitis Symposium: Hepatitis B Virus Infection in the Dental Profession. *J Am Dent Assoc,* 1985; 110:617-26.

[39] Prevention of Bacterial Endocarditis: Committee Report of the American Heart Association. *J Am Dent Assoc,* 1985; 110:98-100.

[40] Johnson CD, Brown RS. How Cocaine Abuse Affects Post-extraction Bleeding *JADA,* Dec. 1993; 124:60-62.

[41] Kapila YL, Kashani H. Cocaine-Associated Rapid Gingival Recession and Dental Erosion. A Case Report. *J. Periodont,* 1997; 56:485-488.

[42] DelloRusso NM, Temple HV. Cocaine Effects on Gingiva (Letter to the Editor). *JADA,* 1982; 104:13.

[43] Garguilo AV Jr, Toto PD, Gargiulo AW. Cocaine-Induced Gingival Necrosis. *Periodontal Case Reports,* 1985; 7(2):44-45.

[44] Quart AM, Butkus-Small C, Klein RS. The Cocaine Connection: Users Imperil Their Gingiva. *JADA,* 1991; 122(1):85-87.

[45] Davis RK, Baer PN. Necrotizing Ulcerative Gingivitis in Drug Addict Patients Being Withdrawn from Drugs. *Oral Surg,* 1971; 31(2):200-204.

[46] Cregler LL, Mark H. Special Report: Medical Complications of Cocaine Abuse. *N Engl J Med,* 1986; 315:1495-1500.

[47] Clapp L, Martin B, Beresfort TP. Sublingual Cocaine: Novel Recurrence of an Ancient Practice, *Clin. Neuropharmacol,* 2004 Mar-Apr, 27(2): 92-4.

[48] Klepinger L, Kuhn JK, Josephus T. Prehistoric Dental Calculus Gives vidence for Coca in Early Coastal Ecuador. *Nature,* 1977; 269:506-507.

[49] Thomson AH, *Ethnographic Odontology; the Inca Peruvians Dent Dig,* January 1903,; IX: 22-48.

[50] Leigh RW. Dental Morphology and Pathology of Pre-Spanish Peru. *Am J Phys Anthropol,* 1937; 22:267-296.

[51] Elzay RP, Allison M, Pezzia A. A Comparative Study of Dental Health Status of Five Pre-Columbian Peruvian Cultures. *Am J. Phys Anthropol,* 1977; 46:135-140.

[52] Turner CG. A prehistoric Peruvian Pathology Suggesting Coca Chewing. *Dental Anthropol Newsletter,* 1993; 7:10-11.

[53] Langsjoen OM. Dental Effects of Diet and Coca-leaf Chewing on the Prehistoric Cultures of Northern Chile. *Am J. Physic Anthropol,* 1996, 101:475-489.

[54] Hamner III JE, Villegas OL. The Effect of Coca Leaf Chewing on the Buccal Mucosa of Aymara and Ouechua Indians in Bolivia. *O Surg O Med O Pathol,* 1969; 38(2):287-295.

[55] Hecht SS, Friedman JL. High Incidence of Cervical Dental Caries Among Drug Addicts. *O Surg O Med O Path,* 1949; 2:1428-1442.

[56] Lowenthal AH. Atypical Caries of the Narcotics Addict. *Dent Survey,* 1967; 43:44-47.

[57] Pallasch TJ, Joseph CE, Oral Manifestations of Drug Abuse. *J Psychoative Drugs,* 1987; 19(4):375-7.

[58] Bassiouny MA. *Cocaine and Oral Health: the Philadelphia Study*, 2005; Manuscript in Progress.

[59] Dawes C. A Mathematical Model of Salivary Clearance of Sugar from the Oral Cavity. *Caries Res*, 1983; 17:321-334.

[60] Dale AC. *Salivary glands*. In: Tencate AR. ed. *Oral Histology. Development, Structure, and Function*. 2nd ed. St. Louis: CV Mosby, 1985; 303-331.

[61] Tabak, L. A. In Defense of the Oral Cavity: Structure, Biosynthesis and Function of Salivary Mucins. *Annu Rev Physiol*, 1995; 57:547-564.

[62] Oppenheim FG, Xu T, McMillan F M. et al. Histatins, A Novel Family of Histidine-Rich Proteins in Human Parotid Secretion. Isolation, Characterization, Primary Structure, and Fungistatic Effects on Candida Albicans. J. Biol Chem, 1988; 263:7472-7477.

[63] Sreebny LM, Schwartz SS. *A Reference Guide to Drugs and Dry Mouth*. 2nd Ed. *Gerodontology*, 1997; 14:33-47.

[64] Amstahl A. Wikstrom M. Oral Microflora in Subjects with Reduced Salivary ecretions *J Dent Res*, 1999; 78:1410-1416).

[65] Schmidt-Nielson B. The Solubility of Tooth Substance in Relation to the Composition of Saliva (Thesis) *Acta Odont Scand* (Suppl.), 1946 2:1-88).

[66] Mandel ID. The Function of Saliva. *J Dent Res*, 1987; 66:623-7.

[67] Levine MI. Development of Artificial Salivas. Crit Rev Oral Biol Med, 1993; 4:279-86.

[68] Moss A. Clinical Implications of Recent Advances in Salivary Research. *J. Esthet Dent*, 1995; 7:197-203.

[69] Edwards M, Creanor SL, Faye RH, Gilmour WH. Buffering Capacities of Soft Drinks: the Potential Influence on Dental Erosion. *J. Oral Rehabil*, 1999; 26(12): 923-7.

[70] Batsakis JG. *Physiology*. In: Cummings CW, Fredrickson JM, Harker LA, Krause CJ, Schuller DE, eds. *Otolaryngology-Head and Neck Surgery*. 2nd *ed*. St.Louis: CV Mosby, 1993:986-96.

[71] Guyton AC. *Textbook of Medical Physiology*. 8th ed. Philadelphia: WB Saunders, 1991:711-3.

[72] Ellis GL, Auglair PL. *The Normal Salivary Glands*. In: *Atlas of Tumor Pathology, Tumor of the Salivary Glands* 3rd series, Editor: Rosai J. Washington DC Armed Forces Institute of Pathology, 1996:1-26.

[73] Jensen SB, Pedersen AM, Reibel J and Nauntofte B. *Xerostomia and Hypofunction of the Salivary Glands in Cancer Therapy Support Care Cancer*, 2003; 11:207-225.

[74] Mosby Medical Encyclopedia1992, p 837.

[75] Holbrook WP. Dental Caries and Cariogenic Factors in Pre-school Urban Icelandic Children. *Caries Res*, 1993; 27:424-430.

[76] Kerr DA. and Ash's Oral Pathology: *An Introduction for General and Oral Hygienists*. 5th edition. Phila: Lea and Febinger, 1986.

[77] Winocur E, Gavish A, Volfin G, Halachmi M, Gazit E. Oral Motor Parafunctions Among Heavy Drug Addicts and Their Effects on Signs and Symptoms of Temporomandibular Disorders. *J Orofac Pain*. 2001; 15(1):56-63.

[78] Friedlander AH, Mills MJ, Gorelick DA. Alcoholism and Dental Management. *O Surg O Med O Path*, 1987; 63:42-6.

[79] Kuriloff D, Kimmelman C. Osteocartilagenous Necrosis of the SinoNasal Tract Following Cocaine Abuse. *Laryngoscope*, 1989; 99:918-24.

[80] Libby D, Klein L, Altorki N. Aspiration of the Nasal Septum: A New Complication of Cocaine Abuse. *Ann Intern Med*, 1992; 116:567.

[81] Schweitzer VG. *Osteolytic Sinusitis and Pneumomediastinum: Deceptive Otolaryngologic Complications of Cocaine Abuse*, 1986; 96:206.

[82] Mattson-Gates G, Jabs A, Hug A. Perforation of the Hard Palate Associated with Cocaine Abuse. *Ann Plast Surg*, 1991; 26:466-8.

[83] Becker G, Hill S. Midline Granuloma Due to Illicit Cocaine Use. *Arch Otol Head Neck Surg*, 1988; 114:90-1.

[84] Seyer BA. Grist W, Muller S. Aggressive Destructive Midfacial Lesion from Cocaine Abuse. *O Surg O Med O Path O Rad Endod*, 2002; 94:465-70.

[85] Villa PD. Midfacial Complications of Prolonged Cocaine Snorting. *J Canad Dent Assoc*, 1999; 65(4):218-23.

[86] Lancaster J, Belloso A, Wilson CA, McCormick M. Rare Case of Naso-Oral Fistula with Extensive Osteocartilaginous Necrosis Secondary to Cocaine Abuse: Review of Otolaryngological Presentations in Cocaine Addicts. *J Laryngol Otol*, 2000; 114(8):630-3.

[87] Talbott JF, Gorti GH, Koch RJ. Midfacial Osteomyelitis in a Chronic Cocaine Abuser: A Case Report. *Ear Nose and Throat J*, 2001; 80(10):738-40, 742-3.

[88] Vilela RJ, Langford C, McCullagh L, Kass ES. Cocaine-Induced Oronasal Fistula with External Nasal Erosion but Without Palate Involvement. *Ear Nose Throat J*, 2002; 81(8):562-3.

[89] Mari A, Arranz A, Gimeno X, Lluch J, Pericot J, Escuder O, Monner A, Piulachs P. Nasal Cocaine Abuse and Centrofacial Destructive Process: Report of Three Cases Including Treatment. *O Surg O Med O Path O Rad Endo*, 2002; 93:435-9.

[90] Gertner E, Hamlar D. Necrotizing Granulomatous Vasculitis Associated with Cocaine Use. *J Rheumatol*, 2002; 29(8):1795-7.

[91] Bassiouny MA, Pollack RL: Esthetic Management of Perimolysis with Porcelain Veneers. *JADA*, Sept 1987; 115:412-417.

[92] Bassiouny MA, Zarrinnia K. Dental Erosion: A Complication of Pervasive Developmental Disorder. *J Clinical Pediatric Dentistry*, 2004; 28 (3):273-78.

[93] Bassiouny MA, Yang G. Influence of Drinking Patterns of Carbonated Beverages on Dental Erosion, *Journal of General Dentistry*, 2005; 53(3):205-210.

[94] Tames SM, Goldenring JM. Madarosis from Cocaine Use. *N Engl J Med*, 1986; 314:1324.

[95] Penarrocha M, Gagan JV, Pannarrocha MA, Silvestre FJ. Cluster Headache and Cocaine Use. *O Surg O Med O Path*, 2000; 90; (3):271-4.

[96] Jonson S, O'Meara M, Young JB. Acute Cocaine Poisoning: Importance of Treating Seizures and Acidosis. *Am J Med*, 1983; 75:1061-4.

[97] Olson K, Benowitz NL, Pentel P, Gay G. Management of Cocaine Poisoning. *Ann Emerg med*, 1983; 12:655-7.

In: Substance Abuse: New Research   ISBN 978-1-60456-834-9
Editors: Ethan J. Kerr and Owen E. Gibson   © 2009 Nova Science Publishers, Inc.

Chapter 2

COCAINE-DEPENDENT PATIENTS WITH ANTISOCIAL PERSONALITY DISORDER

Nena Messina, David Farabee and Richard Rawson*

UCLA Integrated Substance Abuse Programs, USA

ABSTRACT

This study compared the efficacy of two commonly used treatment approaches (cognitive–behavioral treatment and contingency management) for the treatment of cocaine dependence among methadone-maintained patients with and without antisocial personality disorder (ASPD). This disorder is strongly associated with substance abuse and recent study findings provide a strong argument against the perception that substance abusers with ASPD are unresponsive to drug treatment.

Method: Patients were randomly assigned to four study conditions including cognitive–behavioral treatment (CBT), contingency management (CM), CBT with CM, or methadone maintenance (also the control condition). The Structural Clinical Interview for Mental Disorders–IV was administered to 108 patients to assess ASPD.

Hypotheses: We hypothesized that ASPD patients in the three treatment conditions (CBT, CM, CBT + CM) would have better treatment responsivity over the 16-week course of treatment than would ASPD patients in the control condition (MM). Moreover, we hypothesized that there would be a cumulative treatment effect among ASPD patients over the course of treatment, with good performance in the CBT condition, better performance in the CM condition, and optimum performance in the CBT + CM condition. Conversely, we hypothesized that the positive treatment effect of CM would decline for the ASPD patients once the incentive was removed (i.e., during the post-treatment outcome period).

Results: A two-way analysis of variance showed that patients with ASPD were more likely to abstain from cocaine use during treatment than patients without ASPD. The strong treatment effect for ASPD patients was primarily due to the CM condition. A

---

* Corresponding Author: Nena Messina, Ph.D., 1640 S. Sepulveda Blvd., Suite 200 Los Angeles, CA. 90025, Phone: (310) 445-0874 ext. 335, Fax: (310) 312-0559, nmessina@ucla.edu, dfarabee@ucla.edu, matrixex@ucla.edu

series of regression analyses showed that ASPD remained significantly related to CM treatment responsivity while controlling for other related factors.

Conclusion: Monetary incentives appear to reduce cocaine use among substance abusers with ASPD more than among those without ASPD. The results of the present study and other recent publications suggest that substance abusers with ASPD may be more responsive to treatment than previously believed.

INTRODUCTION

Antisocial personality disorder (ASPD) is a personality disorder officially recognized by the American Psychiatric Association and often associated with substance abuse and criminal behavior. The key features of the disorder are outlined in the *Diagnostic and Statistical Manual of Mental Disorders,* fourth edition, commonly known as the DSM-IV. The essential feature of this disorder is "a pervasive pattern of disregard for, and violation of, the rights of others that begins in childhood or early adolescence and continues into adulthood" (American Psychiatric Association, 1994: 645). Common signs of childhood development of ASPD are lying, stealing, fighting, resisting authority, and cruelty to animals. Aggressive sexual behavior, drinking and drug abuse are common in adolescence. Adult manifestations include illegal behavior, deceitfulness, recklessness, violence, job troubles, and marital difficulties. (For a complete description of ASPD, see Messina, 2002.)

Previous research indicates that this disorder is also strongly associated with excessive substance abuse in adulthood, with about 40% to 50% of substance abusers meeting the criteria for ASPD (Messina, Wish, & Nemes, 1999; Tims, DeLeon, & Jainchill, 1994) and approximately 90% of persons diagnosed with ASPD being substance abusers (Gerstley, Alterman, McLellan, & Woody, 1990). In light of the prevalence of ASPD among substance-abusing populations, it became imperative that effective treatment strategies be identified. Thus, the recurring association among ASPD, substance abuse, and crime led to a variety of treatment outcome evaluations for substance abusers with this disorder. Yet, there is a widely held belief among treatment providers that persons with ASPD will not respond well to treatment as a direct result of the symptoms of their disorder (e.g., habitual lying and lack of emotional insight). In fact, treatment providers and therapists alike often state that patients with ASPD will manipulate their therapy for their own self-serving needs (Abram, 1989; Davidson & Neale, 1990; Evans & Sullivan, 1990; Forrest, 1992). As one expert notes: "If it is to their advantage to act cured, they will do so, but they will return to former patterns of behavior at the first opportunity" (Coon, 1983: 465). This belief was substantiated by a frequently cited report that stated that, compared to other types of patients, antisocial opioid abusers responded poorly to both routine drug abuse counseling and specialized psychotherapy (Woody, McLellan, Luborsky, & O'Brien, 1985).

Results from more recent studies that have empirically assessed the relationship between ASPD and substance abuse treatment outcomes have not supported the previous findings regarding this disorder and treatment response (Brooner, Kidorf, King, & Stoller, 1998; Gil, Nolimal, & Crowley, 1992; Messina et al., 1999; Silverman et al., 1998). Gil et al. (1992) compared the treatment outcomes of 55 consecutively admitted methadone maintenance patients with ASPD (42%) and those without ASPD. Although the findings were limited by the small sample and ambiguous design, no significant differences were found between those with and those without ASPD on any 12-month outcome variable (e.g., treatment retention, urine test results, therapy session attendance). It appeared that ASPD patients did as well as those without ASPD in a traditional methadone maintenance program. However, a lack of difference did not necessarily imply good treatment responsivity. The authors reported low overall retention in this sample of clients.

Valliant (1975) had previously speculated that structured behavioral programs with incentives for participation might produce the best results for antisocial opioid patients. Evans and Sullivan (1990) also stated that "[it] is highly unlikely that antisocials will develop genuine remorse and altruistic reasons for staying clean and sober. However, they may be interested if it will help them win at poker, make more money, or stay out of jail" (p. 104).

Brooner and his colleagues (1998) directly tested Valliant's hypothesis regarding the use of incentives. Forty opioid abusers with co-occurring ASPD were randomly assigned to an experimental treatment condition combining methadone maintenance and contingency management techniques (i.e., a structural behavioral intervention using rapid delivery of positive and negative contingencies) or a control condition (i.e., standard methadone maintenance). In the experimental condition, take-home methadone doses and dose alterations were contingent on drug-free urine specimens and counseling session attendance. Preliminary findings did not reveal significant differences between the groups; yet, both groups showed marked reductions in heroin and cocaine use during the 17-week outcome evaluation. The authors contend that these findings are not only contrary to what is commonly thought about ASPD clients in traditional methadone treatment, but also about ASPD clients in enhanced methadone (i.e., methadone maintenance combined with contingency management) treatment programs as well. However, this study was limited by a small sample and by the absence of a non-ASPD control group.

Other contingency management approaches include giving vouchers that are exchangeable for goods and services in response to drug-free urine specimens. Silverman et al. (1998) compared the treatment responsiveness of 59 methadone maintenance patients with ASPD (19%) and without ASPD who were participating in voucher-based cocaine abstinence reinforcement therapy. Patients were randomly assigned to two levels of voucher-based interventions or a control group in which vouchers were given on a noncontingent basis. The authors found that both contingent interventions significantly increased abstinence from cocaine and opiates, compared with the control group. Moreover, a diagnosis of ASPD was unrelated to treatment outcomes. However, the small sample size (and low prevalence of ASPD) may have rendered any differences in outcomes between substance abusers with ASPD and those without ASPD difficult to detect.

Another study explored the relationship of ASPD and treatment outcomes in therapeutic communities (TCs) with random assignment of (primarily cocaine dependent) respondents to two residential programs differing primarily in length (Messina et al., 1999). TCs often rely on cognitive behavioral methods to change existing behavior patterns. Clients diagnosed as having ASPD (n=166) were compared to 172 clients with no ASPD on three outcome measures. After controlling for relevant factors, clients with ASPD were as likely to complete treatment as other clients and they exhibited the same patterns of reduced drug use and criminal activity as did non-ASPD clients.

The findings from the above recent studies could indicate that ASPD is not a strong predictor of treatment nonresponsivity, as previously believed.The implications of these findings are important in light of the fact that substance abusers with ASPD are more likely than those without ASPD to engage in violent and serious criminal behaviors (Abram, 1989; Brooner, Schmidt, Felch, & Bigelow, 1992). However, the empirical literature assessing the relationship between ASPD and substance abuse treatment outcomes is lacking, and the existing research is limited by small sample sizes, nonrandom designs, and/or the absence of an appropriate control group. The present study sought to examine the relationship between ASPD and substance abuse treatment responsivity by addressing these primary weaknesses of the literature.

This study directly compares the efficacy of two commonly used treatment approaches (cognitive behavioral treatment and contingency management) for the treatment of cocaine dependence among methadone-maintained patients *with and without* ASPD. These two treatment approaches represent two of the most promising psychological-behavioral approaches for the treatment of substance abuse. However, the rationales for these two approaches differ considerably. Cognitive behavioral treatment (CBT) strategies are based upon social learning principles (Bandura, 1977). These techniques include a wide range of treatment strategies designed to prevent relapse to drug use. The primary focus of CBT is maintaining a habit-changing process. This process is twofold: to prevent the occurrence of initial lapses to drug use after one has embarked on a program of habit change, and to prevent any lapse from escalating into total relapse (Marlatt & Gordon, 1985).

Contingency management (CM) techniques, on the other hand, are founded on principles of operant conditioning (Skinner, 1938). The CM techniques create systems of incentives and disincentives to motivate behavior change. Some positive incentive strategies include take-home methadone doses and cash incentives for drug-free urine specimens. One of the most promising applications of CBT and CM is in the area of cocaine abuse treatment. Cocaine abuse continues to be a serious public health problem and is an important factor in drug-related crime and violence (Everingham & Rydell, 1994). Moreover, cocaine abuse among methadone-maintained patients continues to be a serious challenge for treatment clinicians (Farabee, Rawson, & McCann, 2002; Rawson, Obert, McCann, & Ling, 1991; Silverman, Chutuape, Bigelow, & Stitzer, 1999). Both CBT and CM have been shown to be effective in treating cocaine-dependent patients (Carroll, 1999; Carroll et al., 1994; Farabee et al., 2002; Foote et al., 1994; Marlatt & Gordon, 1985; Silverman et al., 1996; Silverman et al., 1998; Silverman et al., 1999).

This study offers an excellent opportunity to compare the relative efficacy of an information-based "talk therapy" (CBT) with a purely operant paradigm (CM) for producing desired behavior change among substance-abusing clients with co-occurring ASPD. Furthermore, this study assesses the relative efficacy of combining these interventions (CBT+CM) for reducing cocaine use among methadone-maintained patients with ASPD. Since all patients are involved in a "platform" condition of methadone maintenance, it is possible to use a study design in which three active cocaine treatment conditions (CBT, CM, and CBT+CM) are compared to a control condition in which patients receive no additional treatment for their cocaine disorder.

Because of the limited literature (both in number and design) regarding substance abuse treatment responsivity for ASPD patients, findings are somewhat difficult to interpret. It is possible that group differences within the methadone maintenance studies have not been found because of the low power generated by the insufficient sample sizes. For example, it is likely that Brooner et al. (1998) would have found a significant difference between the ASPD patients in the experimental (CM) condition and the ASPD patients in the control condition had they used a larger sample. (By our calculations, their preliminary study generated a power of only .07, with an effect size of .15). The ASPD patients in the CM condition had a larger number of drug-free urine specimens, on average, than did the ASPD patients in the control condition. Monetary incentives for cocaine abstinence could be a strong external motivator for patients with ASPD.

Monetary incentives *combined* with drug-relapse education and peer support (i.e., CBT) might prove to be a strong treatment intervention for co-disordered patients.

Therefore, we hypothesized that ASPD patients in the three treatment conditions (CBT, CM, CBT+CM) would have better treatment responsivity over the 16-week course of treatment than would ASPD patients in the control condition (i.e., methadone maintenance only). Moreover, we hypothesized that there would be a cumulative treatment effect among ASPD patients over the course of treatment, with good performance in the CBT condition, better performance in the CM condition, and optimum performance in the CBT+CM condition.

$$[CBT] < [CM] < [CBT + CM]$$

Conversely, we hypothesized that the positive treatment effect of CM would decline for the ASPD patients once the incentive is removed (i.e., during the posttreatment outcome period). Because it has been speculated that ASPD patients have little internal motivation, it is reasonable to hypothesize that they will be less likely to remain abstinent in the absence of external incentives. Because the available literature assessing the relationship between ASPD and treatment outcomes is lacking, we also posed the more general research question: Is a diagnosis of ASPD a significant predictor of treatment outcomes?

METHOD

The data for this study is from the "Behavioral/Cognitive Behavioral Trial for Cocaine Abuse Project", a treatment outcome study for methadone-maintained, cocaine-dependent patients. The main treatment outcome report for this project can be found in Rawson et al. (2002). The current chapter focuses on the ASPD diagnosis and its relation to treatment outcomes.

Patients

Study participants were volunteers from two licensed narcotic treatment programs in Los Angeles, California (Matrix Institute and West Los Angeles Treatment Program). To be eligible for the study, all candidates were required: (1) to have been on methadone maintenance treatment at one of the two clinics for a minimum of 90 days; (2) to meet DSM-IV criteria for cocaine dependence; and (3) to show evidence of cocaine use (cocaine-metabolite positive urine sample) during the month prior to study enrollment. Individuals were ineligible if they (1) were also dependent upon alcohol or benzodiazepines to the point of requiring withdrawal medication; (2) if they had received specific treatment for cocaine in the previous 30 days; or (3) if they were court-mandated to treatment.

During a 30-month recruitment period, 120 individuals met study eligibility criteria, were enrolled in the study, and were randomly assigned into one of the four study conditions (CBT, CM, CBT+CM, or MM). [†] At admission, slightly more than half (56%) of the sample was male and the mean age was 43. With respect to race/ethnicity, 38% of the sample were White, 31% African American, 28% Hispanic, and 6% "other." The majority of patients (72%) had completed at least 12 years of school. A small percentage (15%) of the sample reported that they had steady employment over the past 3 years. Among the four conditions, none of the between-group differences in patient characteristics was statistically significant. Similar to the demographic profiles, self-reported prevalence of past-month drug and alcohol use did not vary significantly by study condition.

Procedures

Random assignment into one of the four study conditions (30 patients in each condition) took place following informed consent procedures and a 2-week baseline data collection period.

Demographic and background information was captured using the Addiction Severity Index (ASI). The ASI is a semi-structured interview instrument used for both clinical and research purposes to determine service needs (McLellan et al., 1992). It is a comprehensive instrument consisting of questions pertaining to demographics, employment, living situation, past and current health status, past and current drug use, past and current drug treatment history, past and current criminal and criminal justice involvement, and past and current mental health status and treatment.

The Structural Clinical Interview for Mental Disorders-IV (SCID) was administered during the first 30 days of study participation by a trained masters- or Ph.D.-level staff person to confirm the substance use diagnosis and to determine the presence of ASPD. The SCID is a semi-structured interview for making Axis I and Axis II diagnoses based on DSM-IV criteria (Kranzler, Rounsaville, & Tennen, 1995). SCID interviews were supervised and reviewed by a Ph.D.-level staff member. A total of 108 clients were evaluated by the SCID diagnostic interview and are the focus of this study (12 patients dropped-out of treatment prior to administration of the SCID). Forty-four percent of the target sample met the DSM-IV criteria for ASPD. The frequency of ASPD among the study patients is consistent with other reports on the psychiatric co-morbidity among methadone maintained-individuals (Rounseville, Eyre, Weissman, & Kleber, 1983; Sievewright & Daly, 1997).

[†] Only four individuals volunteered for study participation in the first 60 days of recruitment. The two study clinics operated on a fee-for-service basis in which patients paid either $140 (Matrix Clinic) or $180 (West LA Clinic) per month for methadone maintenance treatment services. Only after a $40 per month methadone program fee-reduction was offered as an incentive for study participation did study recruitment become adequate. Thus, the group of individuals who participated in this study can be characterized as having relatively low motivation to stop their cocaine use as defined by the requirement of a $40 per month incentive to encourage study participation.

Treatment Interventions

CBT procedures. The CBT procedure consisted of a total of 48 group sessions (3 per week for 16 weeks). Typical groups had four to eight patients. Each group session was scheduled to be 90 minutes in duration, and the material for each session was provided in a workbook. Each workbook presented a concept or a brief written exercise that explained or illustrated an aspect of cognitive-behavioral therapy. This method has been found in previous work by Rawson, Obert, McCann, Smith, and Scheffey (1989) to help stimulant users achieve and maintain abstinence. Many of the concepts were distilled from Marlatt and Gordon (1985) and/or are consistent with the National Institute on Drug Abuse manual on CBT (Carroll, 1999). Each session was led by a master's level therapist who had received 40-60 hours of supervised training in delivering the materials in a standardized manner. All sessions were audiotaped and reviewed by a counseling supervisor. Feedback was given to the therapist to shape and reinforce consistency.

The session format consisted of the topic being introduced by the staff member/group leader, the sheet being read aloud by the leader or a participant volunteer, and group members being given approximately 5 to 10 minutes to discuss the relevance of the topic to him/herself. Those individuals who were unwilling to discuss the topic were allowed to sit and listen. At the end of the topic discussion (typically 45-60 minutes into the session), each individual was asked to discuss his/her drug use/nonuse over the previous time period since the last group. The group leader and other group members verbally reinforced those reporting no use, less use, and/or the initiation of some new prosocial behavior. Finally, each member was asked to describe his/her behavioral plan for the time period leading up to the next session. Plans that included activities based upon the cognitive behavioral principles presented in the treatment groups received praise from the group leader and other members.

CM procedures. Patients in the CM-only condition were required to provide three urine samples per week and meet briefly (2-5 minutes) with the CM technician. The meetings with the CM technician covered four topics: (1) a review of the results of the urine test (tested immediately using enzyme multiplied immunoassay tests [EMIT]); (2) the delivery of the appropriate paper voucher certificate, if earned; (3) a discussion of how the voucher or accumulated voucher account could be redeemed; and (4) the delivery of the earned items when the vouchers were redeemed. On occasions when vouchers were earned, the CM technician provided praise and encouragement for successful performance. Patients who provided samples positive for stimulants (there were no contingencies for drug use other than stimulants) were not "scolded" or punished (other than the punishment of withholding the voucher).

The voucher value was based upon an escalating schedule that was similar to that used in previous studies (Higgins et al., 1993, 1994). The initial voucher value started at $2.50 per stimulant-negative sample, increasing in value by $1.25 with each successive negative sample, and with a $10 bonus for three consecutive stimulant-negative samples. The maximum voucher value was $46.25 per sample (excluding the $10 bonus). Across the course of the entire 16 weeks, the maximum possible earning (48 consecutive stimulant-free samples) was $1,277.50. Cash was never given to patients. As the voucher account increased in value as a result of stimulant-free urine samples, patients were encouraged to "spend" their savings on items that could support drug-free activities.

Patients in all study conditions received identical methadone maintenance (MM) services. The average dose of methadone at baseline was 72 milligrams for the CBT group, 62 milligrams for the CM group, 68 milligrams for the CBT+CM group, and 71 milligrams for the MM-only group. Participation in the study had no effect on the nature of their MM treatment. There were very clear rules for the termination of patients from the study. Termination could be a result of: (1) study completion (16-weeks); (2) missing two consecutive weekly data collection visits; or (3) missing either six consecutive CBT groups or six consecutive urine samples. Therefore, a consistent 2-week absence from protocol participation was the criterion for study termination across all study conditions.

Study Measures

The cocaine treatment intervention lasted 16 weeks for all conditions. Cocaine use, as measured by urinalysis, was the principal dependent measure during and after treatment. All study patients were required to give three urine samples per week throughout the 16-week study period and at each of the three follow-up interviews (17, 26, and 52 weeks). All samples were analyzed for metabolites of cocaine (benzoylecognine, BE) and methamphetamine. (Methamphetamine was included as a target along with cocaine to prevent "stimulant switching"; however, the frequency of methamphetamine use in this population was almost nonexistent. Hence, the study findings are specific to cocaine). A 300 ng/ml urinary BE cutoff was used to define a positive sample. All samples were analyzed on-site using EMIT (SYVA) reagent test procedures. All samples were monitored (i.e., collected in bottles equipped with temperature strips, and the bathrooms where samples were collected did not have hot water to prevent tampering). In addition, approximately 33% of all samples were collected under observation. Observation of urine specimens was conducted on a random basis. All subjects were breath alcohol tested at the time of the collection of each urine sample.

Follow-up urine specimens were analyzed for cocaine, methamphetamine, metabolites of illicit opiates, benzodiazepines, barbiturates, and cannabinoids. Ninety percent of the sample provided urine specimens at the 17-week follow-up, 83% provided specimens at the 26-week follow-up, and 83% provided specimens at the 52-week follow-up. There were no significant differences in follow-up rates between those with and those without ASPD across the four study conditions at any of the follow-up periods (percentages shown below).

- *17-Week Follow-Up*: Non-ASPD CBT = 86%; ASPD CBT = 93%; Non-ASPD CM = 92%; ASPD CM = 93%; Non-ASPD CBT+CM = 89%; ASPD CBT+CM = 100%; Non- ASPD control = 87%; ASPD control = 83%.
- *26-Week Follow-Up*: Non-ASPD CBT = 79%; ASPD CBT = 93%; Non-ASPD CM = 83%; ASPD CM = 87%; Non-ASPD CBT+CM = 89%; ASPD CBT+CM = 86%; Non-ASPD control = 73%; ASPD control = 75%.

Table 1. Sample Characteristics at Admission, by ASPD Status (N = 108)

Characteristics	No ASPD (N = 60) %	ASPD (N = 48) %	Total (N = 108) %
Gender			
Male	43**	71**	56
Female	57	29	44
	100%	100%	100%
Race/Ethnicity			
White	43	31	38
Black	40**	21**	31
Hispanic/Other	17	48	31
	100%	100%	100%
Mean Age at Admission (SD)	43.7 (7.6)	43.5 (8.1)	43
Education			
Less than 12 years	18*	40*	28
High-school Degree or more	82	60	72
	100%	100%	100%
Full Time Employment Past 3 Years	17	13	15
Study Condition			
CBT	23	29	26
CM	20	31	25
CBT+CM	32	15	24
MM	25	25	25
	100%	100%	100%

*$p < .05$. **$p < .01$.

52-Week Follow-Up: Non-ASPD CBT = 79%; ASPD CBT = 86%; Non-ASPD CM = 75%; ASPD CM = 93%; Non-ASPD CBT+CM = 95%; ASPD CBT+CM = 71%; Non-ASPD control = 73%; ASPD control = 83%.

Data Analysis

The distribution of demographic and drug-use characteristics by ASPD status was evaluated using chi-square analysis and t-tests. Similarly, the distribution of SCID-I and II diagnoses across study conditions was evaluated by chi-square analysis. In-treatment cocaine use measures were analyzed using a Two-Way Analysis of Variance (ANOVA). To control for inflated alpha error, Tukey-Kramer tests were used for all post hoc comparisons. In addition, a series of regression analyses were conducted to assess in-treatment cocaine use while controlling for pre-existing differences between those with and those without ASPD.

To assess cocaine and heroin use following treatment, separate chi-square analyses were conducted for those with and those without ASPD at each of the follow-up time periods. All statistical tests were considered significant at p ≤ .05 and were two-tailed.

RESULTS

Demographic characteristics for ASPD and non-ASPD patients were similar across the four study conditions; however, small cell sizes limited reliable statistical inference. Although patients were randomly assigned to the study conditions, they were not randomly assigned by ASPD diagnosis. To further explore any pre-existing differences, all ASPD patients were compared with all non-ASPD patients with regard to their demographic and drug use characteristics.

Table 2. Self-Reported Drug/Alcohol Use 30 Days Prior to Admission, by ASPD Status (N = 108)

Substance Use 30 Days Prior to Admission	No ASPD (N = 60) %	ASPD (N = 48) %	Total (N = 108) %
Alcohol Use	57	60	58
Alcohol Use to Intoxication	23	35	29
Marijuana	30	27	29
Heroin Use	58*	79*	68
Other Opiates	08**	31**	18
Cocaine Use	100	98	99
Amphetamines	03	08	06

*p < .05. **p < .01.

Consistent with previous literature, patients diagnosed with ASPD were significantly more likely to be male (71% vs. 43%, p < .01) and to have less than a high school education (40% vs. 18%, p < .05) than non-ASPD patients (see Table 1). With regard to ethnicity, patients with ASPD were significantly more likely than non-ASPD patients to be Hispanic (48% vs. 17%, p < .01). No significant differences between those with and those

Table 3. SCID-I and II Diagnoses, by Study Condition (N = 108)[a]

Diagnoses[b]	CBT	CM	CBT+CM	MM	Total
	(N=28) %	(N=27) %	(N=26) %	(N=27) %	(N=108) %
SCID-I					
Substance Use Disorder	100	100	100	100	100
Mood Disorder	18	33	23	19	23
Anxiety Disorder	18	37	27	19	25
SCID-II					
Antisocial Personality Disorder (ASPD)	50	56	27	44	44
All Diagnoses					
Substance Use Disorder Only	29	23	50	36	34
Substance Use and Other Axis I Disorders	21	22	23	19	21
Substance Use and ASPD	36	22	12	26	24
Substance Use, ASPD, and Other Axis I Dis.	<u>14</u>	<u>33</u>	<u>15</u>	<u>19</u>	<u>21</u>
	100%	100%	100%	100%	100%

[a] N's vary slightly due to missing data.
[b] Only diagnoses prevalent in 5% or more of the sample are shown.
Note. Differences are not significant.

without ASPD were found with regard to age or employment, and patients with ASPD were equally distributed among the study conditions.

Comparisons of demographic characteristics of *ASPD-patients only* across the four study conditions were also conducted. No significant differences were found with regard to age, gender, race/ethnicity, or high school education (results are not shown).

Table 2 displays the self-reported drug and alcohol use patterns by ASPD status during the 30 days prior to study admission. Those with ASPD were significantly more likely to have used heroin (79% vs. 58%, $p < .05$) and other opiates (31% vs. 8%, $p < .01$) during this time period, than non-ASPD patients. No other substance-use differences were found. Cocaine (99%) and heroin (68%) were most likely to be used during the 30 days prior to study admission, followed by alcohol (58%), marijuana (29%), other opiates (18%), and amphetamines (6%).

Table 3 displays the prevalence of ASPD, substance use disorder, and other SCID-I psychiatric disorders by study condition. Only those diagnoses prevalent in more than 5% of the sample are shown. There were no significant differences among the four study conditions with regard to prevalence of psychiatric disorders. All subjects met the criteria for substance use disorder and almost half (44%) had co-occurring ASPD. Of those evaluated by the SCID, 34% had no disorders other than substance use, 21% had substance use and other Axis I disorders, 24% had substance use with co-occurring ASPD, and 21% had substance use disorder, co-occurring ASPD, and other Axis I disorders. (All analyses combine clients with substance use disorder only and those with other Axis I disorders into the non-ASPD group.)

In-Treatment Performance

Treatment retention. Treatment retention is frequently an important outcome indicator and is sometimes used as one measure of treatment efficacy. In this study, the value of treatment retention as a dependent measure was compromised by the necessity to reduce patients' monthly methadone program fees by $40 to promote study enrollment. Therefore, not surprisingly, there was no significant difference in study retention for patients with and those without ASPD across four study conditions. The average number of weeks in treatment for the ASPD group was 14.7 (SD = 3.4), ranging from 12 to 16. The average number of weeks in treatment for the non-ASPD group was 13.2 (SD = 4.9), ranging from 10 to 15 weeks.

Cocaine-abstinence during treatment. The primary dependent measure in this study was cocaine use as measured by urine toxicology. Since retention in treatment was not significantly different for those with and without ASPD across study conditions, the most direct measure of cocaine use across the 16 weeks of the trial was the number of *cocaine-negative* urine samples given by each participant during their 48 opportunities to give samples (3 times per week for 16 weeks). There were no significant differences between those with and those without ASPD across the four study conditions with regard to the rates of missing urines.

Table 4. Treatment Effectiveness Scores for In-Treatment Cocaine-Free Urine Samples, by Study Condition and ASPD Status

ASPD Status	CBT	CM*	CBT+CM	MM
No ASPD				
Mean TES for Cocaine (s.d)	17.6 (17.9)$_a$	25.5 (20.7)$_a$	24.2 (21.1)$_a$	14.5 (16.9)$_a$
		ASPD		
Mean TES for Cocaine (S.D.)	24.8 (15.6)$_a$	39.4 (11.4)$_b$	37.7 (13.3)$_{ab}$	9.3 (11.3)$_c$

Note. Subscripts represent the results of pairwise comparisons between study conditions; means that *do not* have a subscript in common are significantly different from each other ($p < .05$).
*The CM condition was the only condition with a significant difference between those with and without ASPD ($p < .05$).

A Two-Way ANOVA was performed to determine differences in the mean number of cocaine-negative samples (CNS) provided by ASPD status and by study condition. The possibility of an interaction effect (ASPD status X study condition) was also explored. We initially asked if ASPD would be a significant predictor of in-treatment responsivity. There was a significant main effect for ASPD status. The mean number of CNS for patients with ASPD (CNS = 27.4, SD = 17.5) was significantly higher than the mean number of CNS for those without ASPD (CNS = 20.5, SD = 19.4) [F (1,107) = 4.74, p < .05), suggesting that ASPD patients performed better during the 16-week treatment course than non-ASPD patients. However, there was no interaction effect between ASPD status and study condition.

We also hypothesized that ASPD patients in the three cocaine treatment conditions (CBT, CM, CBT+CM) would have better outcomes than ASPD patients in the control condition (MM). This hypothesis was supported. Pairwise comparisons of the mean number of CNS indicated that ASPD patients in each of the treatment conditions had significantly higher scores than those in the control condition (CBT = 24.8; CM = 39.4; CBT+CM = 37.7; vs. MM = 9.3, p < .05). The same pattern was found among the study conditions for the non-ASPD group, but differences were not statistically significant (see Table 4).

The above findings indicate that ASPD patients responded positively to the three cocaine treatment conditions; however, we also hypothesized a cumulative treatment effect for ASPD patients, with optimum performance in the CBT+CM condition (CBT< CM < CBT+CM). This hypothesis was not supported. Pairwise comparisons did show that the mean number of CNS for the ASPD patients in the CM condition was significantly higher than the mean number of CNS for the ASPD patients in the CBT-only condition (CBT = 24.8 vs. CM = 39.4, p < .05). However, no differences were found for the ASPD patients in the CBT+CM condition compared with the ASPD patients in the CM or CBT-only groups (shown in Table 4).

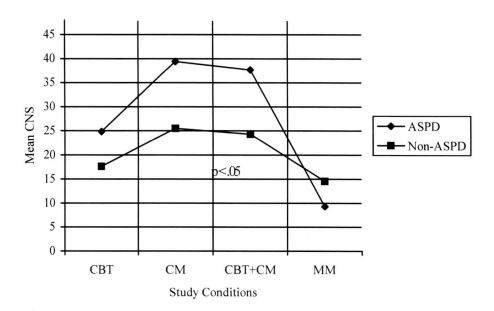

Figure 1. Cocaine-Negative Specimens Provided During Treatment (N=108)

Moreover, ASPD patients in the CM condition performed significantly better than the non-ASPD CM patients (ASPD/CM CNS = 39.4 vs. non-ASPD/CM CNS = 25.5, p < .05). The differences in CNS means were not significant for ASPD and non-ASPD patients in any of the other study conditions (shown in Figure 1).

The above bivariate analyses, however, do not take into account pre-existing differences between those with and without ASPD that might be related to in-treatment performance. Initially, no demographic differences were found between those with and those without ASPD in any of the treatment conditions; however, when we compared *all* of the ASPD patients with *all* of the non-ASPD patients (see Tables 1 and 2), some pre-existing differences were evident (i.e., gender, race, high school education, and opiate use). Therefore, we decided to further explore the association of ASPD with CM treatment using multivariate analyses. Because the total number of patients in the CM condition fell below 30, we were limited in the number of independent variables (or predictors) that could be included in the multivariate analyses (Keppel, 1991). Thus, we conducted a series of regressions pairing ASPD with each of the above characteristics. In all of these pairings, a diagnosis of ASPD remained significantly related to the mean number of CNS (p<.01). We further confirmed the *lack* of an association of ASPD to in-treatment performance among the other study conditions (analyses not shown).

Post-Treatment Performance

Cocaine urinalysis results for ASPD patients at each follow-up period. We hypothesized that the positive treatment effect of CM would decline for the ASPD patients once the incentives were removed (i.e., no vouchers were given during the posttreatment outcome periods). This hypothesis was not supported. ASPD patients in the CM conditions continued to abstain from cocaine use throughout the three follow-up time periods. Figure 2 shows that ASPD patients in the CM-only condition were as likely as those in the other study conditions to have cocaine-free urine specimens at weeks 17, 26, and 52. In fact, over 70% of the CM-only group provided cocaine-free specimens at each follow-up time period. Overall, differences in percentages of cocaine-free specimens between the treatment groups and the control group were not significant at weeks 17 and 26. However, percentages were significantly different at week 52, indicating that between 65% and 80% of the ASPD patients in any of the three treatment conditions were abstaining from cocaine use at the 52-week follow-up period, compared to 20% in the control condition ($p < .05$).

Cocaine urinalysis results for non-ASPD patients at each follow-up period. The rates of cocaine abstinence for the non-ASPD patients did not follow the same trends as those for the ASPD patients. Figure 3 shows that the percentages of cocaine-free specimens were similar across the four study groups for each follow-up time period (i.e., no significant differences were found). However, the CBT-only group was the only treatment group that showed substantial increases in abstinence over the three follow-up time periods (33%, 64%, and 81% respectively).

Post-treatment responsivity. To assess overall differences in posttreatment performance between those with and those without ASPD, we created a posttreatment responsivity measure that totaled the percentages of patients who had cocaine-free urine specimens at all three of the follow-up periods. Figure 4 shows the posttreatment results by study condition for those with and those without ASPD. Among non-ASPD patients, there were no significant differences in cocaine negative specimens at each of the three follow-up time periods.

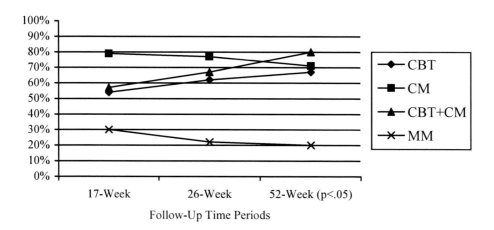

Figure 2. Cocaine-Free Urine Specimens During Follow-Up [ASPD Patients].

In contrast, the ASPD patients in the three cocaine treatment conditions showed large differences in continued abstinence from cocaine compared with those in the control condition ($p < .05$). Over half of the ASPD patients in the CM-only condition had cocaine-

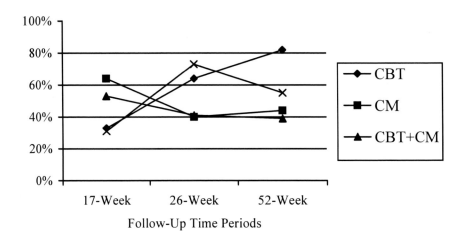

Figure 3. Cocaine-Free Urine Specimens During Follow-Up [Non-ASPD Patients].

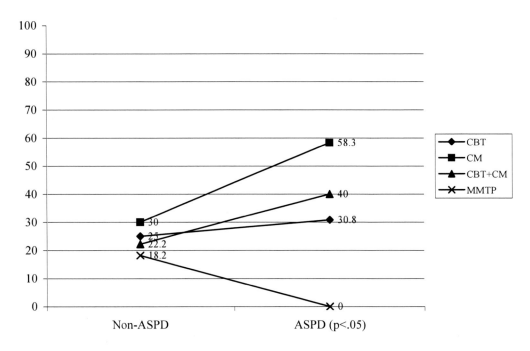

Figure 4: Percentage of Cocaine-Free Urine Specimens at All Three Follow-Up Periods (N=91).

free urine results at each follow-up interview (58%), followed by those in the CBT+CM condition (40%), and those in the CBT-only condition (31%). None of the MM-only group had three consecutive cocaine-free urine results.

Because the posttreatment findings regarding cocaine use were not as expected, we explored the possibility that ASPD patients were more likely than non-ASPD patients to be using heroin at the follow-up time periods. These results are shown below.

Post-treatment heroin urinalysis results. Overall, study patients were less likely to abstain from heroin use, compared to cocaine use, at the three follow-up time periods regardless of treatment group or ASPD status (see Figures 5 and 6). However, abstinence rates were not trivial. At the 26-week follow-up, between 40% and 50% of the ASPD patients tested negative for heroin, whereas between 50% and 60% of the non-ASPD patients tested negative for heroin. In addition, non-ASPD patients in the CBT-only condition were significantly more likely to abstain from heroin at the 17-week follow-up compared with those in the other treatment conditions (CBT = 75% vs. CM = 36% vs. CBT+CM = 35% vs. MM = 23%, p < .05).

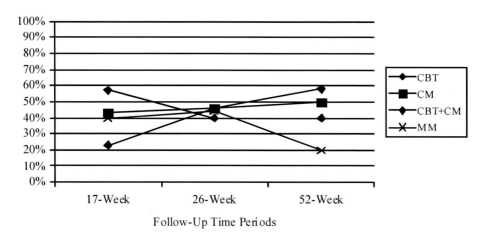

Figure 5: Heroin-Free Urine Specimens During Follow-Up [ASPD Participants].

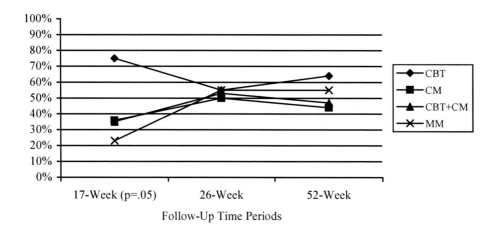

Figure 6: Heroin-Free Urine Specimens During Follow-Up[Non-ASPD Participants].

CONCLUSION

Recent findings of successful treatment outcomes for methadone-maintained patients with ASPD provides a strong argument against the perception that substance abusers with

ASPD are unresponsive to drug treatment (Brooner et al., 1998; Gil et al., 1992; Silverman et al., 1998). However, these studies have been limited by small sample sizes and ambiguous designs. The current study sought to overcome the limitations of the previous research. The primary goal of this study was to determine the efficacy of two commonly used treatment approaches, separately and combined, for the treatment of cocaine dependence in methadone-maintained patients with co-occurring ASPD.

In-Treatment Responsivity

Three major trends of in-treatment responsivity are evident. First, in contrast to previous findings (and beliefs), we found that a diagnosis of ASPD was significantly and positively related to treatment responsivity. Those with ASPD were more likely to abstain from cocaine use during treatment than those without ASPD. Second, ASPD patients in each of the treatment conditions performed significantly better than ASPD patients in the control condition, whereas no differences in performance by study condition were found for the non-ASPD patients. Third, the strong treatment effect for ASPD patients was primarily due to the CM condition. During the 16-week course of treatment, those in the CM condition were significantly more likely to abstain from cocaine use than those in the CBT-only condition. In contrast, abstinence levels in the combined treatment group (CBT+CM) fell between the CBT- and CM-only levels and did not differ significantly from either. Furthermore, ASPD patients in the CM condition were significantly more likely to abstain from cocaine use than non-ASPD patients in the CM condition, even after controlling for pre-existing differences.

As earlier theorists hypothesized (Evans & Sullivan, 1990; Valliant, 1975), monetary incentives appear to be a successful treatment intervention for reducing cocaine use among substance abusers with co-occurring ASPD, and a more successful intervention than for those without ASPD. Furthermore, patients with ASPD responded significantly better to this type of intervention than ASPD patients in "talk-based therapy." The larger question, however, was whether the positive treatment effects of the CM intervention would continue beyond the course of treatment, once the incentive was removed.

Post-Treatment Responsivity

Four major results are evident from our posttreatment outcomes. First, and contrary to our hypothesis, ASPD patients in the CM conditions continued to abstain from cocaine use throughout the three follow-up periods. Although differences in cocaine abstinence between the groups were not significant, ASPD patients in the CM conditions appeared to maintain the highest levels of posttreatment cocaine abstinence. In addition, comparable numbers of ASPD and non-ASPD patients were abstaining from heroin at the follow-up time periods. Second, ASPD patients in all three treatment conditions were significantly more likely to abstain from cocaine use at the 52 week follow-up than those in the control condition. Third, a clear pattern of posttreatment performance between the treatment groups was not evident for the non-ASPD patients. Non-ASPD patients in the CM conditions appeared to do well at the first follow-up, but their performance declined substantially during the remaining follow-up periods. In contrast, non-ASPD patients in the CBT-only group were the only treatment group whose performance increased over the follow-up time periods. And fourth, ASPD patients in each of the treatment conditions were significantly more likely to test negative for cocaine at *all* three of the follow-up periods than those in the MM-only condition, whereas no differences were found for non-ASPD patients. Most importantly, ASPD patients in the CM condition were twice as likely as non-ASPD patients in the CM condition to have negative urine test results for cocaine at all follow-up periods.

These findings provide a strong argument against the perception that substance abusers with ASPD are unresponsive to drug treatment. Consequently, these findings are important in light of treatment program exclusionary criteria and current public policy. Many substance abuse treatment programs across the nation exclude persons with ASPD on the assumption that they will not respond well to treatment efforts (Messina et al., 1999). Furthermore, a diagnosis of ASPD is among the exclusionary criteria for Maryland's newly constructed Public Mental Health System, and ASPD is the only personality diagnosis deemed untreatable within this system of health service delivery (Brooner et al., 1998). The results of the present study and other recent publications suggest that substance abusers with ASPD may be more responsive to treatment than previously believed.

Study Strengths

The primary strength of our study was the rigorous study design. Random assignment of patients across study conditions created comparable groups. As a result, any differences between group performance tend to reflect the effect of the treatment intervention, rather than error variance (Bordens & Abbott, 1991). Random assignment also eliminated the issue of self-selection, which can be affected by such client attributes as personal motivation, perception of treatment modality, and treatment availability (Hser, 1995). In addition, the "platform" condition of methadone maintenance made it possible to use a study design with a true control condition.

Another strength of our study was the high prevalence rate of ASPD (45%), which is similar to other estimates of ASPD among methadone-maintained patients (ranging from 25% to 54%; Rounsaville, Eyre, Weissman, & Kleber, 1983). The high prevalence of this disorder within our sample allowed us to make comparisons of ASPD patients across study conditions, as well as between those with and those without ASPD. Thus, we were able to assess the treatment responsivity of ASPD patients in each treatment condition and compare their performance to those without ASPD.

The use of objective measures of drug use to assess treatment outcomes was an additional strength of this study. Self-reported drug use may be considerably less valid than previously reported (Messina, Wish, Nemes, & Wraight, 2000). For example, Wish, Hoffman, and Nemes (1997) found that among substance-abusing populations, clients were more likely to truthfully report heroin use than cocaine use. The authors further suggest that self-reports may be less valid at follow-up than at intake.

Study Limitations

Some limitations of this study should also be kept in mind when interpreting the results. The primary limitation is the sample size. Although our study had a larger sample than previous research among methadone-maintained patients, our posttreatment comparisons were limited by small cell sizes due to the four study conditions. However, we were able to improve power as compared to our calculations for Brooner's (1998) study. (Power calculation for our study =.47, effect size = .37; power calculation for Brooner = .07, effect size = .15).

Another limitation of this study (and others) is the existence of other psychiatric disorders among the sample. Patients with and without ASPD may have been diagnosed with various other psychiatric disorders. It is difficult to know the degree to which the various combinations of other disorders confounded the distinction between those with and those without ASPD, or if the presence of additional psychiatric disorders in patients with ASPD moderates the effect of the ASPD diagnosis on treatment response. However, recent findings from a large sample of methadone-maintained patients (N = 518) demonstrated minor differences between patients with ASPD only and patients with ASPD and other psychiatric disorders (King, Kidorf, Stoller, Carter, & Brooner, 2001). ASPD-only patients exhibited higher rates of heroin use during treatment, whereas ASPD patients with additional disorders exhibited higher rates of benzodiazepine use. No differences between the two groups were found for cocaine use during treatment.

An additional roadblock facing those who study and treat ASPD is the lack of agreement about a basic definition and the use of different definitions. There is much controversy among social scientists and clinicians over the proper measurement of ASPD among substance abusers. Although social scientists most often use diagnostic interviews that follow DSM-IV criteria to assess ASPD (such as the SCID-II), many have raised concerns about possible limitations of the DSM (Messina, Wish, Hoffman, & Nemes, 2001). It has been suggested that the DSM criteria for ASPD focus on behavioral characteristics instead of underlying personality traits and do not require that ASPD occur independently of substance abuse (Gerstley et al., 1990). Rounsaville et al. (1983) suggest that clients whose antisocial activities are independent of the need to obtain drugs are "primary antisocial addicts" and those whose antisocial activities are directly related to drug use are "secondary antisocial addicts." The authors speculated that secondary antisocial addicts might have better treatment responses. If most of our sample members were secondary antisocial addicts, it could account for their more positive treatment outcomes.

Summary

The relationships between ASPD, substance abuse, and crime is the nexus of a major social problem and understanding the interactions among these patterns of behavior will help identify the individuals and groups who most need effective intervention. The findings from the current study and other recent literature indicate that substance abusers with co-occurring ASPD can benefit from drug treatment programs. Furthermore, methadone-maintained ASPD patients participating in CM interventions show substantial reductions in cocaine use beyond the intervention period. It is therefore suggested that treatment programs make efforts to attract and retain substance abusers with a diagnosis of ASPD. Future research should continue to explore the many issues surrounding the diagnosis of ASPD, as well as its relationship to treatment outcomes.

ACKNOWLEDGMENTS

We are grateful to the staff and the patients at the Matrix Institute and the West Los Angeles Treatment Program for their participation. We would like to thank Alice Huber, Christie Thomas, Vikas Gulati, Al Hasson, and Michael McCann for their assistance with the conduct of this study.

REFERENCES

American Psychiatric Association (APA). (1994). *Diagnostic and Statistical Manual of Mental Disorders, 4th Edition (DSM-IV)*. Washington, DC.

Abram, K. M. (1989). The effect of co-occurring disorders on criminal career: Interaction of antisocial personality, alcoholism, and drug disorders. *International Journal of Law and Psychiatry, 12*, 133-148.

Bandura, A. (1977). Self-efficacy: Toward a unifying theory of behavioral change. *Psychological Review, 84*, 191-215.

Bordens, K., & Abbott, B. (1991). *Research design and methods: A process approach* (2nd Ed.). Mountain View, CA: Mayfield Publishing Company.

Brooner, R., Kidorf, M., King, V., & Stoller, K. (1998). Preliminary evidence of good treatment response in antisocial drug abusers. *Drug and Alcohol Dependence, 49*, 249-260.

Brooner, R., Schmidt, C., Felch, L., & Bigelow, G. (1992). Antisocial behavior of intravenous drug abusers: Implications for diagnosis of antisocial personality disorder. *American Journal of Psychiatry, 149*, 482-487.

Carroll, K. (Ed.) (1999). A cognitive-behavioral approach: Treating cocaine addiction. *Therapy Manuals for Drug Addiction*. Rockville, MD: National Institute on Drug Abuse, U.S. Department of Health and Human Services, National Institutes of Health.

Carroll, K.M., Rounsaville, B.J., Nich, C., Gordon, L.T., Wirtz, P.W., & Gawin, F.H. (1994). One year follow-up of psychotherapy and pharmacotherapy for cocaine dependence: Delayed emergence of psychotherapy effects. *Archives of General Psychiatry, 51*, 989-997.

Coon, Dennis. (1983) *Introduction to Psychology: Exploration and Application*. 3rd ed. Los Angeles: West Publishing Company.

Davison, G. C., & Neale, J. M. (1990). *Abnormal psychology* (5th ed.). New York: Wiley & Sons.

Evans, K., & Sullivan, J. (1990). *Dual diagnoses: Counseling mentally ill substance abusers*. New York: The Guilford Press.

Everingham, S., & Rydell, C. (1994). *Modeling the demand for cocaine*. Santa Monica, CA: RAND.

Farabee, D., Rawson, R., & McCann, M. (2002). Adoption of drug avoidance activities among patients in contingency management and cognitive-behavioral treatments. *Journal of Substance Abuse Treatment, 23,* 343-350.

Foote, J., Seligman, M., Magura, S., Handelsman, L., Rosenblum, A., Lovejoy, M., Arrington, K., & Stimmel, B. (1994). An enhanced positive reinforcement model for the severely impaired cocaine abuser. *Journal of Substance Abuse Treatment, 11*(6), 525-539.

Forrest, G. G. (1992). *Chemical dependency and antisocial personality disorder: Psychotherapy and assessment strategies.* New York: The Hawthorne Press.

Gerstley, L. J., Alterman, A. I., McLellan, A. T., & Woody, G. E. (1990). Antisocial personality disorder in patients with substance abuse disorders: A problematic diagnosis? *American Journal of Psychiatry, 147*(2), 173-178.

Gil, K., Nolimal, D., & Crowley, T. (1992). Antisocial personality disorder, HIV risk behavior and retention in methadone maintenance therapy. *Drug and Alcohol Dependence, 30*(3), 247-252.

Higgins, T., Budney, J., Bickel, K., Foerg, F., Donham, R., & Badger, J. (1994). Incentives improve outcome in outpatient behavioral treatment of cocaine dependence. *Archives of General Psychiatry, 51*(7), 568-576.

Higgins, T., Budney, J., Bickel, K., Hughes, R., Foerg, F., & Badger, J. (1993). Achieving cocaine abstinence with a behavior approach. *American Journal of Psychiatry, 150,* 763-769.

Hser, Y. (1995). Drug treatment counselor practices and effectiveness: An examination of literature and relevant issues in a multilevel framework. *Evaluation Review, 19*(4), 389-408.

Keppel, G. (1991). *Design and analyses: A researcher's handbook.* Prentice Hall: Englewood Cliffs, New Jersey.

King, V., Kidorf, M., Stoller, M., Carter, J., & Brooner, R. (2001). Influence of antisocial personality subtypes on drug abuse treatment response. *Journal of Nervous and Mental Disease, 189,* 593-601.

Kranzler, H., Rounsaville, B., & Tennen, H. (1995). *Validity of the SCID in substance abuse patients* (NIDA Research Monograph, 2, 35). Rockville, MD: National Institute on Drug Abuse.

Marlatt, G. & Gordon, J. (Eds.). (1985). *Relapse prevention: Maintenance strategies in the treatment of addictive behaviors.* New York: Guilford Press.

McLellan, A.T., Kushner, H., Metzger, D., Peters, R., Smith, I., Grissom, G., Pettinati, H., & Argeriou, M. (1992). The fifth edition of the Addiction Severity Index. *Journal of Substance Abuse Treatment, 9,* 199-213.

Messina, N. (2002). The antisocial personality. In Levinson, D. (Ed.). *Encyclopedia of Crime and Punishment*, vol.1. Great Barrington, Mass.: Berkshire Reference Works.

Messina, N., Wish, E., Hoffman, J., & Nemes, S. (2001). Diagnosing antisocial personality disorder among substance abusers: The Structured Clinical Interview for the DSM-III-R versus the Millon Clinical Multiaxial Inventory. *The American Journal of Drug and Alcohol Abuse,27*(4), 699-717.

Messina, N., Wish, E., & Nemes, S. (1999). Therapeutic community treatment for substance abusers with antisocial personality disorder. *Journal of Substance Abuse Treatment, 17*(1-2), 121-128.

Messina, N., Wish, E., Nemes, S., & Wraight, B. (2000). Correlates of underreporting of post-discharge cocaine use among therapeutic community clients. *Journal of Drug Issues, 30*(1), 119-132.

Rawson, R., Huber, A., McCann, M., Shoptaw, S., Farabee, D., Reiber, C., & Ling, W. (2002). A comparison of contingency management and cognitive-behavioral approaches for cocaine dependent methadone maintained individuals. *Archives of General Psychiatry, 59,* 817-824.

Rawson, R., Obert, J., McCann, M., & Ling, W. (1991). Psychological approaches to the treatment of cocaine dependency. *Journal of Addictive Diseases, 11,* 97-120.

Rawson, R., Obert, J., McCann, M., Smith, P., and Scheffey, H. (1989). *The neurobehavioral treatment manual, Matrix.* Beverly Hills, CA.

Rounsaville, B., Eyre, S., Weissman, M., & Kleber, H. (1983). The antisocial opiate addict. In B. Stimmeo (Vol. Ed.). *Psychosocial constructs: Alcoholism and substance abuse,* (pp. 29-43). New York: Hawthorne Press.

Skinner, B. (1938). *The behavior of organisms: An experimental analysis.* Englewood Cliffs, NJ: Prentice-Hall.

Seivewright, N., & Daly, C. (1997). Personality disorder and drug use: A review. *Drug and Alcohol Review, 16,* 235-250.

Silverman, K., Chutuape, M.A., Bigelow, G., & Stitzer, M. (1999). Voucher-based reinforcement of cocaine abstinence in treatment-resistant methadone patients: Effects of reinforcement magnitude. *Psychopharmacology, 146,* 128-138.

Silverman, K., Higgins, S., Montoya, I., Cone, E., Schuster, C., & Preston, K. (1996). Sustained cocaine abstinence in methadone maintenance patients through voucher-based reinforcement therapy. *Archives of General Psychiatry, 53,* 409-415.

Silverman, K., Wong, C., Umbricht-Schneiter, A., Montoya, I., Schuster, C., & Preston, K. (1998). Broad beneficial effects of cocaine abstinence reinforcement among methadone patients. *Journal of Consulting and Clinical Psychology, 66*(5), 811-824.

Tims, F. M., DeLeon, G., & Jainchill, N. (Eds.). (1994). *Therapeutic community: Advances in research and application* (NIDA Research Monograph No.144). Rockville, MD: National Institute on Drug Abuse.

Valliant, G. (1975). Sociopathy as a human process: A viewpoint. *Archives of General Psychiatry, 32,* 178-183.

Wish, E., Hoffman, J., & Nemes, S. (1997). The validity of self-reports of drug use at treatment admission and at follow-up: Comparisons with urinalysis and hair assays. In L. Harris (Ed.), *The validity of self-reports: The implications for survey research* (NIDA Research Monograph No. 167, pp. 200-225). Rockville, MD: National Institute on Drug Abuse.

Woody, G., McLellan, A.T., Luborsky, L, & O'Brien, C. (1985). Sociopathy and psychotherapy outcome. *Archives of General Psychiatry, 42,* 1081-1086.

In: Substance Abuse: New Research
Editors: Ethan J. Kerr and Owen E. Gibson

ISBN 978-1-60456-834-9
© 2009 Nova Science Publishers, Inc.

Chapter 3

DRUG ABUSE AND NEURO-AIDS

Avindra Nath[1,2,], Kurt F. Hauser[3], Mark Prendergast[4] and Joseph Berger[5]*

Departments of [1]Neurology, [2]Neuroscience,
Johns Hopkins University, Baltimore, Maryland, USA;
[3]Departments of Anatomy and Neurobiology, [4]Psychology,
[5]Neurology and Internal Medicine, University of Kentucky,
Lexington, Kentucky, USA.

ABSTRACT

In certain populations around the world, the HIV pandemic is driven by drug abuse. Mounting evidence suggests that these patient populations may have accelerated and more severe neurocognitive dysfunction as compared to non-drug abusing HIV infected populations. Many drugs of abuse are CNS stimulants, hence it stands to reason that these drugs may synergize with neurotoxic substances released during the course of HIV infection. Clinical and laboratory evidence suggest that the dopaminergic systems are most vulnerable to such combined neurotoxicity although multiple regions of the brain may be involved. Identifying common mechanisms of neuronal injury is critical to developing therapeutic strategies for drug abusing HIV-infected populations. This chapter reviews 1) the current evidence for neurodegeneration in the setting of combined HIV infection and use of methamphetamine, cocaine, heroin or alcohol, 2) the proposed underlying mechanisms involved in this combined neurotoxicity, and 3) future directions for research. This manuscript also suggests therapeutic approaches based on our current understanding of the neuropathogenesis of dementia due to HIV infection and drugs of abuse.

Keywords: HIV, dementia, methamphetamine, cocaine, alcohol, opiates, heroin

* Correspondence concerning this article should be addressed to Avindra Nath MD, Department of Neurology, 600 N. Wolfe St, Pathology 509, Baltimore, MD 21287. Tele: 443-287-4656; e-mail: anath1@jhmi.edu.

INTRODUCTION

Drug abuse and HIV are truly interlinked epidemics. Nearly two and one half million Americans use heroin and as many as 30 % of injecting drug users are HIV seropositive. Drug abuse also accounts for nearly half of the HIV infections in women in United States, however, the effect of drug abuse on incidence, rate of progression, or severity of HIV dementia is not entirely clear. However, studying the combined effects of drug abuse and HIV on the brain has been challenging. These patients are often poly-drug abusers. Moreover, the amounts and frequency of drug use vary widely amongst patient groups and within single individuals and these patients are often co-infected with hepatitis C (Murrill et al, 2002) making it difficult to determine the degree to which the drugs may alter brain function. Nonetheless, several patient based studies have been performed and many are currently underway. In this chapter, we review the clinical, pathological and pathophysiological studies which when taken together clearly show that drug abuse in conjunction with HIV infection has synergistic effects on brain function.

EPIDEMIOLOGY AND CLINICAL MANIFESTATIONS

Unlike HIV-seronegative older adults whose rates of drug abuse and mood disorders decline substantially compared with younger adults, this decline is not observed for older HIV seropositive adults (Rabkin et al., 2004). Although the number of studies addressing both the cognitive dysfunction in HIV seropositive individuals and the role of drugs of abuse in their genesis remain limited, the weight of evidence suggests a synergistic effect between HIV and drug abuse on cognitive embarrassment. An early study found no major differences in cognitive functioning amongst asymptomatic HIV-infected persons with or without a history of drug abuse (Concha et al., 1997). However, a later study showed that a history of injection drug use and presentation with prominent psychomotor slowing were associated with more rapid neurologic progression (Bouwman et al., 1998). Furthermore, in some HIV infected drug abusers an accelerated form of HIV dementia may be observed (Nath et al., 2001).

Long-term methamphetamine use has also been associated with neuronal damage as determined by case reports (Bartzokis et al., 1999b; Pascual-Leone and Dhuna, 1990; Pascual-Leone et al., 1990; Weiner et al., 2001), animal models , pathological materials (Wilson et al., 1996a; Wilson et al., 1996b), and magnetic resonance spectroscopy brain imaging (Ernst et al., 2000). Autopsy studies confirm injury to dopaminergic neurons in methamphetamine as well as cocaine abusers (Wilson et al., 1996a; Wilson et al., 1996b). Although infrequent, cocaine use has been associated with persistent dyskinesias including choreoathetoid movements and tics (Bartzokis et al., 1999b; Pascual-Leone and Dhuna, 1990; Weiner et al., 2001) and seizures (Pascual-Leone et al., 1990). Interestingly, some investigators have proposed the use of psychostimulants in the treatment of HIV dementia (Brown, 1995); however, the effects of these drugs on cerebral function in the setting of HIV infection has not been well studied.

Since common drugs of abuse including cocaine, amphetamines, and opiates, all have dopaminergic activation properties, this suggests that these drugs may accelerate the loss of an already compromised dopaminergic system in patients with HIV infection. We recently reported a patient with HIV dementia and a history of cocaine and methamphetamine use who developed a progressive resting tremor, dystonia and athetoid movements (Nath et al., 2001). Furthermore, preliminary studies suggest that intravenous drug abusers with HIV infection had more severe neuronal loss and shrunken neuronal cells in the substantia nigra, compared to patients who died of AIDS without a history of drug abuse (Reyes et al., 1991).

Many features of AIDS dementia mirror symptoms observed in the setting of dopamine deficient states, e.g., Parkinson's disease. Evidence for involvement of the dopaminergic systems in HIV dementia includes the clinical features of the illness, the neuronal loss of deep nuclear structures as determined by magnetic resonance spectroscopy and pathological materials, the shared neurochemistry of the disorders (Berger and Arendt, 2000). Furthermore, patients with AIDS, when treated with even mild dopaminergic blocking drugs, such as prochlorperazine, perpherazine, trifluperazine, low dose haloperidol, thiothixine, chlorpromazine, or metoclopramide, can develop severe parkinsonism (Edelstein and Knight, 1987; Hollander et al., 1985; Hriso et al., 1991; Kieburtz et al., 1991; Mirsattari et al., 1999; Mirsattari et al., 1998). In one study, a comparison was made with psychotic patients without HIV infection receiving neuroleptics (Hriso et al., 1991). The likelihood of developing parkinsonian symptoms was 2-4 times higher in patients with AIDS when controlled for mean drug dose and body weight. Such symptoms developed in 50% of AIDS patients who received less than 4 mg/kg of chlorpromazine equivalents per day and 78% of those who received more than 4 mg/kg per day (Hriso et al., 1991). These observations suggest an already compromised dopaminergic system in HIV-infected individuals receiving these drugs.

The principal source of dopamine and its metabolites in the cerebrospinal fluid is from the dopaminergic system in the brain; dopamine levels in the CSF are thus good reflection of the integrity of dopaminergic neurons. CSF neurotransmitter levels provide a sensitive indicator of neuronal dysfunction and abnormalities can be detected in the asymptomatic phases of neurological disease (Hornykiewicz, 1998). Similarly, CSF homovanillic acid levels are diminished in patients with AIDS and more severely so in patients with AIDS dementia (Berger et al., 1994; Larsson et al., 1991). A study of monoamine metabolites in CSF of asymptomatic SIV infected rhesus macaques showed increased levels of 3,4-dihydroxyphenylacetic acid in the CSF suggesting increased dopamine turnover in early stages of infection (Koutsilieri et al., 1997b).

Alcohol abuse and/or dependence is frequently observed in HIV-infected individuals and likely represents a significant risk factor for HIV infection (Weinhardt et al., 2001). Individuals who abuse alcohol often engage in high-risk sexual behavior (Baldwin et al, 2000) and have significant compromise of immune function, resulting from direct immunotoxicity and nutritional deficiency (Dingle and Oei, 1997; Watzl and Watson, 1992). This latter point, in particular, may suggest that HIV-positive individuals who abuse alcohol are at increased risk for both the development of AIDS and other HIV-related symptoms, such as HIV-associated dementia complex (Pillai et al., 1991; Tabakoff, 1994; Tyor and Middaugh, 1999).

Studies exploring possible interactions between alcohol abuse and development of HIV-1 related symptoms are, to date, inconclusive. A small number of studies have examined cognitive function in alcoholics infected with HIV and find no evidence of a link between greater neuropsychological impairment and HIV-1 positive status (Bornstein et al., 1993; Heaton et al., 1995). However, as Basso and Bornstein (Basso and Bornstein, 2000) correctly point out, these studies and related neuroimaging studies (McArthur et al., 1990; Meyerhoff et al., 1995) did not conduct the critical comparisons between neuropsychological function in alcoholic and non-alcoholic HIV-1 seropositive individuals. Comparisons in these studies were typically conducted between seropositive and seronegative patients. Further, these studies did not account for individual differences in the patients' history of alcohol detoxification, a factor that can dramatically affect neuropsychological functioning (Craig and Mosier, 1978). It is unclear, then, if the presence of alcoholism worsens the neuropathological and behavioral effects of HIV-1 infection in seropositive individuals. Recent studies suggest that opiate use may be associated with the development of asymptomatic peripheral neuropathies in HIV infected patients (Morgello et al., 2004), but this area has not been well studied.

NEUROPATHOLOGY IN HIV INFECTED DRUG ABUSERS

Neuropathological studies, in general, have shown significant differences in the brains of HIV seropositive drug abusers when compared to a control HIV-seropositive population. However, these differences were not consistently demonstrated; perhaps reflective of differences in the study populations and techniques employed. Bell and colleagues demonstrated a marked severity of HIV encephalitis (HIVE) in drug abusers (Bell et al., 1998). A particularly striking involvement of dopaminergic neurons has been reported (Reyes et al., 1991). Drug users with HIVE tend to have more activated microglia than non-drug-using comparison groups, particularly in the thalamus (Arango et al., 2004; Tomlinson et al., 1999). In another study, the same group of investigators found that GFAP-reactive astrocytes in both grey and white matter were significantly more numerous in drug using patients with HIVE when compared to HIV negative drug users or HIV seropositive drug users without HIVE. They were numerous in only one subject who was treatment-naïve suggesting that in this population, HIV infected astrocytes may serve as a reservoir for the virus (Anderson et al., 2003). Drug abuse has no significant effect on B cell infiltrates into the brain of HIV infected patients (Anthony et al., 2004). The above studies have been reported from a cohort in Edinburgh where the population is predominantly an opiate abusing cohort. In a methamphetamine abusing cohort from San Diego, similarly a severe microglial reaction was found in patients with drug abuse and HIVE when compared to patients with HIVE who were non-methamphetamine users. However, in contrast they found that the methamphetamine-using patients with HIVE showed significantly lower gp41 scores suggesting less numbers of HIV infected macrophages/microglia and less severe forms of encephalitis but a higher frequency of ischemic events, and a more pronounced loss of synaptophysin and calbindin immunoreactivity, suggesting damage to non-pyramidal neurons (Langford et al., 2003)

EFFECT OF DRUG ABUSE ON HIV REPLICATION

The "opiate cofactor hypothesis" has been proposed as a mechanism in the pathogenesis of AIDS (Donahoe and Vlahov, 1998), and is based on experimental findings that opioids can modulate HIV propagation in immune cells and suppress immune function. By contrast, the effects of opiates disease progression in non-human primate models of HIV have been less straightforward (Donahoe, 2004), although in recent, carefully controlled studies, chronic, morphine has been shown to markedly increase viral loads in plasma and CSF (Kumar et al., 2004). Opioid drugs and HIV proteins act synergistically to destabilize immune function by affecting monocytes and lymphocytes. Subsets of leukocytes express mu, delta, and kappa opioid receptors, as well as endogenous opioid peptides such as enkephalins, and opioids can modulate neuroimmune function through complex (direct and indirect) actions that involve both peripheral and central neural and non-neural mechanisms (Bidlack, 2000; Chang et al., 1998; McCarthy et al., 2001; Mellon and Bayer, 1998). Although the effects of opioids on immune function have been previously reviewed (Adler et al., 1993; Peterson et al., 2001; Sharp et al., 1998), an emerging concept is that the opioid system can have dichotomous (positive and negative) effects on HIV infection and/or replication in immunocytes. For example, mu receptor stimulation increases HIV expression in monocytic cells (Peterson et al., 1999; Peterson et al., 1993), while kappa receptor activation can have the opposite, inhibitory effect on HIV expression in monocytic and lymphocytic cells (Chao et al., 1996; Chao et al., 2001; Peterson et al., 2001). Mu and kappa receptors have been noted to mediate opposing actions in other systems (Bohn et al., 2000). Interestingly, mu-opioid receptor activation can increase the expression of cytokine receptors, that serve as co-receptors for HIV in susceptible cells including CCR3, CCR5, and CXCR4, while kappa-opioid receptor stimulation can increase CCR2, while decreasing CCR5, expression (Rogers and Peterson, 2003). To add to this complexity, there is evidence for bi-directional heterologous interactions between opioid and chemokine receptors (Rogers et al., 2000) (Rogers and Peterson, 2003). Thus, although opioids can be pro- or anti-inflammatory depending on the particular opioid receptor and cell type that are affected, the typical/net consequence of mu-opioid receptor activation is to suppress immune function thereby promoting disease progression.

EFFECT OF HIV AND DRUGS OF ABUSE ON NEURONAL FUNCTION

In vitro studies show that when neuronal cell lines are exposed to either dopamine, cocaine, or morphine along with supernatants from HIV infected cells, significant neuronal cell death and oxidative stress occurs (Koutsilieri et al., 1997a). An acute exposure to methamphetamine and cocaine may be sufficient to cause neurotoxicity (Turchan et al., 2001). The mechanism by which these substances synergize remains elusive. As demonstrated in these studies, at least in part the mechanism involves mitochondrial dysfunction. Since both gp120 and Tat have been shown to cause toxicity to dopaminergic cells and similarly methamphetamine and cocaine also cause toxicity to dopaminergic systems, we characterized the dopaminergic neurons and receptors in our culture system. We found that only a small proportion of these cells underwent cell death when exposed to HIV proteins and these drugs of abuse (Turchan et al., 2001). This suggests that there must be additional factors, which need to be identified, that cause some neurons in drug abusing individuals to be vulnerable to HIV.

Cocaine

One possible mechanism for cocaine-HIV protein synergy is oxidative stress. Mitochondria have been proposed as critical cellular targets for cocaine toxicity, and prior studies have found that cocaine can decrease mitochondrial respiration and increase the production of reactive oxygen species in animals (Boess et al., 2000). We have found that Tat may produce oxidative damage in vivo (Askenov et al., 2001). Increased oxidative modifications of proteins occur soon following the injection of Tat into the rat striatum and may be an important mechanism for Tat neurotoxicity. Thus, both cocaine and Tat target the mitochondria, producing oxidative stress, suggesting the possibility for synergistic interactions in producing mitochondrial dysfunction and ultimately cell death. This provides a basis for searching for antioxidant compounds that may decrease or prevent oxidative damage produced by cocaine and HIV interactions.

Methamphetamine

Methamphetamine synergizes with Tat in vivo. Methamphetamine-treated animals demonstrated a 7% decline in striatal dopamine levels while Tat-treated animals showed an 8% reduction. Exposure to both methamphetamine + Tat caused an almost 65% reduction in striatal dopamine. This same treatment caused a 56% reduction in the binding capacity to the dopamine transporter. It should be pointed out that the dose of methamphetamine used in this study did not induce hyperthermia, thus increasing the relevance of this animal model with respect to human disease (Maragos et al., 2002). Microdialysis studies in this animal model show that the synergistic response is accompanied by marked decreases in dopamine release in the striatum (Cass et al., 2003).

The combined effects of methamphetamine and HIV proteins may affect a number of regions within the brain and there maybe some differences in the underlying mechanisms in the different regions. For example, administration of Tat or METH resulted in stimulation of cellular oxidative stress and activation of redox-regulated transcription factors in the cortical, striatal, and hippocampal regions of the mouse brain. In addition, DNA-binding activities of NF-kappaB, AP-1, and CREB in the frontal cortex and hippocampus were more pronounced in mice injected with Tat plus METH compared to the effects of Tat or METH alone. Intercellular adhesion molecule-1 gene expression also was upregulated in a synergistic manner in cortical, striatal, and hippocampal regions in mice which received injections of Tat combined with METH compared to the effects of these agents alone. Moreover, synergistic effects of Tat plus METH on the tumor necrosis factor-alpha and interleukin-1beta mRNA levels were observed in the striatal region (Flora et al., 2003).

Opiates

In the CNS, heroin acts largely via its conversion to morphine, making morphine the most commonly used drug of choice to study opiate effects in vivo and in vitro. Besides their immunomodulatory actions, opioids may directly modulate the response of neurons and macroglia to HIV infection. Interestingly, depending on the target tissue, particular opioid receptor type involved, and pharmacodynamics of receptor activation, opioids can have paradoxical neuroprotective or neurodegenerative effects. The divergent actions likely result from the fact that opioid receptors are highly promiscuous in their interactions with particular intracellular signaling pathways, and opioid receptor-effector coupling differs greatly among cell types (Hauser et al., 1998). In some experimental systems, opioids can be protective (Hauser et al., 1999; Meriney et al., 1991; Polakiewicz et al., 1998). For example, selective a mu opioid receptor agonist stimulates anti-apoptotic effectors downstream to the phosphoinositide 3-kinase (PI-3-K)-dependent signaling cascade in CHO cells stably transfected with mu opioid receptors (Polakiewicz et al., 1998). Morphine may exaggerate HIV-envelope protein gp120-induced early proliferative increases in kidney fibroblasts (Singhal et al., 1998a), and opioids can protect against the detrimental effects of gp120 (Stefano, 1999). More often, however, opioids exaggerate the effects of preexisting, non-opioid proapoptotic or proinflammatory signals, respectively; thereby either reducing cell viability directly (Goswami et al., 1998; Yin et al., 1997), or indirectly through the release of cytotoxic inflammatory intermediaries from immune cells. Mu opioid drugs with abuse liability, such as heroin, morphine, and fentanyl, respectively, can induce toxicity in cerebellar Purkinje cells in vitro (Hauser et al., 1994) and in the limbic system of rats at high dosages (Kofke et al., 1996). Fentanyl has been shown to exacerbate the effects of ischemia-induced damage to the basal ganglia (Kofke et al., 1999). Morphine can induce apoptosis through a caspase-3-dependent pathway in primary human microglia and neurons in vitro (Hu S., et al., 2002). Typically, however, opioids are not intrinsically toxic and morphine alone is rarely toxic to most neuronal types (Gurwell et al., 2001; Hauser et al., 2000). By contrast, there is burgeoning data suggesting that nontoxic concentrations of opioids can significantly exacerbate cell losses if combined with pro-apoptotic agents (Nair et al., 1997; Singhal et al., 1999; Singhal et al., 1997; Singhal et al., 1998b; Yin et al., 1999). Mu agonists enhance staurosporine or wortmannin-induced apoptosis in embryonic chick neurons or neuronal cell lines (Goswami et al., 1998).

Alternatively, opioids may lower the threshold of susceptibility of dopaminergic neurons to viral damage by affecting dopamine turnover. Endogenous opioids, and/or opiate drugs such as morphine or heroin, can activate dopaminergic neurons through several different mechanisms of action (review, Kreek, 2001). Opioids can decrease dopamine levels though the disinhibition of interneurons that synapse on dopaminergic neurons, such as in the ventral tegmental area. Opioids may also modulate the cellular response to dopamine. For example, opioid receptor activation reportedly increases D2, but not D1, dopamine receptor binding sites in the rat striatum (Rooney et al., 1991), which may have considerable functional consequences (De Vries et al., 1999; Vanderschuren et al., 1999). Conversely, in another study, repeated intermittent exposure to morphine increases dopamine D1-receptor-induced adenylyl cyclase activity in rat striatal neurons *in vitro* (Schoffelmeer et al., 1997). Another highly significant issue related to HIV susceptibility is the disruption in dopaminergic function that occurs with the development of tolerance and dependence, or during withdrawal (Koob, 2000). Chronic opiate drug exposure is typically accompanied by disruption of second messenger cascades, altered patterns of gene activation, and increased oxidative stress (Hauser et al., 1998; Koob, 2000; Kreek and Koob, 1998), which may further enhance the vulnerability of neurons to HIV infection.

Several investigators have provided evidence that opioids and HIV-1 Tat protein are synergistically toxic to neurons through a direct action on neural cell targets. Importantly, we have observed synergistic Tat-opioid drug toxicity in human and mouse neural cells, using distinct, yet complementary, experimental approaches (Gurwell et al., 2001); (Turchan et al., unpublished observations). Importantly, the enhanced toxicity is mediated through specific opioid receptors, since the neurodegenerative effects of morphine are concentration-dependent and can be reversed by opioid receptor antagonists (Gurwell et al., 2001). Recent studies from our laboratories demonstrate that the coordinate effects are caused by mitochondrial toxicity through actions involving Akt/PKB, PI-3 kinase, and caspases 1, 3 and 7 activation in human neurons (Turchan et al., unpublished observations). A majority of the neurons in our cultures possess mu, delta, and/or kappa receptor immunoreactivity suggesting that opioids and Tat are acting directly. Alternatively, because a small number of contaminating glia may be present, we cannot be certain that some aspects of the neurotoxicity seen result from opiate-HIV actions via glial intermediaries. Subpopulations of striatal astrocytes (Stiene-Martin et al., 1998), and microglia (Chao et al., 1996) can express opioid receptors. Lastly, opioid drugs with abuse liability act by mimicking endogenous opioid peptides. Thus, besides directly modify the neural response to HIV, opiate drugs may act by affecting endogenous opioid peptide levels, which may further modify the response of the CNS to HIV.

Alcohol

Several deleterious effects of chronic ethanol intake occur that are directly neurotoxic and may render the CNS susceptible to other forms of injury, such as that seen in HIVE. For example, chronic ethanol intake can stimulate the production of reactive oxygen species (Brooks, 1997), inhibition of neuronal growth factors (Walker et al., 1993), and reduced local cerebral glucose utilization (Johnson-Greene et al., 1997). Not surprisingly, long-term ethanol abuse in humans is often associated with the development of mild-moderate neurological abnormalities, including impairment of executive function, even in the absence of Korsakoff's syndrome (Diamond and Messing, 1994).

There is reason to postulate that chronic alcoholism may alter neuronal function and sensitize some glutamatergic receptor systems (eg. N-methyl-D-aspartate (NMDA)) to the neurotoxic effects of Tat, gp120, or other HIV-1 proteins. In vitro studies of Tat and gp120 indicate that over activity of NMDA-type glutamate receptors, in addition to that of α-amino-3-hydroxy-5-methyl-4-isoxazole propionate-type receptors, likely contributes to the neurotoxic effects of these HIV-1 proteins [see (Epstein and Gelbard, 1999; Lipton, 1998; Nath and Geiger, 1998; Tyor and Middaugh, 1999). Thus, the presence of pharmacological factors that can produce a heightened sensitivity of glutamatergic receptor systems may promote HIV-1 related neurotoxicity.

It is clear that adaptive neuronal changes occur during long-term ethanol exposure that appears to sensitize the brain to excitatory amino acid neurotransmission during withdrawal from ethanol intake (review; Littleton and Little, 1994). An extensive literature has demonstrated that chronic ethanol exposure to animals or primary neuronal cell cultures produces compensatory increases in the density and sensitivity of NMDA-type glutamate receptors in cortical and hippocampal regions (Devaud and Morrow, 1999; Prendergast et al, 2000; Rudolph et al., 1998). This has been reported to result in NMDA receptor-mediated elevations in $[Ca^{2+}]$ during ethanol withdrawal (Hu and Ticku, 1995). The potentiation of

NMDA receptor-mediated neuronal death during ethanol withdrawal can readily be blocked by NMDA receptor channel blockers (Ahern et al., 1994; Chandler et al., 1993; Prendergast et al., 2000) indicating that chronic ethanol exposure may sensitize the CNS to the neurotoxic effects of HIV-1 proteins that directly or indirectly stimulate function of this excitatory amino acid receptor system, particularly during periods of reduced ethanol intake.

EFFECT OF HIV AND DRUGS OF ABUSE ON GLIAL CELL FUNCTION

Opioid receptors are widely expressed by macroglia and macroglial precursors. Sustained exposure to morphine and Tat viral protein induces the preferential death of glial precursors and a small but significant proportion of astrocytes. The increased cell death is mediated by mu-opioid receptors and accompanied by the activation of caspase-3 (Khurdayan et al., 2004). Recent findings suggest that a major consequence of opiate-HIV interactions is to disrupt astroglial function and implicate astroglia as catalysts triggering early destabilizing and proinflammatory effects of opiates in HIV-infected individuals. Combined opiate and Tat exposure synergistically destabilize intracellular calcium and increase oxyradical production (El-Hage et al., 2005; El-Hage, Nath, Hauser, unpublished) in cultured striatal astroglia, while causing massive coordinate increases in the release of proinflammatory chemokines. This includes monocyte chemoattractant protein-1 (MCP-1) and RANTES. MCP-1, in particular, when released by CNS-resident astrocytes triggers an influx of monocyte/macrophages and microglial activation. Assuming the recruitment of macrophages/microglia to infected CNS loci is exacerbated in opiate-abusers; this would likely exaggerate losses in neuronal function and neurotoxicity, synaptic losses, and may eventually culminate in synaptic losses and neuronal death. Considering the unremitting and debilitating consequences of HIV by itself, when combined with chronic opiate abuse, this is likely to augment the progression of the disease in the CNS. The combined effects of other drugs of abuse with HIV on glial cell function have yet to be studied.

EFFECT OF HIV AND DRUGS OF ABUSE ON BLOOD BRAIN BARRIER FUNCTION

The combined effects of HIV and drugs of abuse on the blood brain barrier has not been well studied. However, an in vitro study showed that cocaine can enhance monocyte migration across the blood brain barrier and induce the expression of adhesion molecules on endothelial cells (Fiala et al., 1998). Similarly, it has been shown that there is disruption of the blood brain barrier in HIV infected patients in vivo (Berger and Avison, 2004) which correlates with early inflammatory changes in the CSF particularly increases in monocyte chemoattractant protein –1 levels (Avison et al., 2004). This has been confirmed autopsy studies from HIV infected patients however drug abuse history of these patients was not known (Petito and Cash, 1992; Power et al., 1993). Several in vitro studies also show that

HIV derived proteins can alter endothelial cell function or disrupt the blood brain barrier (Andras et al., 2003; Pu et al., 2003; Toborek et al., 2003).

THERAPEUTIC STRATEGIES

Drug abusing HIV infected patients pose unique challenges for the treating physician. Pharmacological interactions may occur between drugs of abuse and antiretroviral therapies (Fabris et al., 2000; Flexner et al., 2001). Treatment of HIV infected patients requires that they take a large number of medications and adhere strictly to complicated dosing schedules to prevent drug resistance. Patients with neurocognitive impairment have greater difficulties meeting such demands, thus it is not difficult to imagine that drug abusing HIV-infected patients with cognitive impairment would be the most challenging of all to treat. Hence, treatment strategies need to include drugs with long half lives, combination medications (where several medications can be combined into a single pill) and use of dietary supplements. Biotechnological approaches that would allow the incorporation of drugs into plants may be one such strategy. Close attention also needs to be given to drug-drug interactions. Lastly, therapeutic vaccines might be an attractive alternative, since immune responses generated may suppress viral replication for several months.

Drug Abuse Intervention

The extent to which drug abstinence would halt or potentially reverse the progression of the resultant HIV-associated encephalopathy in drug abusing individuals is uncertain, but a logical topic for future study. If abstinence cannot be achieved, then interventions that limit drug use, or negate drug effects at the cellular or molecular level (Robinson and Berridge, 2000), might be beneficial. For example, in heroin abusing populations, even though replacing one opiate with another may not be ideal, methadone or buprenorphine treatment programs are likely to be beneficial by limiting and regulating opiate exposure. Some of the detrimental effects of intravenous heroin abuse may be attributable to high, fluctuating opiate levels and a failure to accommodate to changes in opioid signal intensity (Kreek and Koob, 1998; Nestler and Aghajanian, 1997). The accompanying disruption in normal function by these high drug levels may increase the susceptibility of cells to HIV protein toxins (Gurwell et al., 2001), while sustained, chronic exposure to more moderate dosages are likely to have fewer side effects. Studies on the molecular basis of addiction hold promise, because they would identify the basis to develop pharmacological ways to prevent craving for drugs of abuse.

Gonadal Hormones

Recently, much attention has been given to the neuroprotective properties of estrogens for both chronic neurodegenerative diseases and acute insults such as stroke. *In vitro* studies also show that estrogens can protect against a number of neurotoxic compounds (Green and

Simpkins, 2000). The mechanisms by which estrogens protect cells can be broadly classified into two categories, receptor mediated and non-receptor-mediated effects. Estrogen receptors are widely expressed in the brain with some regional differences (Gundlah et al., 2000). Estrogen deficiency has been implicated as a risk factor in the development of several neurodegenerative diseases (Manly et al., 2000; Saunders-Pullman et al., 1999; Slooter et al., 1999) and estrogen replacement may result in improvement of cognitive function (Asthana et al., 1999). The mechanisms by which estrogens protect neurons are currently under intense investigation and may involve receptor-mediated mechanisms or non-receptor-mediated, antioxidative effects. For these reasons, we assessed the combined effects of HIV proteins and the drugs of abuse methamphetamine and cocaine, on neuronal function and determined the extent to which estrogen might protect against these neurotoxic substances (Turchan et al., 2001). We observed that 17β-estradiol at concentrations that are achieved physiologically or can easily be obtained pharmacologically protected against the combined insult of HIV proteins and drugs of abuse. Protection was noted against both cell death and mitochondrial impairment. The protection was specific since no protection was noted with 17α-estradiol. In subsequent experiments, we determined if this protection was mediated via estrogen receptors. The estrogen receptor antagonist ICI 182,780 completely, and tamoxifen partially reversed the neuroprotective effects of 17β-estradiol using cell death as an end point. However these compounds were unable to reverse the neuroprotective effects of estrogen on mitochondrial membrane potential, suggesting that the mitochondrial effects of estrogen are non-receptor mediated. Thus, the toxic effects on mitochondria and neuronal cell survival seems to be independently regulated. However, it seems that 17β-estradiol can protect against both these effects by receptor and non-receptor mediated mechanisms (Turchan et al., 2001).

Antioxidants and Neuroprotectants

It is becoming abundantly clear that oxidative stress plays an important role in the neuropathogenesis of HIV infection. As discussed above, HIV proteins and drugs of abuse may synergize to cause mitochondrial toxicity and generate oxidative stress in susceptible neurons. It is thus necessary to determine the degree to which antioxidants can protect HIV infected drug abusing patient populations from developing neurodegeneration. Antioxidants are an attractive approach since they are easily available as dietary supplements and are present is several plants which includes a variety of plant estrogens that do not have feminizing effects. Some novel compounds are also under development that have both anti-retroviral and antioxidant properties (Turchan et al., 2003). A clinical trial is currently underway with L-deprenyl in patients with HIV dementia. This drug has multiple effects on the central nervous system. It is a specific monoamine oxidase B (MAO-B) inhibitor, it has antioxidant effects, reduces the euphoric effects of cocaine and normalizes blood flow in cocaine addicts. In preliminary studies, it has also been shown to slow the progression of HIV dementia and hence might be an ideal candidate for clinical trials in HIV infected drug abusers (Bartzokis et al., 1999a).

SUMMARY

This review has attempted to familiarize the reader with a broad body of knowledge that focuses chiefly on the synergistic effects of HIV and drugs of abuse in the pathogenesis of HIV dementia. This data was drawn from a broad range of studies including clinical assessments, magnetic resonance spectroscopy, CT and MR imaging, and histopathological observations determined at postmortem examination. Clearly, additional research in this important line of investigation is sorely needed.

REFERENCES

Adler MW, Geller EB, Rogers TJ, Henderson EE, Eisenstein TK (1993). Opioids, receptors, and immunity. *Adv. Exp. Med. Biol. 335*: 13-20.

Ahern KB, Lustig HS, Greenberg DA (1994). Enhancement of NMDA toxicity and calcium responses by chronic exposure of cultured cortical neurons to ethanol. *Neurosci. Lett. 165*: 211-4.

Anderson CE, Tomlinson GS, Pauly B, Brannan FW, Chiswick A, Brack-Werner R, Simmonds P, Bell JE (2003). Relationship of Nef-positive and GFAP-reactive astrocytes to drug use in early and late HIV infection. *Neuropathol. Appl. Neurobiol. 29*: 378-88.

Andras IE, Pu H, Deli MA, Nath A, Hennig B, Toborek M (2003). HIV-1 Tat protein alters tight junction protein expression and distribution in cultured brain endothelial cells. *J. Neurosci. Res. 74*: 255-65.

Anthony IC, Crawford DH, Bell JE (2004). Effects of human immunodeficiency virus encephalitis and drug abuse on the B lymphocyte population of the brain. *J. Neurovirol. 10*: 181-8.

Arango JC, Simmonds P, Brettle RP, Bell JE (2004). Does drug abuse influence the microglial response in AIDS and HIV encephalitis? *Aids 18 Suppl. 1*: S69-74.

Askenov MY, Hasselrot U, Bansal AK, Wu G, Nath A, Anderson C, Mactutus CF, Booze RM (2001). Oxidative damage induced by the injection of HIV-1 Tat protein in the rat striatum. *Neurosci. Letters 305*: 5-8.

Asthana S, Craft S, Baker LD, Raskind MA, Birnbaum RS, Lofgreen CP, Veith RC, Plymate SR (1999). Cognitive and neuroendocrine response to transdermal estrogen in postmenopausal women with Alzheimer's disease: results of a placebo- controlled, double-blind, pilot study. *Psychoneuroendocrinology 24*: 657-77.

Avison MJ, Nath A, Greene-Avison R, Schmitt FA, Bales RA, Ethisham A, Greenberg RN, Berger JR (2004). Inflammatory changes and breakdown of microvascular integrity in early human immunodeficiency virus dementia. *J. Neurovirol. 10*: 223-32.

Baldwin JA, Maxwell CJ, Fenaughty AM, Trotter RT, Stevens SJ (2000). Alcohol as a risk factor for hiv transmission among american indian and alaska native drug users. *Am. Indian Alsk. Native Ment. Health Res. 9*: 1-16.

Bartzokis G, Beckson M, Newton T, Mandelkern M, Mintz J, Foster JA, Ling W, Bridge TP (1999a). Selegiline effects on cocaine-induced changes in medial temporal lobe metabolism and subjective ratings of euphoria. *Neuropsychopharmacology 20*: 582-90.

Bartzokis G, Beckson M, Wirshing DA, Lu PH, Foster JA, Mintz J (1999b). Choreoathetoid movements in cocaine dependence. *Biol. Psychiatry. 45*: 1630-5.

Basso MR, Bornstein RA (2000). Neurobehavioural consequences of substance abuse and HIV infection. *J. Psychopharmacol. 14*: 228-37.

Bell JE, Brettle RP, Chiswick A, Simmonds P (1998). HIV encephalitis, proviral load and dementia in drug users and homosexuals with AIDS. Effect of neocortical involvement. *Brain 121*: 2043-52.

Berger JR, Arendt G (2000). HIV dementia: the role of the basal ganglia and dopaminergic systems. *J. Psychopharmacol. 14*: 214-21.

Berger JR, Avison M (2004). The blood brain barrier in HIV infection. *Front. Biosci. 9*: 2680-5.

Berger JR, Kumar M, Kumar A, Fernandez JB, Levin B (1994). Cerebrospinal fluid dopamine in HIV-1 infection. *AIDS 8*: 67-71.

Bidlack JM (2000). Detection and function of opioid receptors on cells from the immune system. *Clin. Diagn. Lab. Immunol. 7*: 719-23.

Boess F, Ndikum-Moffor FM, Boelsterli UA, Roberts SM (2000). Effects of cocaine and its oxidative metabolites on mitochondrial respiration and generation of reactive oxygen species. *Biochem. Pharmacol. 60*: 615-23.

Bohn LM, Belcheva MM, Coscia CJ (2000). Mu-opioid agonist inhibition of kappa-opioid receptor-stimulated extracellular signal-regulated kinase phosphorylation is dynamin-dependent in C6 glioma cells. *J. Neurochem. 74*: 574-81.

Bornstein RA, Fama R, Rosenberger P, Whitacre CC, Para MF, Nasrallah HA, Fass RJ (1993). Drug and alcohol use and neuropsychological performance in asymptomatic HIV infection. *J. Neuropsychiatry Clin. Neurosci. 5*: 254-9.

Bouwman FH, Skolasky RL, Hes D, Selnes OA, Glass JD, Nance-Sproson TE, Royal W, Dal Pan GJ, McArthur JC (1998). Variable progression of HIV-associated dementia. *Neurology. 50*: 1814-20.

Brooks PJ (1997). DNA damage, DNA repair, and alcohol toxicity--a review. *Alcohol. Clin. Exp. Res. 21*: 1073-82.

Brown GR (1995). The use of methylphenidate for cognitive decline associated with HIV disease. *Int. J. Psychiatry. Med. 25*: 21-37.

Cass WA, Harned ME, Peters LE, Nath A, Maragos WF (2003). HIV-1 protein Tat potentiation of methamphetamine-induced decreases in evoked overflow of dopamine in the striatum of the rat. *Brain Res. 984*: 133-142.

Chandler LJ, Newsom H, Sumners C, Crews F (1993). Chronic ethanol exposure potentiates NMDA excitotoxicity in cerebral cortical neurons. *J. Neurochem. 60*: 1578-81.

Chang SL, Wu GD, Patel NA, Vidal EL, Fiala M (1998). The effects of interaction between morphine and interleukin-1 on the immune response. *Adv. Exp. Med. Biol. 437*: 67-72.

Chao CC, Gekker G, Hu S, Sheng WS, Shark KB, Bu DF, Archer S, Bidlack JM, Peterson PK (1996). kappa opioid receptors in human microglia downregulate human immunodeficiency virus 1 expression. *Proc. Natl. Acad. Sci. U S A. 93*: 8051-6.

Chao CC, Gekker G, Sheng WS, Hu S, Peterson PK (2001). U50488 inhibits HIV-1 expression in acutely infected monocyte-derived macrophages. *Drug Alcohol Depend. 62*: 149-54.

Concha M, Selnes OA, Vlahov D, Nance-Sproson T, Updike M, Royal W, Palenicek J, McArthur JC (1997). Comparison of neuropsychological performance between AIDS-free injecting drug users and homosexual men. *Neuroepidemiology 16*: 78-85.

Craig JR, Mosier WM (1978). Clinical and laboratory findings on admission to an alcohol detoxification service. *Int. J. Addict. 13:* 1207-15.

De Vries TJ, Schoffelmeer AN, Binnekade R, Vanderschuren LJ (1999). Dopaminergic mechanisms mediating the incentive to seek cocaine and heroin following long-term withdrawal of IV drug self-administration. *Psychopharmacology. (Berl) 143*: 254-60.

Devaud LL, Morrow AL (1999). Gender-selective effects of ethanol dependence on NMDA receptor subunit expression in cerebral cortex, hippocampus and hypothalamus. *Eur. J. Pharmacol. 369*: 331-4.

Diamond I, Messing RO (1994). Neurologic effects of alcoholism. *West J Med 161*: 279-87.

Dingle GA, Oei TP (1997). Is alcohol a cofactor of HIV and AIDS? Evidence from immunological and behavioral studies. *Psychol. Bull. 122*: 56-71.

Donahoe RM (2004). Multiple ways that drug abuse might influence AIDS progression: clues from a monkey model. *J. Neuroimmunol. 147*: 28-32.

Donahoe RM, Vlahov D (1998). Opiates as potential cofactors in progression of HIV-1 infections to AIDS. *J. Neuroimmunol. 83*: 77-87.

Edelstein H, Knight RT (1987). Severe parkinsonism in two AIDS patients taking prochlorperazine [letter]. *Lancet 2*: 341-2.

El-Hage N, Gurwell JA, Singh IN, Knapp PE, Nath A, Hauser KF (2005). Synergistic increases in intracellular Ca^{2+}, and the release of MCP-1, RANTES, and IL-6 by astrocytes treated with opiates and HIV-1 Tat. *Glia 50:*91-106.

Epstein LG, Gelbard HA (1999). HIV-1-induced neuronal injury in the developing brain. *J. Leukoc. Biol. 65*: 453-7.

Ernst T, Chang L, Leonido-Yee M, Speck O (2000). Evidence for long-term neurotoxicity associated with methamphetamine abuse: A 1H MRS study. *Neurology 54*: 1344-1349.

Fabris P, Tositti G, Manfrin V, Giordani MT, Vaglia A, Cattelan AM, Carlotto A (2000). Does alcohol intake affect highly active antiretroviral therapy (HAART) response in HIV-positive patients? *J. Acquir. Immune Defic. Syndr. 25*: 92-3.

Fiala M, Gan XH, Zhang L, House SD, Newton T, Graves MC, Shapshak P, Stins M, Kim KS, Witte M, Chang SL (1998). Cocaine enhances monocyte migration across the blood-brain barrier. Cocaine's connection to AIDS dementia and vasculitis? *Adv. Exp. Med. Biol. 437*: 199-205.

Flexner CW, Cargill VA, Sinclair J, Kresina TF, Cheever L (2001). Alcohol use can result in enhanced drug metabolism in HIV pharmacotherapy. *AIDS Patient Care STDS 15*: 57-58.

Flora G, Lee YW, Nath A, Hennig B, Maragos W, Toborek M (2003). Methamphetamine potentiates HIV-1 Tat protein-mediated activation of redox-sensitive pathways in discrete regions of the brain. *Exp. Neurol. 179*: 60-70.

Goswami R, Dawson SA, Dawson G (1998). Cyclic AMP protects against staurosporine and wortmannin-induced apoptosis and opioid-enhanced apoptosis in both embryonic and immortalized (F-11kappa7) neurons. *J. Neurochem. 70*: 1376-82.

Green PS, Simpkins JW (2000). Neuroprotective effects of estrogens: potential mechanisms of action. *Int. J. Dev. Neurosci. 18*: 347-58.

Gundlah C, Kohama SG, Mirkes SJ, Garyfallou VT, Urbanski HF, Bethea CL (2000). Distribution of estrogen receptor beta (ERbeta) mRNA in hypothalamus, midbrain and temporal lobe of spayed macaque: continued expression with hormone replacement. *Brain Res. Mol. Brain Res. 76*: 191-204.

Gurwell JA, Nath A, Sun Q, Zhang J, Martin KM, Chen Y, Hauser KF (2001). Synergistic neurotoxicity of opioids and human immunodeficiency virus-1 Tat protein in striatal neurons in vitro. *Neuroscience 102*: 555-63.

Hauser KF, Foldes JK, Turbek CS (1999). Dynorphin A (1-13) neurotoxicity in vitro: opioid and non-opioid mechanisms in mouse spinal cord neurons. *Exp. Neurol. 160*: 361-75.

Hauser KF, Gurwell JA, Turbek CS (1994). Morphine inhibits Purkinje cell survival and dendritic differentiation in organotypic cultures of the mouse cerebellum. *Exp. Neurol. 130*: 95-105.

Hauser KF, Harris-White ME, Jackson JA, Opanashuk LA, Carney JM (1998). Opioids disrupt Ca2+ homeostasis and induce carbonyl oxyradical production in mouse astrocytes in vitro: transient increases and adaptation to sustained exposure. *Exp. Neurol. 151*: 70-6.

Hauser KF, Houdi AA, Turbek CS, Elde RP, Maxson W, 3rd (2000). Opioids intrinsically inhibit the genesis of mouse cerebellar granule neuron precursors in vitro: differential impact of mu and delta receptor activation on proliferation and neurite elongation. *Eur. J. Neurosci. 12*: 1281-93.

Heaton RK, Grant I, Butters N, White DA, Kirson D, Atkinson JH, McCutchan JA, Taylor MJ, Kelly MD, Ellis RJ, et al. (1995). The HNRC 500--neuropsychology of HIV infection at different disease stages. HIV Neurobehavioral Research Center. *J. Int. Neuropsychol. Soc. 1*: 231-51.

Hollander H, Golden J, Mendelson T, Cortland D (1985). Extrapyramidal symptoms in AIDS patients given low-dose metoclopramide or chlorpromazine [letter]. *Lancet 2*: 1186.

Hornykiewicz O (1998). Biochemical aspects of Parkinson's disease. *Neurology 51*: S2-9.

Hriso E, Kuhn T, Masdeu JC, Grundman M (1991). Extrapyramidal symptoms due to dopamine-blocking agents in patients with AIDS encephalopathy. *Am. J. Psychiatry. 148*: 1558-61.

Hu S, Sheng WS, Lokensgard JR, Peterson PK (2002). Morphine induces apoptosis of human microglia and neurons. *Neuropharmacology 42:*829-36.

Hu XJ, Ticku MK (1995). Chronic ethanol treatment upregulates the NMDA receptor function and binding in mammalian cortical neurons. *Brain Res. Mol. Brain Res. 30*: 347-56.

Johnson-Greene D, Adams KM, Gilman S, Koeppe RA, Junck L, Kluin KJ, Martorello S, Heumann M (1997). Effects of abstinence and relapse upon neuropsychological function and cerebral glucose metabolism in severe chronic alcoholism. *J. Clin. Exp. Neuropsychol. 19*: 378-85.

Khurdayan VK, Buch S, El-Hage N, Lutz SE, Goebel SM, Singh IN, Knapp PE, Turchan-Cholewo J, Nath A, Hauser KF (2004). Preferential vulnerability of astroglia and glial precursors to combined opioid and HIV-1 Tat exposure in vitro. *Eur. J. Neurosci. 19*: 3171-82.

Kieburtz KD, Epstein LG, Gelbard HA, Greenamyre JT (1991). Excitotoxicity and dopaminergic dysfunction in the acquired immunodeficiency syndrome dementia complex. Therapeutic implications. *Arch. Neurol. 48*: 1281-4.

Kofke WA, Garman RH, Garman R, Rose ME (1999). Opioid neurotoxicity: fentanyl-induced exacerbation of cerebral ischemia in rats. *Brain Res. 818*: 326-34.

Kofke WA, Garman RH, Stiller RL, Rose ME, Garman R (1996). Opioid neurotoxicity: fentanyl dose-response effects in rats. *Anesth. Analg. 83*: 1298-306.

Koob GF (2000). Neurobiology of addiction. Toward the development of new therapies. *Ann. N Y Acad. Sci. 909*: 170-85.

Koutsilieri E, Gotz ME, Sopper S, Sauer U, Demuth M, ter Meulen V, Riederer P (1997a). Regulation of glutathione and cell toxicity following exposure to neurotropic substances and human immunodeficiency virus-1 in vitro. *J. Neurovirol. 3*: 342-9.

Koutsilieri E, Gotz ME, Sopper S, Stahl-Hennig C, Czub M, ter Meulen V, Riederer P (1997b). Monoamine metabolite levels in CSF of SIV-infected rhesus monkeys (Macaca mulatta). *Neuroreport 8*: 3833-6.

Kreek MJ (2001). Drug addictions. Molecular and cellular endpoints. *Ann. N. Y. Acad. Sci. 937*: 27-49.

Kreek MJ, Koob GF (1998). Drug dependence: stress and dysregulation of brain reward pathways. *Drug. Alcohol. Depend. 51*: 23-47.

Kumar R, Torres C, Yamamura Y, Rodriguez I, Martinez M, Staprans S, Donahoe RM, Kraiselburd E, Stephens EB, Kumar A (2004). Modulation by morphine of viral set point in rhesus macaques infected with simian immunodeficiency virus and simian-human immunodeficiency virus. *J. Virol. 78*: 11425-8.

Langford D, Adame A, Grigorian A, Grant I, McCutchan JA, Ellis RJ, Marcotte TD, Masliah E (2003). Patterns of selective neuronal damage in methamphetamine-user AIDS patients. *J. Acquir. Immune Defic. Syndr. 34*: 467-74.

Larsson M, Hagberg L, Forsman A, Norkrans G (1991). Cerebrospinal fluid catecholamine metabolites in HIV-infected patients. *J. Neurosci. Res. 28:* 406-9.

Lipton SA (1998). Neuronal injury associated with HIV-1: approaches to treatment. *Annu. Rev. Pharmacol. Toxicol. 38*: 159-77.

Littleton J; Little H (1994). Current concepts of ethanol dependence. *Addiction 89*: 1397-412.

Manly JJ, Merchant CA, Jacobs DM, Small SA, Bell K, Ferin M, Mayeux R (2000). Endogenous estrogen levels and Alzheimer's disease among postmenopausal women. *Neurology 54*: 833-7.

Maragos WF, Young KL, Turchan JT, Guseva M, Pauly JR, Nath A, Cass WA (2002). Human immunodeficiency virus-1 Tat protein and methamphetamine interact synergistically to impair striatal dopaminergic function. *J. Neurochem. 83*: 955-63.

McArthur JC, Kumar AJ, Johnson DW, Selnes OA, Becker JT, Herman C, Cohen BA, Saah A (1990). Incidental white matter hyperintensities on magnetic resonance imaging in HIV-1 infection. Multicenter AIDS Cohort Study. *J. Acquir. Immune. Defic. Syndr. 3*: 252-9.

McCarthy L, Wetzel M, Sliker JK, Eisenstein TK, Rogers TJ (2001). Opioids, opioid receptors, and the immune response. *Drug Alcohol Depend. 62*: 111-123.

Mellon RD, Bayer BM (1998). Evidence for central opioid receptors in the immunomodulatory effects of morphine: review of potential mechanism(s) of action. *J. Neuroimmunol. 83*: 19-28.

Meriney SD, Ford MJ, Oliva D, Pilar G (1991). Endogenous opioids modulate neuronal survival in the developing avian ciliary ganglion. *J. Neurosci. 11*: 3705-17.

Meyerhoff DJ, MacKay S, Sappey-Marinier D, Deicken R, Calabrese G, Dillon WP, Weiner MW, Fein G (1995). Effects of chronic alcohol abuse and HIV infection on brain phosphorus metabolites. *Alcohol Clin. Exp. Res. 19*: 685-92.

Mirsattari SM, Berry ME, Holden JK, Ni W, Nath A, Power C (1999). Paroxysmal dyskinesias in patients with HIV infection. *Neurology 52*: 109-14.

Mirsattari SM, Power C, Nath A (1998). Parkinsonism with HIV infection. *Mov. Disord. 13*: 684-9.

Morgello S, Estanislao L, Simpson D, Geraci A, DiRocco A, Gerits P, Ryan E, Yakoushina T, Khan S, Mahboob R, Naseer M, Dorfman D, Sharp V (2004). HIV-associated distal sensory polyneuropathy in the era of highly active antiretroviral therapy: the Manhattan HIV Brain Bank. *Arch. Neurol. 61*: 546-51.

Murrill CS, Weeks H, Castrucci BC, Weinstock HS, Bell BP, Spruill C, Gwinn M (2002). Age-specific seroprevalence of HIV, hepatitis B virus, and hepatitis C virus infection among injection drug users admitted to drug treatment in 6 US cities. *Am. J. Public Health. 92*: 385-7.

Nair MP, Schwartz SA, Polasani R, Hou J, Sweet A, Chadha KC (1997). Immunoregulatory effects of morphine on human lymphocytes. *Clin. Diagn. Lab. Immunol. 4*: 127-32.

Nath A, Geiger JD (1998). Neurobiological Aspects of HIV infections: neurotoxic mechanisms. *Prog. Neurobiol. 54*: 19-33.

Nath A, Maragos W, Avison M, Schmitt F, Berger J (2001). Accelerated HIV dementia with methamphetamine and cocaine use. *J. Neurovirol. 7*: 66-71.

Nestler EJ, Aghajanian GK (1997). Molecular and cellular basis of addiction. *Science 278*: 58-63.

Pascual-Leone A, Dhuna A (1990). Cocaine-associated multifocal tics. *Neurology 40*: 999-1000.

Pascual-Leone A, Dhuna A, Altafullah I, Anderson DC (1990). Cocaine-induced seizures. *Neurology 40*: 404-7.

Peterson PK, Gekker G, Hu S, Lokensgard J, Portoghese PS, Chao CC (1999). Endomorphin-1 potentiates HIV-1 expression in human brain cell cultures: implication of an atypical mu-opioid receptor. *Neuropharmacology 38*: 273-8.

Peterson PK, Gekker G, Lokensgard JR, Bidlack JM, Chang A, Fang X, Portoghese PS (2001). kappa-Opioid receptor agonist suppression of HIV-1 expression in CD4(+) lymphocytes. *Biochem. Pharmacol. 61*: 1145-51.

Peterson PK, Gekker G, Schut R, Hu S, Balfour HH, Jr., Chao CC (1993). Enhancement of HIV-1 replication by opiates and cocaine: the cytokine connection. *Adv. Exp. Med. Biol. 335*: 181-8.

Petito CK, Cash KS (1992). Blood-brain barrier abnormalities in AIDS: immunohistochemical localization of serum proteins in postmortem brain. *Ann. Neurol. 32*: 658-666.

Pillai R, Nair BS, Watson RR (1991). AIDS, drugs of abuse and the immune system: a complex immunotoxicological network. *Arch. Toxicol. 65*: 609-17.

Polakiewicz RD, Schieferl SM, Gingras AC, Sonenberg N, Comb MJ (1998). mu-Opioid receptor activates signaling pathways implicated in cell survival and translational control. *J. Biol. Chem. 273*: 23534-41.

Power C, Kong PA, Crawford TO, Wesselingh S, Glass JD, McArthur JC, Trapp BD (1993). Cerebral white matter changes in AIDS dementia: alterations of the blood-brain barrier. *Ann. Neurol. 34*: 339-350.

Prendergast MA, Harris BR, Blanchard JA, 2nd, Mayer S, Gibson DA, Littleton JM (2000). In vitro effects of ethanol withdrawal and spermidine on viability of hippocampus from male and female rat. *Alcohol. Clin. Exp. Res. 24*: 1855-61.

Pu H, Tian J, Flora G, Lee YW, Nath A, Hennig B, Toborek M (2003). HIV-1 Tat protein upregulates inflammatory mediators and induces monocyte invasion into the brain. *Mol. Cell Neurosci. 24*: 224-37.

Rabkin JG, McElhiney MC, Ferrando SJ (2004). Mood and substance use disorders in older adults with HIV/AIDS: methodological issues and preliminary evidence. *Aids 18 Suppl. 1*: S43-8.

Reyes MG, Faraldi F, Senseng CS, Flowers C, Fariello R (1991). Nigral degeneration in acquired immune deficiency syndrome (AIDS). *Acta Neuropathol. 82*: 39-44.

Robinson TE, Berridge KC (2000). The psychology and neurobiology of addiction: an incentive-sensitization view. *Addiction 95 Suppl. 2*: S91-117.

Rogers TJ, Peterson PK (2003). Opioid G protein-coupled receptors: signals at the crossroads of inflammation. *Trends Immunol. 24*: 116-21.

Rogers TJ, Steele AD, Howard OM, Oppenheim JJ (2000). Bidirectional heterologous desensitization of opioid and chemokine receptors. *Ann. N. Y. Acad. Sci. 917*: 19-28.

Rooney KF, Armstrong RA, Sewell RD (1991). Increased dopamine receptor sensitivity in the rat following acute administration of sufentanil, U50,488H and D-Ala2-D-Leu5-enkephalin. *Naunyn. Schmiedebergs. Arch. Pharmacol. 343*: 458-62.

Rudolph JG, Lemasters JJ, Crews FT (1998). Effects of chronic ethanol exposure on oxidation and NMDA-stimulated neuronal death in primary cortical neuronal cultures. *Alcohol. Clin. Exp. Res. 22*: 2080-5.

Saunders-Pullman R, Gordon-Elliott J, Parides M, Fahn S, Saunders HR, Bressman S (1999). The effect of estrogen replacement on early Parkinson's disease. *Neurology 52*: 1417-21.

Schoffelmeer AN, Hogenboom F, Mulder AH (1997). Kappa1- and kappa2-opioid receptors mediating presynaptic inhibition of dopamine and acetylcholine release in rat neostriatum. *Br. J. Pharmacol. 122*: 520-4.

Sharp BM, Roy S, Bidlack JM (1998). Evidence for opioid receptors on cells involved in host defense and the immune system. *J. Neuroimmunol. 83*: 45-56.

Singhal PC, Kapasi AA, Reddy K, Franki N, Gibbons N, Ding G (1999). Morphine promotes apoptosis in Jurkat cells. *J. Leukoc. Biol. 66*: 650-8.

Singhal PC, Reddy K, Franki N, Sanwal V, Gibbons N (1997). Morphine induces splenocyte apoptosis and enhanced mRNA expression of cathepsin-B. *Inflammation 21*: 609-17.

Singhal PC, Sagar S, Reddy K, Sharma P, Ranjan R, Franki N (1998a). HIV-1 gp120 envelope protein and morphine-tubular cell interaction products modulate kidney fibroblast proliferation. *J. Investig. Med. 46*: 243-8.

Singhal PC, Sharma P, Kapasi AA, Reddy K, Franki N, Gibbons N (1998b). Morphine enhances macrophage apoptosis. *J. Immunol. 160*: 1886-93.

Slooter AJ, Bronzova J, Witteman JC, Van Broeckhoven C, Hofman A, van Duijn CM (1999). Estrogen use and early onset Alzheimer's disease: a population-based study. *J. Neurol. Neurosurg. Psychiatry. 67*: 779-81.

Stefano GB (1999). Substance abuse and HIV-gp120: are opiates protective? *Arch. Immunol. Ther. Exp. 47*: 99-106.

Stiene-Martin A, Zhou R, Hauser KF (1998). Regional, developmental, and cell cycle-dependent differences in mu, delta, and kappa-opioid receptor expression among cultured mouse astrocytes. *Glia 22*: 249-59.

Tabakoff B (1994). Alcohol and AIDS--is the relationship all in our heads? *Alcohol. Clin. Exp. Res. 18*: 415-6.

Toborek M, Lee YW, Pu H, Malecki A, Flora G, Garrido R, Hennig B, Bauer HC, Nath A (2003). HIV-Tat protein induces oxidative and inflammatory pathways in brain endothelium. *J. Neurochem. 84*: 169-79.

Tomlinson GS, Simmonds P, Busuttil A, Chiswick A, Bell JE (1999). Upregulation of microglia in drug users with and without pre-symptomatic HIV infection. *Neuropathol. Appl. Neurobiol. 25*: 369-79.

Turchan J, Anderson C, Hauser KF, Sun Q, Zhang J, Liu Y, Wise PM, Kruman I, Maragos W, Mattson MP, Booze R, Nath A (2001). Estrogen protects against the synergistic toxicity by HIV proteins, methamphetamine and cocaine. *BMC Neurosci. 2*: 3.

Turchan J, Pocernich CB, Gairola C, Chauhan A, Schifitto G, Butterfield DA, Buch S, Narayan O, Sinai A, Geiger J, Berger JR, Elford H, Nath A (2003). Oxidative stress in HIV demented patients and protection ex vivo with novel antioxidants. *Neurology 60*: 307-14.

Tyor WR, Middaugh LD (1999). Do alcohol and cocaine abuse alter the course of HIV-associated dementia complex? *J. Leukoc. Biol. 65*: 475-81.

Vanderschuren LJ, Wardeh G, De Vries TJ, Mulder AH, Schoffelmeer AN (1999). Opposing role of dopamine D1 and D2 receptors in modulation of rat nucleus accumbens noradrenaline release. *J. Neurosci. 19*: 4123-31.

Walker DW, Heaton MB, Lee N, King MA, Hunter BE (1993). Effect of chronic ethanol on the septohippocampal system: a role for neurotrophic factors? *Alcohol. Clin. Exp. Res. 17*: 12-8.

Watzl B, Watson RR (1992). Role of alcohol abuse in nutritional immunosuppression. *J. Nutr. 122:* 733-7.

Weiner WJ, Rabinstein A, Levin B, Weiner C, Shulman LM (2001). Cocaine-induced persistent dyskinesias. *Neurology 56*: 964-5.

Weinhardt LS, Carey MP, Carey KB, Maisto SA, Gordon CM (2001). The relation of alcohol use to HIV-risk sexual behavior among adults with a severe and persistent mental illness. *J. Consult. Clin. Psychol. 69*: 77-84.

Wilson JM, Kalasinsky KS, Levey AI, Bergeron C, Reiber G, Anthony RM, Schmunk GA, Shannak K, Haycock JW, Kish SJ (1996a). Striatal dopamine nerve terminal markers in human, chronic methamphetamine users. *Nat. Med. 2*: 699-703.

Wilson JM, Levey AI, Bergeron C, Kalasinsky K, Ang L, Peretti F, Adams VI, Smialek J, Anderson WR, Shannak K, Deck J, Niznik HB, Kish SJ (1996b). Striatal dopamine, dopamine transporter, and vesicular monoamine transporter in chronic cocaine users. *Ann. Neurol. 40*: 428-39.

Yin D, Mufson RA, Wang R, Shi Y (1999). Fas-mediated cell death promoted by opioids. *Nature 397*: 218.

Yin DL, Ren XH, Zheng ZL, Pu L, Jiang LZ, Ma L, Pei G (1997). Etorphine inhibits cell growth and induces apoptosis in SK-N-SH cells: involvement of pertussis toxin-sensitive G proteins. *Neurosci. Res. 29*: 121-7.

In: Substance Abuse: New Research
Editors: Ethan J. Kerr and Owen E. Gibson

ISBN 978-1-60456-834-9
© 2009 Nova Science Publishers, Inc.

Chapter 4

DRUG ABUSE

Manoel Jorge Nobre and Vanessa Moreno Castilho

Faculty of Philosophy, Sciences and Letters of Ribeirao Preto,
University of Sao Paulo, Brazil

INTRODUCTION

Drug dependence, or addiction, is a relapsing disorder characterized by the loss of control of drug intake, or compulsion to take the drug, associated with the appearance of a withdrawal syndrome after a discontinuation of its long-term use. Several authors have pointed out the need to define the phenomenon of addiction in behavioral terms establishing that, in a general way, addiction is a relapsing disorder that leads to a compulsive drug use, despite the harmful effects in some aspects of the person's functioning. Actually, with the progress in basic and clinical research, evidenced by the rapid advances at the molecular, cellular, neural and behavioral levels, the study of drug dependence has raised important conceptual issues that have helped the neurobiological research to better understand the changes in the neural mechanisms underlying the development of addiction, and the expression of the withdrawal symptoms.

Drugs of abuse produce, initially, a state of pleasure characterized by its positive reinforcing properties, and that is the reason they are taken. However, its repetitive administration leads to a natural adaptation of the central nervous system, including long-lasting changes. As the user's body adjusts to the drug, a bigger amount of it needs to be taken each time to get to the same first results. This can quickly lead to the use of more and more of the drug and, consequently, to addiction or dependence, characterized by the appearance of a behavioral repertoire toward an excessive drug intake, whenever the drug ingestion is interrupted. This means that, in addicts, drug-seeking behavior becomes compulsive. If a user stops taking the drug withdrawal symptoms appears, as the nervous system needs to adjust functioning without the drug. It may take weeks before the nervous system is back to normal, and during this time there is great temptation to use the drug again and then, discontinue the withdrawal symptoms. In fact, relapse is possible even after long periods of abstinence, even years after cessation of drug use (Figure 10.1). In this chapter, we will briefly discuss some basic neurobiological, motivational and behavioral processes that drive an individual from an impulsive to a compulsive disorder and, the importance of affective symptoms, such as fear and anxiety, as the promoting factors of relapsing.

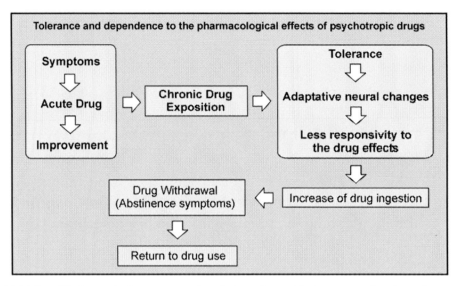

Figure 10.1. The addiction cycle from acute to chronic ingestion and its importance in relapse (return to drug intake after a period of abstinence).

NEURAL ADAPTATION

Drug seeking behavior and drug self-administration in both animals and humans, can be triggered by drugs of abuse themselves, or can be facilitated by prolonged exposition to stressful events. Chronic ingestion of drugs of abuse leads to long-lived alterations in the brain function, and the fundamental types of mechanisms appear to be similar: chronic drug administration induces prolonged changes in the brain function (neural plasticity), by influencing the signal transduction pathways of the brain, including the regulation of neural gene expression. This type of functional organization reflects adaptation to the environment. In this sense, long-lasting activity-dependent changes in the efficacy of synaptic transmission, play an important role in the development of neural circuits and may mediate many forms of learning and memory that serves an adaptive process, shared by virtually all organisms. So, if the environment stays approximately the same, the functional organization also remains unaltered. On the other hand, any changes in the environment lead to a homeostatic imbalance reflected by physiological modifications in the neural systems that trigger plastic changes to facilitate re-adaptation. That is what drug abuse does: functional and probably structural changes in the brain functioning.

In parallel with drugs that produce physical addiction, many drugs of abuse also cause psychological dependence, that is, in some situations the individual maintains the behavior upon which their presentation is contingent. Most addictive drugs, like amphetamine, cocaine, morphine and ethanol, and in some cases benzodiazepines, support self administration. This pattern of responding may vary depending upon the schedule of delivery, the organisms' prior history and the type of stimuli presented (type of drug, cues presented during reinforcement, etc).

In a general way, the phenomenon of neural adaptation to continuous administration of any drug could be observed from the following hypothetical constructs: the appearance of tolerance or sensitization to the effects of the drug, the raising of an abstinence syndrome after the treatment has been discontinued (withdrawal), and the appearance of feelings of craving. We will see briefly now, each one of these constructs.

TOLERANCE

Tolerance and physical dependence develop after chronic administration of any one of an array of mood-altering substances. Tolerance is a phenomenon often defined as a gradual decrease in responsiveness (over days or weeks) to a drug dose, after its continuous administration in such a way that the dose must be increased to produce the same initial effect and thus, more drug is needed. Tolerance and dependence develop as the nerve cells counteract the drug's psychoactive effects, chemically and structurally. Tolerance is a complex generalized phenomenon that involves many independent physiological and behavioral mechanisms (Figure 10.2).

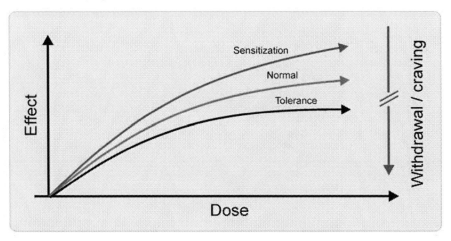

Figure 10.2. Shifts in a dose-response curve during tolerance and sensitization. There is a shift of the dose-response curve to the right or to the left in the tolerance and sensitization, respectively, that is, for a given dose there is a lower or a greater effect in comparison with the initial dose. Cessation of drug intake leads to craving and withdrawal syndrome.

The tolerance can be pharmacodynamic (or functional tolerance), physiological (or adaptation by homeostatic mechanisms), pharmacokinetic (metabolic) and conditioned (behavioral). Of importance for this chapter is the classically conditioned tolerance in which a stimulus repeatedly paired with the drug administration can evoke, alone, conditioned responses that are conflicting with the drug effect, by compensatory mechanisms. The conditioned tolerance can be explained by a compensatory response (CR) in which the conditioned stimuli presented during the drug administration acquire the capacity to elicit the compensatory response, by compensatory mechanisms, or the cues present in the context at the moment of the drug ingestion add to the drug effects generating a compensatory response, which is a tolerance response to the drug effects (Figure 10.3).

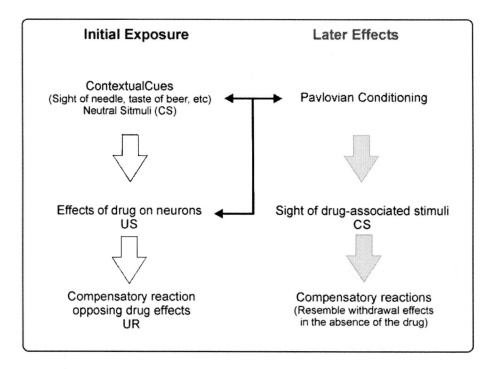

Figure 10.3. Main effects of chronic drug use and the importance of Pavlovian conditioning in the learned tolerance. An initial exposure to drug (on acute ingestion) leads to its reinforcing effects on the central nervous system that promotes a raised compensatory response, that is, a compensatory response of the organism opposed to the drug effect. In parallel, environmental cues, initially harmless (e.g. sight of a needle), begin to sum up to the drug effects. After a long-period administration and in function of a Pavlovian-like conditioning, the simple presentation of a cue-related drug raises a similar compensatory response and all the disagreeable effects, similarly to what happens during drug withdrawal.

SENSITIZATION

Sensitization is defined as the enhancement of a directly elicited drug effect, through adaptive processes, and appears to represent facilitation within a system, making it easier to elicit the response in future occasions. Like tolerance, sensitization of a drug effect can become linked to the events that co-occurred when the effect was originally elicited, being thus possible to come under selective event control.

WITHDRAWAL

The term withdrawal defines a group of symptoms that result from an abrupt interruption of a chronic drug treatment. The abrupt interruption of the chronic administration of a drug of abuse leads to the instatement of a withdrawal syndrome characterized by the raise of a lot of physical and negative affective symptoms, such as dysphoria, anhedonia and anxiety. This type of phenomenon can also be induced by pharmacological means or by the use of specific antagonists. For example, an opioid withdrawal syndrome can be induced in morphine-dependent rats by the administration of an opioid antagonist, such as naltrexone. In the same way, a benzodiazepine withdrawal syndrome can be produced by a single injection of flumazenil, a benzodiazepine antagonist.

During withdrawal of a drug of abuse, the individual becomes obsessed with obtaining the drug for a sense of well being. Chemically dependent people become inflexible in their behavior toward the drug, despite the adverse consequences. The intensity of this felt "need" or dependence may vary from mild craving, to an intense overwhelming obsession. In most cases, the withdrawal symptoms are opposed to the original symptoms, or represent an exacerbation of the symptoms which generated the need of that drug. Because of this, it is common to say that the withdrawal symptoms are a rebound effect in the physiological systems modified by the drug. For example, alcohol depresses the central nervous system, withdrawal stimulates it. Amphetamine is a stimulant of the central nervous system, so amphetamine withdrawal causes depression. Benzodiazepines are anxiolytic drugs; nevertheless diazepam withdrawal is characterized by intense anxiety.

The time required to produce physical dependence may vary among the drugs. Withdrawal symptoms can develop in a single day with large quantities of central nervous system depressants. For most drug users, development of physical dependence is gradual, occurring over weeks, months, or years of chronic administration.

CRAVING

Generally, craving is defined as an excessive "yearning" to experiment the effects of some drug, or a very strong desire for a drug or for its intoxicating effects, and it is thought to develop, at least partially, as a result of associations resulting from Pavlovian conditioning that rise when the person is confronted with a conditioned stimulus associated with the drug effects. In fact, even stimuli presented during a single cocaine experience may elicit drug-seeking for up one year. Craving is one of the most important symptoms of the withdrawal syndrome and frequently represents the most common cause of relapse. Nevertheless, the occurrence of craving and relapse can be facilitated by other factors, like stress. In fact, stress plays a crucial role in relapse, although complex and influenced by multiple sources.

NEURAL SYSTEMS AND DRUG DEPENDENCE

After a chronic exposition to drugs of abuse, many changes begin to occur in the brain, particularly at the brainstem and limbic structures. In fact, drugs of abuse act characteristically on a particular system in the brain to achieve its rewarding effects. Initially, the reinforcing properties of the drug seem to act according to the paradigm of the operant conditioning in which its rewarding effects facilitate further exposure to the drug.

In general, the factors that lead an individual from a simple acute ingestion of any psychoactive drug, to an incontrollable "craving" for it, could be described in three steps: Initially, almost always because of social or cultural pressures, the individual takes the drug (alcohol, for example). The contact and ingestion (acute use) of the drug raises an affective (psychological) and physical (somatic and autonomic) welfare that causes a temporary organic unbalancing. In this stage the subject responds to the drug and to the drug-related stimuli in a controlled manner, not dissimilar from normal motivated responding. Following repeated ingestion (chronic use), an homeostatic process begins to occur, promoting a neural adaptation. At the same time, all the cues presented during reinforcement (drug ingestion) begin to add to the drug effect leading to tolerance. With repeated drug exposure, the subject enters progressively in the stage of drug abuse. The repeated associations of drug reward and drug-related stimuli result in the attribution of excessive motivational value to the drug-associated stimuli. At this moment, the subject can still control the drug intake in the absence of the drug-related stimuli. Their presence, however, elicits drug-seeking, associated sometimes to mild drug need (craving). In this stage, abstinence results in a negative emotional state that maintains the motivational relationship between the subject and the drug in the intervals, when drug-conditioned incentives are not available. In the post-addiction stage, abstinence symptoms progressively disappear but Pavlovian associations remain as powerful incentives for reinstatement of drug self-administration, so that the presence of a mild drug-related cue is sufficient to evoke craving.

THE DOPAMINERGIC SYSTEM

Most drugs of abuse act on ancient and remarkably conserved neural mechanisms, associated with positive emotions that evolved to mediate incentive behavior. Heroin, cocaine, alcohol, marijuana, amphetamine, and their synthetic analogs activate mesolimbic dopamine-containing neurons and associated opioid receptors, in mammalian brains, a system that may be a "common neural currency" for reward and a substrate for regulating motivation. In fact, the discovery of neural circuits responsible for the modulation of the reinforcing effects of drugs of abuse starts, initially, from a classical experiment conducted by Olds and Milner (1954) that, accidentally, revealed the involvement of the mesolimbic-dopaminergic pathway in the reward effects induced by electrical intracranial self-stimulation in rats (Figure 10.4). They found that electrical stimulation of this brain area has a potent reinforcing effect, which means that the subject will repeat any behavior which results in pleasurable sensation.

The reinforcing effects of brain electrical stimulation have been found in a variety of animals. The discovery has also been confirmed in humans. Since then, these regions are called pleasure or reward centers in the brain. There are reward centers in the hypothalamus, septal regions and in the temporal lobes of the cerebral hemispheres. For instance, when the septal region is stimulated in conscious patients undergoing neurosurgery, they experience feelings of pleasure, optimism, euphoria, and happiness.

Since the discovery that most drugs of abuse (except benzodiazepines) increase the release of dopamine in the brain, there has been an intense interest in the long-length mesolimbic-dopaminergic pathway, the main dopaminergic system in the brain. The most important source of dopaminergic innervation in the central nervous system is found in the mesencephalon, basically three cell groups named, A8, A9 and A10. The A8 and A10 groups compose the ventral tegmental area (VTA), and the A9 group belongs to the *substantia nigra pars compacta* (SNpc). It is well known that the mesencephalic dopaminergic neurons localized in these areas give rise to massive ascending projections, divided in two main systems: the *nigro-striatal* that originates mainly from A9 group neurons, and the mesolimbic dopaminergic system that originates from the A10 group. In a general way, the nigro-striatal pathway is a motor control pathway and the mesolimbic system is the so-called reward pathway (Figure 10.5).

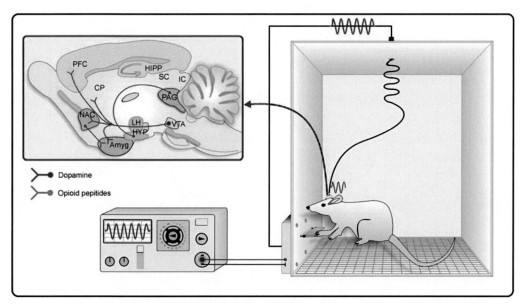

Figure 10.4. Brain self-stimulation in rats. Brain electrical stimulation by an electrode inserted into the medial forebrain bundle (the brain reward system) enhances rat lever pressing behavior. Since the animal prefers the region of the test apparatus where the stimulation is received, it may be inferred that the rat has a pleasurable experience. To test this hypothesis, researchers have elaborated an experiment to determine whether the rat would learn to perform arbitrary behaviors to obtain brief pulses of brain stimulation. Amyg = amygdala, CP= caudate-putamen, Hipp = hippocampus, Hyp = hypothalamus, IC = inferior colliculus, LH = lateral hypothalamus, Nac = nucleus accumbens, PAG = ventral periaqueductal gray, PFC = prefrontal cortex, SC = superior colliculus.

The dopaminergic neurons from the VTA project to the basal forebrain, mainly to the prefrontal cortex, *nucleus accumbens* (NAcc), olfactory tubercle, amygdala and limbic cortices through the medial forebrain bundle (Figure 10.5). This system is commonly activated by natural reinforcers, such as water, food and sex, and is the primary site of action of drugs like alcohol, stimulants (such as cocaine) and opioids. As an example, the reinforcing effects of cocaine and amphetamines are the result of the drug-induced alterations in dopamine NAcc; opiates, nicotine and THC act by interacting with dopamine and opioid peptides systems in the ventral tegmental area, NAcc and amygdala.

Many studies have revealed the essential role of the ventral tegmental area in reward. Some works utilizing the self-administration technique showed that animals self-administer drugs directly in this structure while the rewarding properties of morphine are probably due to its action in opioid receptors present in the dopaminergic neurons.

The *nucleus accumbens* (NAcc) is the other structure clearly involved in the reinforcing effects of psychoactive drugs. This forebrain region is also known by the name of ventral striatum and is the main target of the dopaminergic projections from VTA, consisting of a ventral shell (target of the mesolimbic dopamine projections) and a dorsal core (the target for

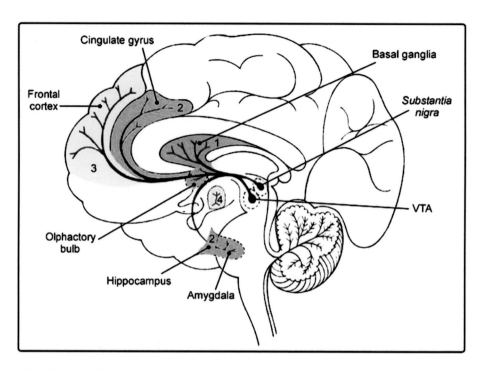

Figure 10.5. The mesolimbic and *nigro-striatal* dopaminergic pathways. The mesolimbic dopaminergic pathway has cell bodies located in the VTA and its axons ascend through the medial forebrain bundle to limbic and cortical structures innervating mainly the NAcc and also the amygdala, hippocampus, septum and olfactory tubercle. The mesolimbic pathway is involved in the control of motor behavior, as well as motivation, emotions and reward. The *nigro-striatal* dopaminergic pathway originates in the SNpc and terminates in the dorsal part of the striatum, the caudate-putamen, also known as the dorsal striatum. A minor part of this pathway projects to the ventral striatum. The *nigro-striatal* pathway contains about 75% of whole brain dopamine, and is involved in the control of posture and motor behavior, as well as learning motor programs and habits.

the nigro-striatal system). It is well documented that the activation of NAcc can facilitate or trigger consumatory behavior (eating) but, its primary role is in the motivational circuitry. Most researchers in the field of drug abuse believe that drug-induced pleasurable effects correlate with an increase in the extracellular dopamine levels within the NAcc and there is some agreement about the mainly function of dopamine in the reinforcing effects of drugs of abuse, but this is not true for benzodiazepines; just to remember, this class of anxiolytic drugs act on specific receptors called GABA-benzodiazepine receptors. For example, differently from other psychoactive drugs, the withdrawal syndrome induced by abrupt interruption of chronic treatment with diazepam seems not to be linked to changes in dopamine transmission in the mesolimbic system. In this way, the behavioral, sensorial and autonomic effects observed during diazepam withdrawal could be a consequence of the activation of other neurotransmitter systems, like the glutamatergic or serotonergic, for example.

A lot of evidence has demonstrated the involvement of the mesolimbic system (comprised of the NAcc, amygdala, and VTA) in the reinforcing properties of drugs of abuse and it has already been demonstrated an increase of dopamine levels in the NAcc after direct electrical stimulation of some brain regions, or after self-administration of many drugs of abuse including ethanol. Thus, it has been of utmost importance to have knowledge on the multiple ways drugs of abuse act on the dopaminergic system. The disclosure of the particular dopaminergic circuit, the type of receptors with which a given drug interacts and its mechanism of action is of great importance in the understanding of the molecular mechanisms underlying its potential of abuse (Box 1). However, not all drugs have their potential of abuse related to the dopaminergic transmission. Indeed, it is very intriguing that though benzodiazepines and alcohol share virtually the same behavioral effects, the symptoms observed after benzodiazepine administration seem not to be related to alterations in dopaminergic processes. Our understanding of the mechanisms of action of benzodiazepines, alcohol and nicotine has been significantly enhanced by the discovery of their brain targets, the $GABA_A$ and the nicotine receptors.

THE GABAERGIC SYSTEM, BENZODIAZEPINES AND ALCOHOL

When benzodiazepine drugs were first introduced in the clinical practice, they were thought to be free of addictive properties, until the 1970´s decade, when it was clear that these types of compounds could produce a withdrawal syndrome after its discontinuation. The study of benzodiazepines and its propensity to produce abstinence is a relevant matter, since a substantial proportion of patients that receive both high and normal doses of benzodiazepines will develop some form of physiological dependence (neuroadaptation induced by a prolonged exposure to the drug).

Benzodiazepines have been prescribed basically by their hypnotic and anxiolytic properties and, also, as sedatives, anticonvulsants, muscle-relaxants, and to treat the symptoms of alcohol withdrawal. However, despite the clinical advantages (mainly their minimal side-effects and a very low risk of overdose), during chronic administration it has been reported physiological withdrawal syndrome, following their abrupt discontinuation, and the return of the original anxiety in a more potent form (named rebound anxiety) sometimes accompanied by psychological (anxiety, irritability, insomnia) and physiological (tremor, palpitations, muscle spasms, gastrointestinal disturbances and even, in some cases, convulsions) symptoms. It has also been reported marked catatonia induced by benzodiazepine abstinence, with high doses and/or long term treatment. The increased anxiety symptoms are not so easy to differentiate from the original pathology, but they can be distinguished in terms of intensity and severity. It is worth mentioning that the high levels of anxiety, and the somatic and autonomic changes, present during abstinence are among the most powerful reasons for resuming drug intake.

Tolerance to benzodiazepines has been mainly attributed to metabolic (pharmacokinetic) or adaptative (pharmacodynamic) changes within the central nervous system after a prolonged exposure to the drug. These effects are mainly an attempt of the central nervous system to return to homeostasis, and keep its normal physiological function. It is considered that the physiological dependence leads to a pattern of physical withdrawal (somatic and autonomic alterations) symptoms, and that the psychological dependence reflects the powerful desire (craving) to obtain the drug during abstinence. Many theories have been elaborated to explain these types of adaptative processes. One of the most widely known argues that chronic drug administration leads to the initiation of adaptive processes that counteract the acute effects of the drug, and that these processes persist after the drug has been cleared from the brain, leaving the opposing forces unopposed (Figure 10.6).

Up to now, not a single specific neurotransmitter binding site for alcohol in the brain has been identified, but it is thought that alcohol can affect the neuronal function by directly interacting with membrane proteins, such as receptors and ion channels. Current research also strongly suggests that alcohol, similar to other drugs of abuse such as benzodiazepines, affects multiple neurotransmitter systems in the brain, causing the neuron to react, by increasing or decreasing its normal functions. Research performed on the GABAergic system has demonstrated that both alcohol and benzodiazepines potentiate chloride influx induced by $GABA_A$ receptors in some regions of the brain. These types of effects can be blocked by previous administration of GABA antagonists, such as picrotoxin or bicuculline and even by benzodiazepine inverse agonists. However, it seems that the $GABA_B$ receptors are also involved in the alcohol effects. In fact, their blockade can powerfully enhance the acute effects of alcohol on $GABA_A$ receptor-mediated inhibitory postsynaptic currents (IPSCs) in the hippocampus of the rat. In this way, $GABA_B$ receptors seem to function as autoreceptors inhibiting $GABA_A$ IPSCs, suggesting that some $GABA_B$ receptor-dependent processes can play an important role in the alcohol sensitivity of GABAergic synapses.

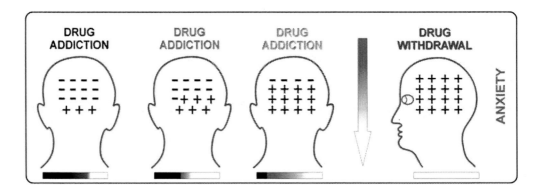

Figure 10.6. Schematic illustration of the main alterations induced by drug of abuse in the brain. In a "normal" condition, and regulated by homeostatic mechanisms, there is a balance between inhibitory and excitatory mechanisms. A long-term drug use (e.g. opioid drugs) leads to an enhancement of the excitatory systems in the brain, as opposed to the depressant effects of the drug. During abstinence, when the organism is drug-free, there is an overload in the brain areas where the drug acted induced by the excitatory mechanisms, mainly mediated by glutamate.

The reinforcing effects of alcohol can explain its ability to function as discriminative stimulus in a lot of operant paradigms. In fact, alcohol is considered to be reinforcing because its ingestion, withdrawal following long-term use, or sometimes just the sight or smell of an alcoholic drink or associated cues, increase the drinking probability. These effects could be explained by the ability of alcohol to interact with the brain reward system, thus stimulating its continued use.

When alcohol is chronically administered, some neurons seem to adapt to its presence by enhancing or reducing their response to a normal stimuli, characterizing an organic form of tolerance. Also, chronic alcohol administration produces behavioral effects similar to that observed during chronic exposure to benzodiazepines and barbiturates. Indeed, chronic alcohol ingestion produces tolerance, dependence and a withdrawal syndrome after its interruption. These types of effects are associated with a decrease in the sensitivity of $GABA_A$ receptors in some areas of the brain, mainly the cerebral cortex, NAcc, the medial septal nucleus and, also, the spinal cord.

THE OPIOID SYSTEM

Since 1806, when the German scientist Sertürner isolated morphine, a very important active principle of opium, this substance has been largely used in the entire world, basically by its anesthetic qualities. Morphine is a very potent analgesic, but it is as addictive as opium. Indeed, besides its analgesic effects, its acute administration produces euphoria, drowsiness and, in a chronic administration, it has a high potential to produce dependence.

The existence of endogenous opioid-like molecules produced by the organism itself was demonstrated in 1970´s, from the observation that the mammalian brain extracts possess opiate-like activity. This fact has stimulated the researches in this field, leading to the isolation and characterization of endogenous opioid peptides, such as the enkephalins (leu- and met-enkephalin), β-endorphins and dynorphins, each one of them derived from its precursors molecules Proenkephalin A (ProEnk), Pro-opiomelanocortin (POMC) and Proenkephalin B, also known by Prodynorphin (ProDyn), respectively.

Tolerance to opioids develops rapidly, although not all their pharmacological effects change with the same speed and magnitude. For example, whereas the analgesic and euphoric effects suffer rapid tolerance, miosis and constipation persist even after prolonged (chronic) use. The level of tolerance depends upon the frequency of use and doses of the drug. After three or four months of use, the dose consumed can be ten times higher than the initial. In fact, the dose utilized by a regular user can be enough to kill a non-tolerant user.

Tolerance to opioid substances seems to be mainly pharmacodynamic since the cells virtually "adapt themselves" to the drug presence. The chronic administration of opioids just moderately reduces the number of opioid receptors *in vivo*. For example, after 6 days of subcutaneous administration of morphine in guinea pigs, the number of μ receptors is 25% reduced, with no alterations in the number of δ or κ receptors. Therefore, the tolerance to opioids is not exclusively linked to the down-regulation of receptors, but mainly to the desensitization process.

Conditioning processes have also been implicated in the development of tolerance to opioids. An environmental stimulus associated with morphine administration elicits compensatory responses. This can be confirmed by some experiments in which rats have received morphine chronic treatment in a distinct environment. The tolerance to the analgesic effects occurred only when the animals were tested in the same context in which they had received the drug, but not when they were tested in a different context.

All the opioid substances produce psychological and physiological dependence expressed, respectively, by the emergence of affective and physical withdrawal symptoms, when the chronic administration of the drug is abruptly discontinued. These symptoms are so unpleasant that they constitute the most important factor that leads the user to persist taking the drug. The physical signs are restlessness, agitation, yawning and chills and a lot of autonomic and somatic changes. The severity of these symptoms depends on the dose utilized, the frequency of administration and the time of drug use. This set of symptoms is accompanied by emotional alterations, such as depression, irritability and high levels of anxiety. The peak of these symptoms generally occurs 26 h after the last administration and disappears between 7 to 10 days. During the abstinence phase, opioid administration blocks all symptoms. It is believed that the withdrawal syndrome occurs when the opioid receptors stop being occupied with the opioid. For this reason, the administration of an opioid antagonist, as naloxone, that removes abruptly the opioid from its receptors, promotes a withdrawal syndrome more severe than that caused by the simple abstinence of the drug.

Opioid Reinforcement, Dependence and Withdrawal Effects

There is some evidence showing that the positive reinforcement produced by opioids depends on the opioid receptors activation in the ventral tegmental area (VTA) and in the NAcc. In this way, rats rapidly learn to press a lever to get morphine injections in the VTA, but not in other areas. Besides, morphine microinjection in the VTA facilitates the intracranial self-stimulation (ICSS) and induces conditioned place preference (CPP). It is believed that exogenous opioids produce its positive reinforcement effects through activation of μ receptors present in the VTA, specifically. The same phenomenon is observed in the NAcc, but this type of behavior requires higher doses of morphine than the ones that maintain the self-administration in the VTA. Similarly to what occurs in the VTA, blockade of μ or activation of κ receptors in the NAcc results in conditioned place aversion (Box 2).

It is believed that many brain regions are responsible for the development and expression of opioid dependence. Studies with microinjection of opioid antagonists in specific brain areas of opioid-dependent animals have been conducted to identify the structures involved in the physical and affective symptoms of abstinence.

The brain structures involved in the physical dependence to opioids seem to be, mainly, the locus coeruleus, central gray and lateral hypothalamus, since the administration of naloxone or metylnaloxonium (a hydrophilic opioid antagonist that is not quickly spread out in the brain), directly in these areas, precipitates the somatic symptoms of withdrawal in morphine-dependent animals.

On the contrary, microinjections of opioid antagonists in the VTA and, especially, in the NAcc and amygdala, precipitate only affective signs of abstinence in dependent animals, expressed by the conditioned aversion to the place, associated with the withdrawal. Moreover, the induction of the affective symptoms of morphine abstinence is correlated with increased activity of neurons in the central nucleus of amygdala and the NAcc (shell).

The chronic use of opioids produces changes in the endogenous opioid systems. In a clinical study, it was observed that human addicts in heroine present plasmatic levels of β-endorphin about 3 times lesser than normal subjects, suggesting that the endorphin system in chronic addicts in heroine is depressed. Morphine-dependent rats present diminished levels of β-endorphin in the plasma, pituitary, hypothalamus and mesencephalon. Thus, the tolerance to the analgesic effect of morphine, for example, could be developed because the reduction in the levels of endogenous opioids would imply in the necessity of greater amounts of morphine to inhibit the transmission in the pain pathways. In this point, abrupt withdrawal of morphine, in conjunction with low levels of endogenous opioid peptides, would disinhibit pain fibers, producing a typical symptom of withdrawal, the hyperalgesia. The same reasoning can be applied to other symptoms of abstinence.

Besides its crucial role in the mediation of positive reinforcing effects of the opioids, alterations in the mesolimbic dopaminergic system are also responsible for the expression of withdrawal symptoms. In morphine-dependent animals, the withdrawal of the drug reduces the rate of firing of the VTA-NAcc neurons in about 30%, decreasing significantly the amount of dopamine released in the NAcc, what possibly is correlated with the affective symptoms of abstinence. However, the importance of the decrease in dopaminergic activity during the expression of physical dependence to opioids also must be considered, since the somatic symptoms of withdrawal can be induced after the blockade of D_2 receptors in the NAcc, or reduced by its activation. As the administration of opioid antagonists in the NAcc does not precipitate somatic symptoms of abstinence, it becomes clear that this structure is not part of the main brain sites for the induction of physical dependence, but it can have an important role in the regulation of the circuits that fire the somatic and affective responses during the opioid withdrawal. The expressive reduction in the release of dopamine in the mesolimbic dopaminergic system can be influenced by the hyperactivity of the noradrenergic system, which exerts an inhibitory influence on the mesencephalic dopaminergic neurons. However, the relations among these systems still need to be elucidated.

MARIJUANA, LYSERGIC ACID AND ECSTASY

Marijuana is one of the most utilized drugs of abuse in the world, even today. Its scientific name is *cannabis sativa* and the main chemical substance responsible for its psychomimetic effects is Δ-9-tetrahydrocannabinol (THC). The effects that marijuana produces in the central nervous system can be divided in physical and psychic effects. Its ingestion leads to very few physical effects like hyperemia, dry mouth and tachycardia Psychological effects will depend on the type of marijuana smoked, and the personal characteristics of the smoker, but generally feelings of welfare, calm, and easy laughing may appear (however, for some people the effects can be disagreeable and the individual may feel anxious, fearful of losing control, trembling and sweating). There is still evident disturbance in the person's capacity for calculating time and space, and also attention deficit and damages in learning and memory capacity. These types of cognitive deficiencies seem to persist after withdrawal. In few cases, chronic ingestion of marijuana produces paranoia and panic disorder.

So far, some studies have identified two cannabinoid-like receptors, the first named type 1, CB1 (and another possible subtype called CB1A that mediates the acute effects of cannabinoids, as well as the development of tolerance) found in the brain, and the second, named type CB2, found in the immune system. CB1 receptors are found in highest concentration, in the brain neurons, are coupled via G proteins, and modulate adenylate cyclase and ion channels. CB2 receptors are found in cells of the immune system, are also coupled via G proteins, but inhibit adenylate cyclase. The CB1 receptor and its variant CB1A, are found mainly in the hippocampus, cerebellum and striatum. The CB2 receptor is found predominantly in the spleen and in haemopoietic cells, what could explain the immunosuppressive actions of marijuana. Similar to endogenous opiates, there is much evidence of the existence of an endogenous ligand for marijuana receptors in the brain, called *anandamide*. It is important to note that marijuana, as well as other drugs of abuse, also seems to generate its effects by increasing the activity of dopaminergic neurons in the VTA.

LSD is an abbreviation of diethylamide of lysergic acid, a synthetic drug that produces intense hallucinations when ingested, and is perhaps the most powerful psychedelic drug ever produced. LSD acts in the brain, producing a series of perceptual distortions that include hallucinations, illusions and disorders of thinking such as paranoia. Similarly to marijuana, its effects can be dependent on contextual and personal factors. In this way, some individuals experiment high excitation and euphoria while others become quiet and passive. LSD does not commonly lead to dependence, and there is not description of an abstinence syndrome if its chronic use is abruptly interrupted.

The chemical effects of LSD are not well understood, but several studies have demonstrated that LSD affects the serotoninergic systems in the brain. In this context, several proposals have emerged. One of them states that LSD is a serotonin (5-HT) receptor antagonist, acting specifically through these receptors, mainly in prosenchephalic structures, blocking 5-HT2 receptors, thus preventing the usual effects of 5-HT. Another possibility is that LSD is actually a 5-HT agonist instead of an antagonist, and also that LSD effects can be the result of 5-HT1 receptors in higher brain structures, which may result in an enhancement of positive mood state, such as euphoria and mood changes.

Ecstasy is the generic name of 3-4methylenedioxymethamphetamine (MDMA), a synthetic derivative of amphetamine that has stimulant, hallucinogenic and mood-improving qualities. Initially this substance was used basically as appetite moderator. To some authors, ecstasy should be considered as a central nervous system stimulant, like cocaine and amphetamine, but it is classified as a psychedelic drug by virtue of its potential for provoking hallucinations. As all psychomimetics, ecstasy is capable of promoting auditory, visual or tactile hallucinations and, at high doses, depersonalization, illusions and floating sensations, among other effects. Besides, the drug also increases the heart rate and blood pressure. Other symptoms such as dry mouth, loss of appetite and euphoria may also appear. During its continuous use the pleasurable affects tend to diminish while the negative ones (confusion, depression anxiety and paranoia) enhance.

Ecstasy is normally consumed in a pill form, and once it reaches its targets in the central nervous system, it virtually causes an explosion of 5-HT in the synapses, increasing the firing of post-synaptic neurons, faster than any other process. Together with serotonin changes, ecstasy also promotes a bizarre functioning of 5-HT transporters which tend to capture dopamine molecules in a neuron where they do not belong. Because dopamine is extremely harmful to serotonin cells, this reuptake error leads to a neural toxicity.

STRESS, ANXIETY AND RELAPSE

Selye (1975) defined stress as the non-specific response of the body to any demand placed upon it to adapt, whether that demand produces pleasure or aversion. In any case, the sympathetic nervous system and the hypothalamic-pituitary adrenal axis are typically activated leading to an increase in the heart rate, rise in the blood pressure and a blood flow to skeletal muscles, increase in the blood glucose and rate of respiration, and dilatation of pupils, preparing the organism for flight or fight, when faced with the stressor.

The characteristic signs of the withdrawal or discontinuity of chronic use of psychostimulants, like d-amphetamine, courses with significant molecular adaptations in the neuronal circuitry of mesolimbic system, such as physiological alterations in the dopaminergic neurons that regulate motivational and emotional processes. This assumption may have a relationship with the fact that some stressful events also stimulate the dopaminergic mesolimbic system. Thus, the same dopaminergic circuits responsible for the pleasurable effects of a given drug acting on the mesolimbic system may also underlie the aversive effects of the drug withdrawal (see Box 3). It has been shown that the characteristic signs of the withdrawal or discontinuity of chronic use of psychostimulants, like d-amphetamine, courses with significant molecular adaptations in the neuronal circuitry of mesolimbic system, such as physiological alterations in the dopaminergic neurons that regulate motivational and emotional processes related to drug abstinence. In this context, it has been firmly demonstrated the ability of a variety of stressors to facilitate the acquisition of a drug self-administration procedure in rats. Rats exposed to tail-pinch, foot-shocks, social defeat, or neonatal isolation procedures, rapidly learn to self-administrate psychostimulants, such as cocaine and amphetamine, and opioids, such as morphine and heroin. In humans, it has been well documented that the reward effect of a drug is powerfully potentiated in individuals with previous history of stress. In fact, previous exposure to stressful situations is a strong factor that could lead an individual to relapse more easily, mainly because, as we shall see, withdrawal of drugs of abuse generates a lot of symptoms of somatic, autonomic and affective aversive nature. The conjunction of all these symptoms plus previous aversive experiences make the individual more predisposed to relapse after a long-term drug use.

In theory, it has been suggested that abstinence of many drugs of abuse that generate dependence, such as benzodiazepines, psychostimulants and opioids, also promotes a lot of aversive symptoms, as dysphoria and irritability accompanied by sensorial and autonomic alterations, similar to those verified in the anxiety. The abrupt discontinuation of a chronic treatment with diazepam, for example, results in a marked withdrawal syndrome characterized by high level of anxiety, insomnia, tremors, weight loss, muscle rigidity, sensorial disturbances and, sometimes, convulsion. These responses are the result of alterations in the $GABA_A$ receptor complex (as the self-administration of diazepam in rats is blocked after systemic injections of GABAergic or benzodiazepine antagonist) and, differently from other drugs of abuse, the emergence of these symptoms seems not to be related to changes in the release of dopamine in the mesolimbic system. In this way, it seems that the behavioral, sensorial and autonomic effects, consequent of benzodiazepine abstinence can be related to the activation of other systems of neurotransmitters, such as the glutamatergic and serotonergic. In fact, pharmacological experiments that utilize specific agonists and antagonists of glutamate receptors have confirmed that mechanisms mediated by excitatory aminoacids can underlie the expression of symptoms of benzodiazepine withdrawal. As an example, previous administration of GYKI-52466 (AMPA antagonist) prevents while CPP (NMDA antagonist) blocks anxiety, convulsion, and muscle spasms induced by withdrawal from chronic treatment with diazepam. These responses are initially modulated by AMPA receptors that, once activated, recruit NMDA receptors, resulting in the expression of withdrawal symptoms. Other studies have demonstrated that alterations promoted by benzodiazepine withdrawal are consequence of a deficit on the GABAergic inhibition exerted by the basolateral amigdaloid nucleus on central nucleus neurons. Chronic administration of benzodiazepines leads also to a decrease of the GABA ability to inhibit serotoninergic neurons, leading to an increase in its release in the basolateral amygdaloid nucleus. Thus, the altered states of fear and anxiety observed during withdrawal from benzodiazepines could be the consequence of a reduction of the control promoted by the neurons of the basolateral amygdala, on the neurons of the central nucleus. The central nucleus neurons project to midbrain areas mainly involved in the somatic and autonomic expression of fear and anxiety such as the periaqueductal gray. This structure participates actively in the expression of fear and defensive behaviors, as well as in vocalization and stress-induced analgesia.

Abstinence from opioids, such as morphine, also causes a similar pattern of affective and homeostatic imbalance. Some studies have demonstrated, for example, that abrupt interruption of opioids, in dependent humans, provokes irritability and extreme anxiety. In animals, opioid abstinence promotes anxiogenic effects in the plus-maze and conditioned place aversion.

The μ opioid receptors seem to have a fundamental role in the opioid addiction, as the knock-out mouse for this receptor do not present withdrawal symptoms after interruption of chronic morphine treatment. Other studies have revealed the involvement of neuropeptides, such as substance P, in the modulation of aversive effects induced by opioid withdrawal. In fact, it is well known that the reward effects of morphine are absent in the knock-out mouse for NK1 neurokininergic receptor. Besides, these receptors are expressed in great number in brain regions involved in depression and anxiety, as well as in other regions, such as the NAcc, that mediates the motivational properties of drugs of abuse, including opioids. There is also much evidence showing that NK1 receptors could be involved in the morphine-related reward processes.

All of these studies pointed out that the abrupt interruption of chronic ingestion of drug of abuse, that has mainly a negative reinforcing effect, induces an homeostatic imbalance leading, as a consequence, to the emergence of a great variety of symptoms, amongst which a pronounced increase in anxiety levels that could underlie the compulsive motivational behavior (craving) observed during withdrawal from drugs of abuse. Still, it is suggested that the symptoms observed during withdrawal from drugs of abuse, that are commonly observed in animals exposed to aversive stimulation, as for instance when facing natural predators, or after electrical or chemical stimulation of brainstem regions belonging to the so-called brain aversive system, such as the amygdala, medial hypothalamus and dorsal periaqueductal may share the same neurobiological mechanisms that are involved in anxiety/fear and, probably, in characteristic aversive states of the withdrawal from drug of abuse. These elements have been taken into account in an integrative model of drug dependence, outlined below.

A Theoretical Model of Drug Abuse

In the view of the operant learning theory, drug use can be viewed as a behavior that is maintained by its consequences. Consequences that strengthen a behavior pattern are reinforcers. Some drugs may reinforce the antecedent drug-taking behavior by terminating some aversive or unpleasant situation (negative reinforcement), as for example, when they alleviate pain or anxiety. Likewise, drugs may reinforce drug abuse by inducing pleasurable effects (positive reinforcement). It has been proposed that the same neural system is responsible for both the negative and positive reinforcing aspects of drug abuse. To support this assumption it appears that people take drugs primarily to avoid the discomfort of drug withdrawal rather than to experience pleasure. Dopaminergic projections from the VTA to the NAcc seem to be the main component of this system. Based on this view, the NAcc would be the main target for both psychostimulant and opiate reinforcement, with both classes activating the dopaminergic pathways linking these two brain structures.

Most studies that have implicated dopamine mechanisms in the reinforcing effects of drugs have used animal models that measure the direct self-administration of the drug, its effects on reward thresholds using intracranial self-stimulation in the medial forebrain bundle, particularly in its connections with the NAcc, and measure also the preferences for the environment paired with the drug administration (place preference). It has been found that psychostimulants and opiate drugs are self-administered intravenously. Decrease in the dose of drugs available to the animal will change the pattern of self-administration so that the interinjection interval decreases and the number of injections increase. Selective agonists and antagonists of these drugs decrease or increase the self-administration respectively, as if the rats were trying to compensate for the gain or the reduction in the reinforcement magnitude. Lesion of the NAcc, with 6-hydroxidopamine, produces a significant reduction in cocaine self-administration. This effect seems to be due to a cooperative action of dopamine on D1 and D2 receptors in the NAcc. Likewise, cocaine injected acutely has been reported to lower self-stimulation thresholds in rats. During cocaine withdrawal following prolonged use, reward thresholds are elevated. Thresholds of intracranial self-stimulation have been hypothesized to reflect the hedonic state of an animal because the animal will readily self-administer stimulation to its own brain. Intracranial self-stimulation is thought to activate the same neural substrates that mediate the reinforcing effects of natural reinforcers (e.g., water and food). Thus, it has been suggested by these findings, that cocaine can alter the function of the reward system in the medial forebrain bundle, and that during the course of cocaine withdrawal, there may be some hypoactivity in the functioning of the dopaminergic reward system.

Regarding opiates drugs, it has been shown that heroin, similarly to cocaine, is readily self-administered intravenously by rats. Rats have been found to maintain stable levels of drug intake on a daily basis, without any major indices of physical dependence. Likewise cocaine decreases in the doses of heroin available to the animal change the pattern of self-administration, i.e. the interinjection interval decreases and the number of injections increases. Similar increases in the number of injections have been obtained by both systemic and central administration of competitive opiate antagonists, such as methylnaloxoniun in the NAcc, suggesting that the animals attempt to compensate for the opiate antagonism, by increasing the amount of drug injected. Opiates are self-administered directly into the source of the mesolimbic dopamine system, the ventral tegmental area, and microinjections of opioids into the VTA lower brain stimulation reward thresholds and produce significant place preference.

It has also been shown that rats self-administer opioid peptides into the region of the nucleus accumbens. Furthermore, place preferences produced by opioids appear to have a major dopaminergic component. These results suggest that neural elements in the region of the nucleus accumbens are responsible for both the reinforcing properties of opiates and psychostimulants. However, the neurochemical mechanisms of these effects seem to be different. Rats trained to self-administer cocaine and heroin every day, receiving 6-hydroxidopamine (6-OHDA) lesions of the NAcc, have shown a time-dependent decrease or extinction of cocaine self-administration, whereas heroin self-administration was not disturbed by this procedure. Thus, the reinforcing actions of opiates may involve both a dopamine-dependent (VTA) and dopamine independent (NAcc) mechanism.

From the evidence obtained so far, it has not been possible to define clearly the neural substrates of the negative reinforcing properties of opiate withdrawal. As stated in the beginning of this chapter, dependence on opiate drugs is defined by a characteristic withdrawal syndrome that appears with the abrupt termination of the opiate administration, or that can be precipitated by the administration of competitive opiate antagonists. Opiate withdrawal in humans is characterized by both motivational symptoms and physical correlates such as nausea, gastrointestinal disturbances, chills, sympathetic reactions, painful flu-like dysphoric state, anxiety, depression, anhedonia, dysphoria and drug craving. As these subjective symptoms are shared by several drugs of abuse, such as alcohol, morphine, cocaine and amphetamine, and based on the fact that in general, during precipitated withdrawal syndrome of these drugs, a dopamine reduction occurs in the NAcc, it has been suggested that a common neurochemical substrate may underlie the aversive subjective symptoms of drugs of abuse. In rats, opiate physical dependence has been characterized by an abstinence syndrome that includes the appearance of ptosis, teeth chattering, wet dog shakes and diarrhea, and this syndrome can be dramatically precipitated in dependent animals by systemic injections of opiate antagonists. Among motivational measures, the disruption of trained operant behavior for food reward, and the development of place aversion following precipitated withdrawal with systemic opiate antagonist administration have been studied.

In opposition to the notion of a same neural system underlying positive and negative reinforcement, it has been proposed that there are two distinct brain systems responsible for drug induced pleasure, and the alleviation of aversive stimulation. A schematic diagram of the functioning of these neural systems is depicted in Figure 10.7. This assumption in based on the observation that non dependent on morphine rats self-administer the drug directly in the VTA, in the absence of subsequent concomitants of abstinence. However, repeated administration of morphine into the periaqueductal gray, but not VTA, causes withdrawal syndrome after challenge with the opioid antagonist naloxone. Thus, drugs of abuse apparently act on this VTA-NAcc pathway to potentiate the drug taking behavior. On the other hand, opiate drugs act in the periaqueductal gray to alleviate three kinds of pain – physical pain, pain of loneliness and social withdrawal, and drug-induced pain of opiate withdrawal. It has been well documented that separate brain sites are responsible for the motivational symptoms and physical correlates of opiate withdrawal, and that some physical correlates may be mediated by peripheral (gut) opiate receptors. For example, the search for neural substrates for motivational symptoms and physical correlates of the withdrawal syndrome has identified several brain structures as being particularly important. Microinjection of methylnaloxoniun into the periaqueductal gray and locus coeruleus precipitates withdrawal syndrome in opiate-dependent rats, characterized by jumping, rearing, and increased locomotor activity. In a recent study using the place aversion paradigm by pairing methylnaloxoniun injection in several brain sites of dependent rats with a particular environment, it has been found that NAcc is the most sensitive site for the intracerebral injections of methylnaloxoniun produce place aversion in dependent rats. In view of these results, it has been suggested that the neurobiological basis for the motivational symptoms is localized in the NAcc, while the physical correlates may be mainly localized in regions such as the periaqueductal gray and *locus coeruleus*.

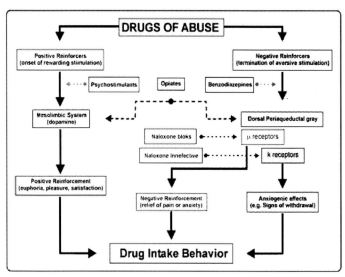

Figure 10.7. A hypothetical model of drug dependence.

From what has been discussed in this chapter it is clear that the positive and negative reinforcing effects of opioids seem to be mediated by different neural systems. In each system, the drug effects also depend on the type of opioid receptor on which it interacts. Activation of μ or δ receptors induces conditioned preference place in the NAcc. Injection of low doses of morphine, directly in the periaqueductal gray, activates only μ receptors and attenuates the aversive consequence of the electrical stimulation of this structure. On the other hand, the activation of κ or the blockade of μ receptors promotes conditioned place aversion. In function of these results many studies have suggested the involvement of opioid mechanisms in the modulation of the aversive behavior in the dorsal mesencephalon. Both autonomic and behavioral consequences, resultant of electrical stimulation of this region are attenuated by the administration of minor tranquilizers, probably through facilitation of GABAergic neurotransmission, that exert a tonic inhibitory control over the neural circuits responsible for the mediation and expression of the defensive behaviors elicited by stimulation of this brain region. Thus it is likely that several neurotransmitters systems may interact to produce the complex array of actions inherent to the positive and negative reinforcing effects of drugs of abuse.

Box 1

Dopamine Receptors

Dopamine is a neurotransmitter that acts as a modulator of the neuronal activity, regulating important and different functions in the brain, such as sensory perception (in the retina and olfactory bulb), prolactin release in the pituitary gland, body temperature, food intake and sexual behavior in the hypothalamus, tuning of sensory motor cues in the basal ganglia, and importantly, the maintenance and expression of qualitative values of novelty in life experiences and, thus motivation and aversion. Dopamine belongs to a group of neurotransmitters called catecholamines. The precursor for the synthesis of DA is the aromatic amino acid tyrosine that is transformed in L-DOPA (L-3,4-dyhidroxyphenylalanine) by the enzyme tyrosine hydroxilase. The decarboxylation of L-DOPA by the enzyme aromatic L-amino acid decarboxylase transforms L-DOPA in dopamine.

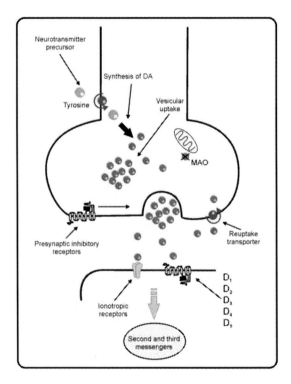

Figure 10A. Schematic representation of a dopaminergic (DA) synapse with the main steps involved in the neurotransmission. It can be seen the synthesis of DA from the amino acid tyrosine (TH) and the storage of DA in vesicles on the pre-synaptic neuron. On the synaptic cleft it is depicted the releasing of the neurotransmitter by exocytose, interaction of the neurotransmitter with the various receptors located on the post-synaptic neuron membrane. The enzymatic degradation of DA by the monoamine oxidase (MAO) and reuptake transporter sites are illustrated on the pre-synaptic neuron. Five types of DA receptors located on the post-synaptic neuron membrane are also indicated (D1, D2. D3, D4, D5).

Drugs of abuse produce their effects interacting with autoreceptors or postsynaptic dopaminergic receptors. There are, at least, five dopamine receptors (D1 to D5), divided in two subfamilies based on its pharmacological and biochemical properties, the D1-like (D1, D5) and the D2-like (D2, D3, D4) receptors. The D1-like receptors (D1 and D5) show pharmacological properties similar to those of the original pharmacologically defined D1 receptor, that is, a high affinity for selective antagonists of this subtype, SCH 23390 and SKF 83566. These receptors also show moderate affinity for typical and selective dopamine agonists, such as apomorphine and SKF 82526, respectively. A D1 receptor antagonist prevents the activation of the dopamine D1 receptor. The D1 receptor is coupled to stimulatory G-proteins, which dissociate from the receptor due to agonist binding, and initiate secondary messenger signaling mechanisms and stimulation of adenylyl cyclase. This causes cell depolarization, which is inhibited by antagonist binding. High levels of D1 receptors are found in the typical dopamine rich neurons of the brain, such as the neostriatum, substantia nigra, NAcc and tubercle olfactory, whereas the distribution of D5 receptors has a much more restricted distribution, and is not well understood.

The D2 receptors are the predominant D2-like subtypes in the brain and are found at high levels in dopamine brain areas. D3 and D4 receptors are found at much lower levels, in a more restricted distribution pattern and almost predominantly in limbic areas of the brain. The D2 receptor is coupled to inhibitory G-proteins, which dissociate from the receptor, due to agonist binding, and inhibit secondary messenger signaling mechanisms. In this way, a D2 receptor antagonist prevents the activation of the dopamine D2 receptor, causing inhibition of down-stream signaling mechanisms. Contrary to the D1-, the D2-like dopamine receptors have been shown to inhibit adenylyl cyclase. This type of receptor is important for mediating the effects of dopamine to control movement, some aspects of behavior in the brain and the prolactin secretion. Whilst the functions of the D3 and D4 receptors are less known, their localization in the limbic areas suggest that they play a role in cognitive, emotional and behavioral functions. The mesolimbic dopaminergic pathway has been implicated in the control of reward mechanisms and in the psychomotor effects of drugs of abuse. This is extended not only to drugs that affect directly the DA receptors, such as cocaine or amphetamines, but also to opiates and alcohol. Cocaine and amphetamines are the most common drugs that affect the DA pathways in the brain, and these drugs reach their effects in a similar manner.

Box 2

The Reinforcing Properties of Opioids Also Depend of other Neurotransmitters

Lots of evidence has implicated the mesolimbic dopaminergic system, specially the VTA – NAcc pathway, in the reinforcing effects of opioids. Intra-VTA morphine or intracerebroventricular β-endorphin microinjections increase the cell firing of dopaminergic neurons in the VTA and, consequently, increase DA release in the NAcc. This increase is mediated by μ receptors located in the cell bodies of VTA neurons. In contrast, the κ receptors activation in NAcc produces the opposite effect, reducing the local DA activity at the same time that produces conditioned place aversion. In agreement with studies utilizing specific dopaminergic ligands, several research groups have proposed that the tonic release of DA, activating mainly D_1 receptors in the NAcc, is necessary to maintain a neutral motivational state. Any alteration that reduces the DA activity mediated by D_1 receptors in this region, for example, the κ pre-synaptic receptors activation in the NAcc, produces aversive effects. On the other hand, any alteration that increases the DA activity, such as the activation of the μ receptors in the VTA, promotes positive reinforcement.

The involvement of dopamine in the opioid reinforcement has been widely confirmed. Neurotoxic lesions of the DA neurons in VTA or NAcc, produced by the neurotoxin 6-OHDA, reduce the CPP induced by μ agonists, as well as the conditioned aversion induced by κ agonists. However, while the self-administration of psychostimulants, like cocaine and amphetamine, is eliminated by VTA and NAcc 6-OHDA lesions, self-administration of heroin is only partially reduced, suggesting the involvement of other neurotransmitter systems in the mediation of the positive reinforcement effects of opioids.

Excitatory amino acids (EAA) seem also to have some involvement in the mediation of opioid reinforcement, but their function is less known. In models of ICSS and self-administration, the blockade of NMDA receptors increases the reinforcing effects of morphine and inhibits the CPP induced by the same drug, perhaps in virtue of the deleterious effects of the NMDA antagonists on learning.

The positive reinforcing effects of opioids must be also dependent on the cholecystokinin (CCK) action, which seems to produce different effects depending on the type of receptor that is activated. The activation of CCK-A receptors favors the establishment of the opioid reinforcement, while the activation of CCK-B receptors disrupts it. However, secure conclusions about this are difficult, because negative results about the role of CCK-B receptors in the opioid reinforcement have just been reported.

Other neurotransmitter systems are probably involved in the positive reinforcing effects of opioids. Histamine, for example, inhibits the positive reinforcement produced by morphine. On the other hand, substance P, acting on NK□ receptors, stimulates the rewarding processes related to morphine. The rewarding effects of morphine are absent in knock-out mice lacking the NK□ receptor. Moreover, these receptors are expressed in brain regions such as the NAcc that mediates the motivational properties of opioids. Serotonin seems to facilitate the reinforcing action of opioids. The NAcc is possibly, the main region involved in this effect, as suggested by the fact that lesions of 5-HT terminals in this area inhibit the CPP induced by morphine.

The development of the opioid dependence is characterized by alterations in other neurotransmitter systems. Much evidence also implicates the noradrenergic system in the expression of the physical dependence. In this respect, the most important cerebral area seems to be the *locus coeruleus*, the greatest group of noradrenergic neurons in the brain. This is the most sensitive region for the precipitation of physical symptoms of withdrawal after microinjection of metylnaloxonium, in dependent animals. The acute morphine administration, that activates μ receptors, hyperpolarizes the neurons of the *locus coeruleus*, reducing the release of noradrenaline (NA) in some areas of the CNS. With its chronic use, it develops tolerance for this effect and normalization of the NA release. During the opioid withdrawal occurs the rebound effect on the release of NA that increases significantly, mainly due to hyperactivity of the *locus coeruleus*. This increase is correlated with the occurrence of the somatic symptoms of abstinence.

The α_2-adrenergic agonists, that inhibit the activity of the *locus coeruleus* neurons, just by acting in inhibitory autoreceptors, reduce the autonomic manifestations and the majority of the somatic symptoms of abstinence. Beyond its role in the physical dependence, the NA system also seems to be involved in the psychological dependence of opioids. In fact, affective symptoms of abstinence, expressed by the conditioned aversion to the place associated with the withdrawal, are blocked by the reduction of the central NA activity, through the administration of α_2-adrenergic agonists or β-adrenergic antagonists.

The hyperactivation of *locus coeruleus* during the morphine withdrawal could be due, mainly, to the afferent excitatory projections, even though intrinsic modifications, consisting in an "up-regulation" of the CAMP pathway, can also be involved. It is believed that these afferent projections originate from the paragigantocelullaris nucleus that excites the *locus coeruleus* neurons through EAA release. The EAA favors the expression of physical dependence of opioids, as the blockade of NMDA receptors attenuates the severity of the somatic symptoms of withdrawal in dependent animals. Moreover, NMDA antagonists also prevent the development of physical dependence when administered together with morphine. The EAA also seems to contribute to the psychological dependence, since the blockade of NMDA receptors reduces the affective symptoms of morphine abstinence.

Box 3

The Spiraling Distress Model

As noted earlier in this chapter the establishment of drug dependence involves the raise of an adaptive process aimed to counter the acute effects of the drug that persist even after the end of the drug treatment. In this condition, to inhibit the action of the drug in the brain there are the raise of neural processes with opposed signs that counteract the drug action so as when the drug administration is interrupted the withdrawal symptoms are expressed.

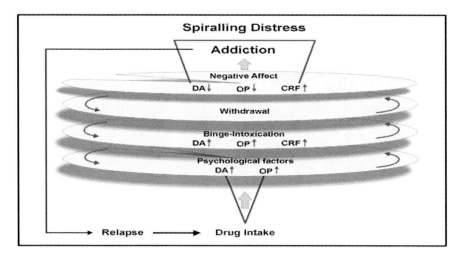

Figure 10B. The spiraling distress model of drug abuse. This model has been proposed by Koob and Le Moal (1997) to explain the involvement of different neural systems in the addiction cycle. The main site for the positive reinforcing effects of drugs of abuse (including psychostimulants, opiates, nicotine, cannabinoids and alcohol) is the mesolimbic dopaminergic system. Initially, there is an enhancement in the activity of this system. During drug withdrawal the brain reward function may be depressed in that the absence of the drug leads to several negative emotional-motivational states as dysphoria, stress, anxiety and even depression. In parallel with a decrease in dopamine levels there is also a decrease in opioid peptides, 5-HT, GABA levels with a concomitant increase in glutamatergic transmission and in CRF levels. DA: dopamine; OP:opioid peptides; CRF: corticotrophin releasing factor.

As proposed by Koob and Le Moal (1997), drug addiction is not only a static or unitary phenomenon but mainly a composition of several elements that constitutes what he called an ever-growing spiral-like pathology. In this case, multiple sources of reinforcement are identified in this cycle suggesting addiction as a break in the homeostatic organic levels induced by a dysregulation in the hedonic homeostatic process. During this process changes in the levels of some neurohormones and neurotransmitters systems have been identified suggesting an organic substrate for addiction that could mediate the appearance of addiction and the symptoms of withdrawal.

The theory considers three main components of the addiction cycle named *preoccupation-anticipation, binge-intoxication and withdrawal negative affects*. Each one of these constructs is linked to specific sources of reinforcement and different neurochemical and endocrine systems that, together, could explain the addiction cycle in a spiraling distress model used to describe the progressive imbalance of the brain-reward dopaminergic-system induced by the continuity of the addiction cycle. It is also possible that the cues present during drug ingestion can generate a secondary reinforcing-like effect, through Pavlovian conditioning. In this context, all the cues present during drug ingestion will be summed up to the drug effects.

It is well-known that the mesocorticolimbic system is the main responsible by the positive-reinforcing effects of drugs of abuse, as demonstrated by the fact that drugs such as opioids and psychostimulants enhance the dopamine transmission in this system. The major components of this circuit are the basal forebrain (mainly composed by NAcc, amygdala, limbic and frontal cortices) and the VTA (A10), the most important source of dopamine in the brain. There are also the presence of opioid peptides, GABA, glutamate and 5-HT neurons in this system.

Stress also plays an important role in the development of addiction since it is well demonstrated that individuals submitted to stressful events or with a previous history of stress are predisposed to drug dependence.

The state of stress induces a lot of physiological changes, amongst them the activation of the hypothalamic-pituitary-adrenal axis, which leads to an increase in the glucocorticoid levels in the bloodstream, the activation of the sympathetic system and the appearance of an emotional behavior in virtue of the activation of the brain emotional systems. The negative reinforcing effect of drugs of abuse is believed to occur through the alleviation of an existing aversive state (e.g. stress, pathological anxiety, or anxiety induced by withdrawal).

The spiraling distress model proposed by Koob assumes that the positive reinforcing effects are largely associated with the binge-intoxication stage and the negative one with negative affects that raise during withdrawal condition. Indeed, withdrawal of drugs of abuse leads to the expression of many negative affective states (a homeostatic dysregulation of the reward systems), amongst which extreme anxiety and a parallel activation of the stress system in the brain. These counteradaptative within-system changes include decreases in dopamine and opiate levels associated with decreases in GABA functions and increase in the glutamatergic transmission in the NAcc during abstinence.

REFERENCES

Alexander EJ. Withdrawal effects of sodium amytal. *Dis Nerv Syst* 12:77-82, 1951.
Ariwodola OJ, Weiner JL. Ethanol potentiation of GABAergic synaptic transmission may be self-limiting: role of presynaptic GABA(B) receptors. *J Neurosci* 24:10679-10686, 2004.

Bals-Kubik R, Ableitner A, Herz A, Shippenberg TS. Neuroanatomical sites mediating the motivational effects of opioids as mapped by the conditioned place preference paradigm in rats. *J Pharmacol Exp Ther* 264:489-495, 1993.

Bozarth MA, Wise RA. Anatomically distinct opiate receptor fields mediate reward and physical dependence. *Science* 224:516-517, 1984.

Cohen BM, Baldessarini RJ. Tolerance to therapeutic effects of antidepressants. *Am J Psychiatry* 142:489-490, 1985.

Di Chiara G, North RA. Neurobiology of opiate abuse. *TIPS* 13:185-193, 1992.

Falk JL. Drug dependence: myth or motive? *Pharmacol Biochem Behav* 19:385-391, 1983.

Givens B, McMahon K. Effects of ethanol on nonspatial working memory and attention in rats. *Behav Neurosci* 111:275-282, 1997.

Graeff FG, Audi EA, Almeida SS, Graeff EO, Hunziker MH. Behavioral effects of 5-HT receptor ligands in the aversive brain stimulation, elevated plus-maze and learned helplessness tests. *Neurosci Biobehav Rev* 14:501-506, 1990.

Harris GC, Aston-Jones G. Involvement of D_2 dopamine receptors in the nucleus accumbens in the opiate withdrawal syndrome. *Nature* 371:155-157, 1994.

Kalant H, LeBlanc AE, Gibbins RJ, Wilson A. Accelerated development of tolerance during repeated cycles of ethanol exposure. *Psychopharmacology* (Berl) 60:59-65, 1978.

Koob GF, Bloom FE. Cellular and molecular mechanisms of drug dependence. *Science* 242:715-723, 1988.

Koob GF. Drugs of abuse: anatomy, pharmacology and function of reward pathways. *TIPS* 13:177-184, 1992.

Koob FG, Le Moal M. Drug abuse: hedonic homeostatic dysregulation. *Science* 278:52-58, 1997.

Koob GF, Le Moal M. Drug abuse: hedonic homeostatic dysregulation. Science 278: 52-58.oob GF, Le Moal M (2001) Drug addiction, dysregulation of reward, and allostasis. *Neuropsychopharmacology* 24:97-129, 1997.

Koob GF. Neuroadaptative mechanisms of addiction: studies on the extended amygdala. *Eur Neuropsychopharmacol* 13:442-452, 2003.

Lu L, Shepard JD, Hall FS, Shaham Y. Effect of environmental stressors on opiate and psychostimulant reinforcement, reinstatement and discrimination in rats: a review. *Neurosci Biobehav Rev* 27:457-491, 2003.

Markou A, Kosten TR, Koob GF. Neurobiological similarities in depression and drug dependence: a self-medication hypothesis. *Neuropsychopharmacology* 18:135-174, 1998.

McKim WA. *Drugs and behavior: an introduction to behavioral pharmacology* (4th edition). New Jersey: Prentice-Hall, p. 246-267, 2000.

Narita M, Funada M, Suzuki T. Regulations of opioid dependence by opioid receptor types. *Pharmacol Ther* 89:1-15, 2001.

O'Brien CP. Drug addiction and abuse. In: *Goodman and Gilman's The Pharmacological Basis of Therapeutics*, Hardman J, Limbird L (eds.). New York: McGraw-Hill, pp. 557-577, 1996.

Oei TPS, Singer G, Jeffreys D, Lang W., Latiff A. Schedule induced self-injection of nicotine, heroin and methadone by naive animals. In: *Stimulus properties of drugs: ten years of progress* (Colpaert FC, Rosencrans JA, eds), pp 503-516. New York: Elsevier, 1978.

Olds J, Milner P. Positive reinforcement produced by electrical stimulation of septal area and other regions of rat brain. *J Comp Physiol Psychol* 47:419-427, 1954.

Pilotto R, Singer G, Overstreet D. Self-injection of diazepam in naive rats: effects of dose, schedule and blockade of different receptors. *Psychopharmacology* (Berl) 84:174-177, 1984.

Ramos BM, Siegel S, Bueno JL. Occasion setting and drug tolerance. *Integr Physiol Behav Sci* 37:165-177, 2002.

Remington B, Roberts P, Glautier S. The effect of drink familiarity on tolerance to alcohol. *Addict Behav* 22:45-53, 1997.

Rosebush PI, Mazurek MF. Catatonia after benzodiazepine withdrawal. *J Clin Psychopharmacol* 16:315-319, 1996.

Sante AB, Nobre MJ, Brandão ML. Place aversion induced by blockade of μ or activation of κ opioid receptors in the dorsal periaqueductal gray matter. *Behav. Pharmacol* 11:583-589, 2000.

Schulteis G, Koob GF. Reinforcement processes in opiate addiction: a homeostatic model. *Neurochem Res* 21:1437-1454, 1996.

Selye, H. Confusion and controversy in the stress field. *J.Hum.Stress* 1:37-44, 1975.

Siegel S. Evidence from rats that morphine tolerance is a learned response. *J Comp Physiol Psychol* 89:498-506, 1975.

Siegel S, Hinson RE, Krank MD, McCully J. Heroin "overdose" death: contribution of drug-associated environmental cues. *Science* 216:436-437, 1982.

Ungerstedt U. Stereotaxic mapping of the monoamine pathways in the rat brain. *Acta Physiol Scand Suppl* 367:1-48, 1971.

Van Ree JM, Gerrits MAFM, Vanderschuren LJMJ. Opioids, reward and addiction: an encounter of biology, psychology and medicine. *Pharmacol Rev* 51:341-396, 1999.

Waldhoer M, Bartlett SE, Whistler JL. Opioid receptors. *Annu Rev Biochem* 73:953-990, 2004.

Woods JH, Katz JL, Winger G. Benzodiazepines: use, abuse, and consequences. *Pharmacol Rev* 44:151-347, 1992.

Woods JH, Winger G. Current benzodiazepine issues. *Psychopharmacology* (Berl) 118:107-115, 1995.

In: Substance Abuse: New Research   ISBN 978-1-60456-834-9
Editors: Ethan J. Kerr and Owen E. Gibson   © 2009 Nova Science Publishers, Inc.

Chapter 5

CROSS-CULTURAL PARENT-CHILD RELATIONS: THE ROLE OF PARENTAL MONITORING IN YOUTH'S SUBSTANCE ABUSE BEHAVIORS IN HUNGARY AND THE UNITED STATES

Bettina F. Piko[1] and Kevin M. Fitzpatrick[2]
[1] University of Szeged, Hungary
[2] University of Arkansas, USA

ABSTRACT

Adolescence is an important development time when there is a significant restructuring in youth's social networks and support systems. A number of studies emphasize the negative role that peer groups play in determining youth's substance use, while still other studies find that youth substance use can be mediated by parental attitudes, family connectedness and monitoring. The main goal of the present study is to explore some of these associations in two different cultural settings. Data were collected among middle and high school students (ages 11-20 years) in Southern Hungary (N = 1240) and students (ages 10-19) living in a mid-sized urban area in Central Alabama, U.S. (N = 1525). The self-administered questionnaires were identical in both places and contained items that asked youth about their substance use (smoking, drinking, illicit drug use), and the parental/family influences in their life such as parental monitoring and parental attitudes towards substance use. Using multiple regression analyses in both samples, results suggest that parental monitoring (e.g., when parents know where their children are) is an important protective factor regardless of culture. Likewise, being beaten by a parent is an important universal risk factor. However, some differences may also be detected, e.g., parental attitudes towards substance use is an important influence only among Hungarian youth, while family structure is a significant predictor of substance use among US adolescents.

Key words: parental monitoring, parental attitudes, youth substance use, cross-cultrual comparison

INTRODUCTION

Adolescence is characterized by an increased experimentation with substance use, namely, smoking, drinking and drug use (Gilvarry, 2000). Among the influencing factors of adolescent substance use, the processes of social networks have always been in the focal point of research (Hawkins, Catalano and Miller, 1992; Piko, 2000; Poikolainen, 2002). Not surprisingly, social networks and social supports have been found to be key variables in predicting adolescents' health and health related behaviors (Frey and Röthlisberger, 1996). Adolescence is a period of life during which there is a restructuring of the social network and support systems (Aneshensel and Gore, 1991; Piko, 2000). During adolescence, youth begin to develop peer-oriented relationships while their link to parents undergoes dramatic changes as well. Although adolescence is definitely characterized by spending more time with peers and less with parents, the restructuring is not merely a question of quantitative change but qualitative change as well. Many researchers emphasize that parent-adolescent relations continue to serve as an adaptive function by providing a secure base for adolescents as they begin exploring new, peer based environments (Paterson, Pryor, and Field, 1995).

The enduring family socialization model suggests a consistent parental influence on adolescents' health related behavior, although parents sometimes may be unaware of the influence of their behaviors or parenting practices on children in this period of life (Christensen, 2004; Norton, Sivarajan-Froelicher, Waters, and Carrieri-Kohlman, 2003). Parenting style is based on two dimensions of parental practices, namely, control (that is, strictness, demandedness) and warmth (attachment, responsiveness, communication). In terms of adolescent development, the best outcomes tend to be those associated with the authoritative parenting style, when a parent is warm yet still expresses a moderate level of control (Radziszewska, Richardson, Dent, and Flay, 1996). This parenting style represents both demanding and responsive parental practices which appear to be protective against adolescent substance use as well (Jackson, Henriksen, and Foshee, 1998; Simons-Morton, Haynie, Crump, Eitel, and Saylor, 2001). In addition to parenting style, parental attitudes towards substance use, that is, approval or disapproval have been found to be a more important correlate of adolescent substance use than parental substance use (Piko, 2001; Sargent and Dalton, 2001).

Regarding adolescent substance use, one aspect of parent-child relations is the monitoring function. Parental monitoring consists of the knowledge of where and with whom youth spend their time with (Li, Feigelman, and Stanton, 2000). Thus, parental monitoring includes an active attempt to control youth (e.g., when parents set a curfew or they have rules established for letting them know where their children are). This funtion is closely connected with parenting practices, therefore, parental monitoring may serve as important protection not only against substance use but also against conduct problems (Deković, 1999). High parental monitoring and involvement have been found to be negatively associated with youth's substance use (Li, Stanton, and Feigelman, 2000; Steinberg, Fletcher, and Darling, 1994).

Another aspect of the parent-child relation is connectedness/attachment such as the utilization of emotional support, proximity, and the quality of affect. Harmony, closeness or support are the elements of parent-child relationships which are extraordinarily important in terms of the maintaining affective ties between parents and adolescents. These aspects are key elements in adolescent adjustment because despite the decreased frequency of interaction during the adolescent years they provide protection against youth's substance use and other problem behaviors (Vazsonyi, 2003). Adolescents with greater family togetherness score lower levels of depression and drug use (Field, Diego, and Sanders, 2002). In addition, adolescents with higher family bonds are less likely to have close friends involved in substance use (Bahr, Marcos, and Maughan, 1995). Another element in parent-child connectedness is the communication between them. Communicating well with parents, that is, talking about problems with them is associated with lower levels of substance use (Stronski, Ireland, Michaud, Narring, and Resnick, 2000). Another study also supports the idea that parents continue to exert an influential role even in late adolescent substance use (Wood, Read, Mitchell, and Brand, 2004). Other studies, however, suggest that in comparison with peer effects, the influences of parental monitoring and attachment to parents are relatively small if significant (Bahr, Hoffmann, and Yang, 2005). Therefore, further research is needed to interpret not only the relative but the absolute role of parental variables in understanding adolescent substance use.

Beyond parental practices, living in high risk families may also enhance the risk of adolescent substance use. Family life events and family structure may serve as risk factors in terms of adolescents' substance use. Children who experience family life events such as parental unemployment, divorce or separation are at an elevated risk to experience emotional and behavioral problems (Harland, Reijneveld, Brugman, Verloove-Vanhorick, and Verhulst, 2002). Domestic violence and being beaten by parents foster children's problem behavior (Formoso, Gonzales, and Aiken, 2000; Jaffee, Moffitt, Caspi, Taylor, and Arseneault, 2002). Another familial risk factor is the non-intact family structure when one or both parents are absent from the home (Ackerman, D'Eramo, Umylny, Schultz, and Izard, 2001). Family structure is particularly important in terms of problem behaviors of children living in economically disadvantaged or minority families (Fitzpatrick, 1997a).

Besides sociodemographics, cultural factors also may influence the frequencies of substance use and the role of these background variables. A number of cross-cultural studies report on the cultural differences in adolescent substance use (Steptoe and Wardle, 1992). Research documents, for example, that smoking is more frequent among European youth than their American counterparts (Brown, 2002). This is particularly true in case of Eastern European youth where smoking has a high rates both among adults and adolescents (Piko, Luszczynska, Gibbons, and Teközel, 2005). The differences in alcohol use is less significant, in addition, drug use is usually more common among American youth than European, particularly Eastern European youth (Piko and Fitzpatrick, 2001). There is much less research regarding the influencing factors of adolescent substance use and the specific roles of parenting practices and other familial variables. Based on previous findings, however, Vazsonyi (2003) raised a universal explanation for the role of family processes in adolescents' problem behavior with very few invariations across different cultures. Chen and colleagues argue that measures of parent-adolescent relationship (e.g., warmth or monitoring) are related to adolescent problem behavior in a highly similar fashion cross-culturally (Chen, Greenberger, Lester, Don, and Guo, 1998). Chirkov and Ryan (2001) explain this similarity by pointing out similar socialization goals and mechanisms to achieve them. Despite possible differences in concrete parenting behavior, parenting goals and practices seem to be rather universal (Rohner and Britner, 2002).

Since adolescence is a critical period of life in terms of further development, we should know more about the parent-child relationship. This is particularly important in the modern world when prolonged puberty has emerged bringing new challenges for adolescents' social network systems. Cross-cultural research definitely aids us in developing a better understanding of family processes during this period of life. Therefore, the main goal of the present study is to give an outline of parental and familial influences of adolescent substance use (namely, smoking, drinking and marijuana use) in two different cultural settings. First, the study is based on a data collection in a sample of American (Southern African-American) youth, and second, a sample of European (Southern Hungarian) youth. Previous findings suggest that socialization processes in European and American adolescents are somewhat different and in fact result in differences in their substance use and problem behaviors (Arnett and Jensen, 1994). In addition, studies also draw attention to the similarities in risk and protective stuctures of the influencing factors suggesting that despite any differences in the amount of problem behaviors, some universal tendencies in the background variables may be justified (Fitzpatrick, Piko and Wright, 2005; Piko, Fitzpatrick, and Wright, 2005). Using two samples from distinct cultural settings, we have the somewhat unique opportunity to detect possible differences and similarities in a number of parenting and familial factors influencing adolescent substance use.

METHODS

Samples

American sample. The sample consists of 1,525 African-American middle and high school students from a single school district in central Alabama. The majority of the residents living in the school district are African-American (60%); over one-third (35%) are from families headed by a female with children under the age of 18; and over one-third are living below the poverty level. Of the sampled students, approximately 49% were males and the median age of the sample was 14 years of age (9th grade), age range: 10-19 years (Mean = 14.0 years, S.D. = 2.3 years). The 2001-2002 average daily attendance (ADA) for the middle and high schools in the system was 2,028 students. Student's participation in the study was voluntary, yielding a response rate of approximately 76%. After approval, written parental permission was obtained. In addition to those students who decided against participation (< 10%), the remaining students likely consisted of youth who were absent, suspended, or no longer attending school in the system.

Hungarian sample. This sample consists of 1,240 middle and high school students (age range: 11-20 years) from seven schools in Szeged, a major metropolitan center of southern Hungary, where data collection was based on random selection of classes. The majority of residents living in Szeged are Caucasian (above 90%). Most students were from two-parent families (66.5%) or lived with a parent and a step-parent (10.8%), only 17.9% of them lived with their mother, 2.3% with their father and 2.5% with other relatives. Of the sampled students, 53% were males and the median age of the sample was 16 years of age (Mean = 15.6 years, S.D. = 2.1 years). Of the 1,500 questionnaires sent out (approximately 13% of the entire student population), 1,240 were returned, giving us a response rate of approximately 84%. Similar to the American sample, student participation was voluntary and confidentiality was emphasized, noting that the data used in the study were for research purposes only.

MEASURES

Three types of *substance use* were included in the analyses: smoking, drinking and marijuana use (Search Institute, 1998). Regarding the frequency of smoking, the following questions were asked: "How much in the past 30 days did you smoke cigarettes?" Response categories were the following: not at all (1), less than 1 a day (2), 1-5 cigarettes a day (3), 6-10 cigarettes a day (4), 11-20 cigarettes a day (5), more than pack a day (6). Regarding alcohol use, a similar question was asked: "How many times in the past 30 days did you drink alcohol (including beer, wine, wine coolers, rum, gin, wodka, whisky, etc.)?" Response categories in terms of drinking were never (1), once or twice (2), 3 to 9 times (3), 10 to 19 times (4), 20 to 39 times (5) and 40 or more times (6). Regarding drug use, the most common form, that is, marijuana use was measured: "How many times in the past 30 days did you smoke marijuana (pot, grass, blunt)?" Response categories were the following: none (1), once or twice (2), 3 to 9 times (3), 10 to 19 times (4), 20 to 39 times (5), and 40 or more times (6).

Among the parental and familial factors, father's and mother's schooling, and family structure were included in the analyses as sociodemographics. A four-level classification of education was used to measure father and mother schooling: primary education = 1; apprenticeship = 2; high school level (General Certificate of Education in Hungary) = 3; and university or college degree = 4. Students were also asked about the family structure, that is, with whom do they live together most of the time? The variable was dichotomized reflecting parental absence/presence (Fitzpatrick, 1997b). In addition, various questions were asked about parenting practices (Ary, Duncan, Biglan, Metzler, Noell, and Smolkowski, 1999; Deković, 1999; Search Institute, 1998). Parental monitoring was measured by using two independent items. First, students were asked whether their parents typically set a curfew for them. Students were also asked whether their parents knew where they were when they were going out with friends. Both variables were coded from 0 = never set/never knew to 4 = always set/knew all the time.

Regarding family cohesion, students were asked the following question: "Thinking about Monday through Friday, how often do you come home after school and there is no adult at home?" Response categories were never (0), rarely (1), once a month (2), 2-4 times a week (3), and every day. In addition, students were asked about sharing a meal together as a family: "How often do you eat dinner with your family?" Responses were never (0), a few times (1), some of the time (2), most of the time (3), and all of the time (4).

As variables of family connectedness/attachment, students were asked how often they talked with their parents/guardians about their personal problems. This variable was coded as 0 = never, 1 = hardly ever, 2 = sometimes, 3 = most of the time and 4 = all of the time. In contrast with this variable, a family risk factor was also asked as a measure of parent-child conflict. Students were asked whether they had ever been beaten by a parent or adult living with them and those ordinal responses were 0 = never, 1 = once or twice, 2 = several times, 3 = alot of times, and 4 = all the time.

Finally, parental disapproval of substance use in general also was included: "How do you think your parents feel about substance use?" This variable was measured by a five-point scale which varied from strongly agree (1) to strongly disagree (5).

PROCEDURE

The data for both samples were collected between the academic years of 2000 and 2001. In both cases, questionnaires were self-administered under close supervision by classroom teachers. Teachers received training and a set of instructions outlining the administration of the survey, confidentiality, and procedures for responding to student's questions. Students filled out questionnaires during the class period. When finished, respondents returned them in sealed envelopes, which were then collected from the participating schools.

DATA ANALYSIS

For statistical analysis, SPSS 12.0 was used and the minimum level of significance was set at .05. The analysis begins with an examination of the descriptive statistics for the substance use variables and parental/familial factors. Student's t-tests and Chi-square tests were initially used to determine significant gender and sample differences. Multiple regression analyses were applied to explore the relative effects of parental and familial factors on the frequency of each type of substance use. Possible gender differences also were detected in the background variables. In addition, results of the two samples were examined separately to explore cross-cultural differences or similarities.

RESULTS

Figure 1 shows the smoking patterns among Hungarian and American youth. A significant difference exists showing more Hungarian students reported cigarette smoking (51%) compared to the frequencies of American youth (23.3%), particularly in terms of heavy smoking (p<.001 by Chi-square test). For example, the percentage of those reporting 6-10 cigarettes/day was 1.0% among American but 12.3% among Hungarian youth. The percentage of those smoking 11-20 cigarettes/day during the past month was 1.2% among Americans but 9.1% among Hungarian youth. Similar patterns may be noticed in terms of alcohol use (see Figure 2): 31.2% of American youth compared to 53% of Hungarian youth reported drinking during the past month (p<.001 by Chi-square test). However, the percentage of regular drinkers (more than 20 times/month) was nearly the same (2.2% among American and 2.4% among Hungarian youth). In contrast to smoking and drinking, marijuana use was more common among American students: 18.8% of them reported using marijuana during the past 30 days in contrast to 6.5% of Hungarian youth (see Figure 3).

Table 1 provides detailed descriptive statistics for the samples broken by gender. Both gender and sample differences in parental and familial variables were calculated.

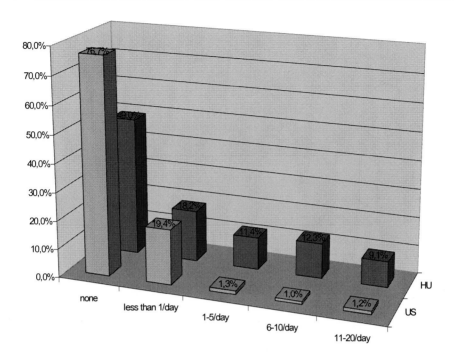

Figure 1. Smoking patterns among Hungarian and American youth.

Table 1. Descriptive statistics by gender for parental and familial factors for Hungarian (n = 1,240) and American youth (n = 1,538).

	HUNGARIAN SAMPLE			AMERICAN SAMPLE		
	Boys	Girls	Gender significance	Boys	Girls	Gender significance
[a]Beaten by parent (Mean, S.D.)	1.4 (0.7)	1.5 (0.8)	N.S.	1.4 (0.8)	1.4 (0.8)	N.S.
[b]Family structure (%)+ Non-intact vs. Intact	30.9 69.1	36.8 63.2	N.S.	70.6 29.4	74.3 25.7	N.S.
[a]Parents set a curfew (Mean, S.D.)	2.8 (1.5)	3.4 (1.5)	p<.001	3.1 (1.5)	3.3 (1.5)	p<.05
[a]Parents know where their children are (Mean, S.D.)+	3.5 (1.3)	4.0 (1.1)	p<.001	3.9 (1.2)	4.3 (1.1)	p<.001
[a]Talking about problems with parents (Mean, S.D.)	2.9 (1.1)	3.4 (1.1)	p<.001	2.8 (1.3)	3.1 (1.3)	p<.001
[a]Eating together as a family (Mean, S.D.)	3.2 (1.2)	3.2 (1.2)	N.S.	3.6 (1.3)	3.4 (1.3)	p<.01
[a]Adult at home after school (Mean, S.D.)+	3.6 (1.8)	3.4 (1.9)	N.S.	2.8 (1.7)	2.6 (1.6)	p<.01
[a]Parental disapproval of substance use (Mean, S.D.)+	4.2 (0.9)	4.2 (0.9)	N.S.	3.6 (1.7)	3.9 (1.6)	p<.001

[a]ANOVA, [b]Chi-square test
+p<.01 for sample differences

There were no significant gender differences in the frequencies of being beaten by a parent or family structure, although this latter variable shows rather large differences between samples. Among American youth, all variables of parental and familial factors show significant gender differences, that is, more girls than boys receive parental monitoring such as the setting of a curfew by parents and likewise girls report that they talk about problems more often with their parents. In the Hungarian sample, similar to their American counterparts, girls report more parental monitoring (e.g., when parents state a curfew and their parents know where they are) and talk more about problems with their parents. However, in contrast with American youth, there were no significant gender differences in having dinner together, the presence of an adult at home after school or parental disapproval of substance use.

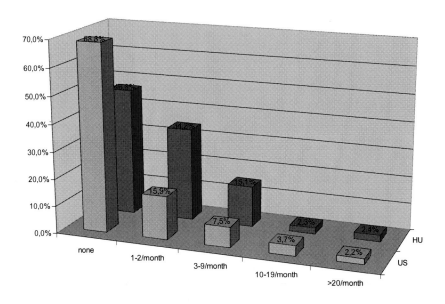

Figure 2. Drinking patterns among Hungarian and American youth.

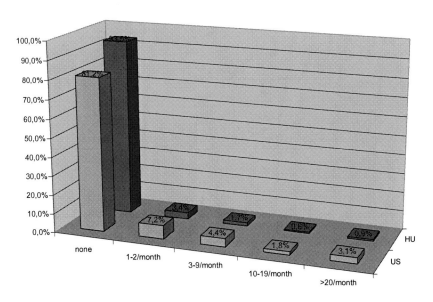

Figure 3. Marijuana use among Hungarian and American youth.

Table 2. Standardized regression estimates for parental and other familial factors in predicting Hungarian youth's smoking (n = 1240).

	WHOLE	BOYS	GIRLS
Parental and other familial factors			
Father schooling	0.06[a]	0.01[a]	0.01[a]
Mother schooling	0.09	0.02	0.01
Family intactness	-0.04	-0.03	-0.06
Beaten by a parent	0.10***	0.10**	0.11*
Having dinner as a family	-0.01	-0.01	-0.02
Adult at home after school	-0.03	-0.08*	-0.02
Talking about problems with parents	-0.01	0.01	-0.01
Parents set a curfew	-0.14***	-0.16***	-0.10*
Parents know where the children are	-0.15***	-0.15***	-0.134**
Parental disapproval of substance use	-0.25***	-0.27**	-0.24***
Constant	1.308***	1.008**	1.422***
R^2	0.17***	0.18***	0.15***

One-tailed t-tests *p < 0.05; **p < 0.01; ***p < 0.001
[a]Standardized regression coefficients

In addition to differences in family structure between the samples (that is, a higher rate of non-intact families in the US sample), American adolescents report more parental monitoring (parents knowing where their children are), while Hungarian youth report a greater frequency of an adult's presence at home after school and greater parental disapproval of substance use.

Table 3. Standardized regression estimates for parental and other familial factors in predicting Hungarian youth's alcohol use (n = 1240).

	WHOLE	BOYS	GIRLS
Parental and other familial factors			
Father schooling	-0.01[a]	0.04[a]	-0.04[a]
Mother schooling	-0.01	-0.02	0.01
Family intactness	-0.01	-0.02	-0.05
Beaten by a parent	0.07**	0.07*	0.10*
Having dinner as a family	-0.02	0.01	-0.07
Adult at home after school	-0.02	-0.03	-0.01
Talking about problems with parents	-0.07*	-0.05	-0.04
Parents set a curfew	-0.20***	-0.22***	-0.15***
Parents know where the children are	-0.14***	-0.12**	-0.15***
Parental disapproval of substance use	-0.23***	-0.18***	-0.32***
Constant	2.179***	2.176**	1.965***
R^2	0.19***	0.14***	0.25***

One-tailed t-tests *p < 0.05; **p < 0.01; ***p < 0.001
[a]Standardized regression coefficients

Table 2 presents regression estimates of smoking among Hungarian youth in the whole sample and broken by gender subgroups. In each case, being beaten by a parent was a positive influence on smoking. Among the negative correlates, parental monitoring (setting a curfew and knowing where youth were) proved to be significant regardless of gender. In addition, those reporting a greater level of parental disapproval of substance use tended to smoke less.

Table 4. Standardized regression estimates for parental and other familial factors in predicting Hungarian youth's marijuana use (n = 1240).

	WHOLE	BOYS	GIRLS
Parental and other familial factors			
Father schooling	-0.01[a]	-0.03[a]	0.07[a]
Mother schooling	0.08*	0.12*	0.07
Family intactness	0.01	0.01	-0.03
Beaten by a parent	0.05	0.05	0.10*
Having dinner as a family	-0.02	-0.06	0.04
Adult at home after school	-0.01	-0.01	-0.03
Talking about problems with parents	-0.02	-0.03	-0.10*
Parents set a curfew	-0.11***	-0.09*	-0.12**
Parents know where the children are	-0.15***	-0.15***	-0.09*
Parental disapproval of substance use	-0.26***	-0.14***	-0.19***
Constant	0.262	0.278	0.001
R^2	0.09***	0.08***	0.12***

One-tailed t-tests *$p < 0.05$; **$p < 0.01$; ***$p < 0.001$
[a]Standardized regression coefficients

Table 5. Standardized regression estimates for parental and other familial factors in predicting American youth's smoking (n = 1538).

	WHOLE	BOYS	GIRLS
Parental and other familial factors			
Father schooling	-0.01[a]	-0.03[a]	-0.03[a]
Mother schooling	0.02	0.02	0.01
Family intactness	-0.07**	-0.07*	-0.06*
Beaten by a parent	0.11***	0.12***	0.09*
Having dinner as a family	-0.01	-0.07*	-0.05
Adult at home after school	-0.05	-0.02	-0.08*
Talking about problems with parents	-0.06*	-0.01	-0.09**
Parents set a curfew	0.01	0.01	0.03
Parents know where the children are	-0.18***	-0.18***	-0.16***
Parental disapproval of substance use	-0.02	-0.01	-0.05
Constant	0.792***	0.955***	0.587***
R^2	0.07***	0.07***	0.07***

One-tailed t-tests *$p < 0.05$; **$p < 0.01$; ***$p < 0.001$
[a]Standardized regression coefficients

Table 3 presents regression estimates of alcohol use among Hungarian youth in similar groupings to the models specified in the earlier tables. Again, being beaten by a parent was a significant predictor. Among the negative influences, parental monitoring and parental disapproval of substance use predicted youth's drinking patterns.

Table 4 displays regression estimates of marijuana use among Hungarian youth. In addition to similar results, compared with the two previous types of substance use (that is, the role of parental monitoring and parental disapproval), some differences were detected. Among boys, there were no more factors acting as significant predictors. Among girls, however, being beaten by a parent was positive, while talking about problems with parents acted as a negative influence.

Table 5 presents regression estimates of smoking among American youth in the whole sample and broken into gender subgroups similar to the Hungarian sample in the earlier table 2. Similar to the results of the Hungarian sample, being beaten by a parent was a positive influence for both sexes. Among the negative influences, parents knowing where youth were and family intactness were signficant predictors for both boys and girls. Having dinner together as a family proved to be significant predictor for boys, while talking about problems with parents and the presence of an adult at home after school were significant predictors for girls. In contrast with the findings of the Hungarian sample, setting a curfew or parental disapproval of substance use were nonsignificant in the American sample.

Table 6. Standardized regression estimates for parental and other familial factors in predicting American youth's alcohol use (n = 1240).

	WHOLE	BOYS	GIRLS
Parental and other familial factors			
Father schooling	0.02[a]	-0.02[a]	0.08*[a]
Mother schooling	-0.01	0.02	-0.05
Family intactness	-0.05*	-0.05	-0.05
Beaten by a parent	0.12***	0.13***	0.11**
Having dinner as a family	-0.05	-0.09*	-0.01
Adult at home after school	-0.07**	-0.03	-0.13***
Talking about problems with parents	-0.05	-0.01	-0.09**
Parents set a curfew	-0.07**	-0.11**	-0.02
Parents know where the children are	-0.15***	-0.10**	-0.19***
Parental disapproval of substance use	-0.03	-0.04	-0.02
Constant	1.153***	1.284**	1.005***
R^2	0.09***	0.09***	0.11***

One-tailed t-tests *p < 0.05; **p < 0.01; ***p < 0.001
[a]Standardized regression coefficients

Table 6 presents regression estimates of alcohol use among American youth in similar groupings to the earlier tables. As found in table 5, being beaten by a parent exerted a positive influence on increasing risk behavior. Among the negative influences, parents knowing where their children were proved to be a significant parental factor for both sexes. In addition, talking about problems with parents and the variable showing an adult's presence at home after school were significant predictors for girls. Among boys, having dinner together as a family and parental setting a curfew were significant predictors.

Table 7 displays regression estimates of marijuana use among American youth. Again, being beaten by a parent exerted a positive influence on risk behavior similar to other regression estimates for both American and Hungarian youth. Among the negative influences, parents knowing where the children were proved to be significant for both sexes. Setting a curfew and parental disapproval of substance use were significant predictors of marijuana use only for boys, talking about problems with parents and family intactness were predictors only for girls.

In addition to these specific differences between drugs, there were also important differences by samples in the amount of variation these models actually explained. Generally, explained variation was greater in the Hungarian samples in each of the substance use models. For example, in terms of smoking, the variations explained proved to be the following: 7% in American youth and 15-18% in Hungarian youth. Regarding alcohol use, it was 9-11% in American youth and 14-25% in Hungarian youth. The percentages were the following in case of marijuana use: 9-12% in Hungarian youth and 7-8% in American youth.

Table 7. Standardized regression estimates for parental and other familial factors in predicting American youth's marijuana use (n = 1240).

	WHOLE	BOYS	GIRLS
Parental and other familial factors			
Father schooling	-0.05*[a]	-0.06[a]	-0.04[a]
Mother schooling	0.03*	0.05	-0.03
Family intactness	-0.05*	-0.04	-0.08*
Beaten by a parent	0.10***	0.14***	0.05
Having dinner as a family	-0.01	-0.01	-0.04
Adult at home after school	-0.01	-0.01	-0.02
Talking about problems with parents	-0.04	-0.01	-0.08*
Parents set a curfew	-0.08**	-0.11**	-0.05
Parents know where the children are	-0.17***	-0.15***	-0.17***
Parental disapproval of substance use	-0.03	-0.08*	-0.02
Constant	0.983***	0.833***	1.042***
R^2	0.07***	0.08***	0.08***

One-tailed t-tests *$p < 0.05$; **$p < 0.01$; ***$p < 0.001$
[a]Standardized regression coefficients

DISCUSSION

Research continues to analyze the background variables of adolescent substance use, particularly those related to youth's social network (Deković, 1999; Hawkins, Catalano, and Miller, 1992; Piko, 2000; Poikolainen, 2002). With tremendous restructuring of the social network and support systems during adolescence a strong influence on youth's lifestyle and health related behaviors has been documented (Frey and Rötlisberger, 1996; Aneshensel and Gore, 1991; Piko, 2000). While there are a number of studies investigating the role of peers, more research is needed to gain a better understanding of the role of parental practices and other familial factors in youth's substance use and problem behaviors (Vazsonyi, 2003). Thus, the main goal of the present study has been to investigate parental and familial influences on the adolescent risk-taking behaviors of smoking, drinking and marijuana use.

The current investigation adds to the literature on parent-adolescent relationship in several ways. First, the study examined various parental and familial factors such as parental monitoring, parental attitudes towards substance use and parent-child connectedness. Second, the study is based on a data collection of youth from two different cultural settings which provides us an opportunity to detect possible differences and similarities in a number of parenting and familial influences of adolescent substance use. The cross-cultural comparison helps us develop a better understanding of the universality versus cultural specificity of parental practices (Chen et al., 1998; Chirkov and Ryan, 2001; Rohner and Britner, 2002).

The most striking findings of our results are the following: 1) There are significant differences in both the frequencies of substance use and the kinds of parental practices; 2) the role of parenting practices in youth's substance use is quite similar in both cultural settings, and 3) although there are similarities in the structure of parental and familial factors which are dominant cross-culturally, some minor differences are observed.

The descriptive statistics show that smoking and drinking are more common among Hungarian while marijuana use is more common among American youth similar to previous studies (Brown, 2002; Piko et al., 2005; Steptoe and Wardle, 1992; Vazsonyi, 2003). Hungarian youth reported greater presence of an adult at home after school and more intact families as well as a greater parental disapproval of substance use. On the other hand, American youth stated that more parents knew where their children were. Being beaten by a parent showed gender differences in none of the samples while parental monitoring was more common among girls in both samples.

We included a number of parental and familial factors in the model explaining youth's substance use. All in all, these factors explain only a small amount of variations in the multivariate model. This is particularly true in case of the American sample (between 7 and 11% altogether) while the variations explained were greater in the analyses for the Hungarian sample (between 9 and 25% altogether). Previous studies also report that parental factors play little role in the development of adolescents' substance use as compared to peer groups effects (Ary et al., 1999; Piko, 2001; Simons-Morton et al., 2001). It seems to be, however, that parental and familial factors are more important determinants of Hungarian adolescents' substance use, particularly in terms of smoking and drinking.

Among the parental and familial factors, being beaten by a parent seems to be a universal positive influence regardless of gender or culture. Those who experience this type of parent-child conflict report higher levels of substance use similar to previous studies (Formoso, Gonzales, and Aiken, 2000; Jaffee et al., 2002). Likewise, a certain form of parental monitoring, that is, when the parents know where their children are, seems to exert a universal negative influence. The other form of parental monitoring, curfew setting by parents seems to be more important for Hungarian youth. This variable was a significant predictor of substance use among Hungarian youth in each case of substance use in both sexes. However, for American youth, this was only a significant predictor of boys' alcohol and drug use, in addition, the relationships that were observed were not as strong. Previous studies also have found that parental monitoring may serve as an important protection against adolescent substance use (Deković, 1999; Li, Feigelman, and Stanton, 2000; Li, Stanton, and Feigelman,

2000; Stenberg, Fletcher and Darling, 1994). The differences may be attributed to a more traditional parenting style found in Hungary (Vazsonyi, 2003).

Another difference in the structure of parental/familial influences lies in the role of family structure. In the Hungarian sample, more children reported living in an intact family and the family structure tended not to play a significant role in their substance use. In the American sample, however, more children live in a non-intact family and the family intactness may serve as a protection against their substance use. Other studies from the U.S. also report on the role of family structure, particularly for children living in economically disadvantaged or minority families (Ackerman et al., 2001; Fitzpatrick, 1997a). In contrast with this variable, parental disapproval seems to be an important influence for Hungarian youth. Another study from Hungary also reports on the importance of parental attitudes towards children's substance use (Piko, 2001). Parental attitudes are much more important determinant of children's substance use than parental behavior in contrast with peer behavior (Simons-Morton et al., 2001). For American youth, parental attitudes do not seem to make a difference.

Other types of parental practices such as talking about problems with parents, having dinner together as a family or the presence of an adult at home after school are more important for American youth. These variables represent certain aspects of family connectedness which may serve as a protection against adolescent substance use (Stronski et al., 2000; Vazsonyi, 2003). This is particularly noteworthing taking into account the high level of non-intact families in the U.S.

Our findings provide important evidence for the role of parental and familial factors in adolescent substance use (Wood et al., 2004). Despite the fact that these effects are relatively lower than those of peer groups, the parent-adolescent relations continue to provide a secure base for adolescents during this period of their development (Paterson, Pryor and Field, 1995). Due to the special characteristics of the samples (a sample of youth from an Eastern European country, and the African-American sample living in a low-income urban setting in the Southern US), the generalizibility of our findings may be limited. Some additional limitations also should be noted here. Because of the cross-sectional study design, our results cannot provide an explanatory (cause and effect) model for understanding externalizing problem behavior. Additionally, the current study of parental/familial influences is based on youth's self-reports. Although we should mention here that previous studies also recommend that studies of parent-child relationships should be based on children's self-reports which reflect their valid perceptions of parental monitoring (Gray and Steinberg, 1999).

As a summary, we think that our data make a valuable contribution toward a better understanding of youth substance use and the role(s) of parental/familial influences. Future studies should continue to examine the relative and absolute effects of parental/familial structure on adolescent substance use within the cross-cultural context. In addition, future research should also consider longitudinal study designs for a more comprehensive explanatory framework for understanding parent-child relationship and its consequences.

REFERENCES

Ackerman, B. P., D'Eramo, K. S., Umylny, L., Schultz, D., and Izard, C. E. (2001). Family structure and the externalizing behavior of children from economically disadvantaged families. *Journal of Family Psychology*, 15, 288-300.

Aneshensel, C. S., and Gore, S. (1991). Development, stress and role restructuring. Social transitions in adolescence. In J. Eckenrode (Ed.), *The social context of coping* (pp. 55-77). New York and London: Plenum Press.

Arnett, J. J., and Jensen, L. A. (1994). Socialization and risk behavior in two countries: Denmark and the United States. *Youth and Society*, 26, 3-20.

Ary, D. V., Duncan, T. E., Biglan, A., Metzler, C. W., Noell, J. W., and Smolkowski, K. (1999). Development of adolescent problem behavior. *Journal of Abnormal Child Psychology*, 27, 141-150.

Bahr, S. J., Hoffmann, J. P., and Yang, X. (2005). Parental and peer influences on the risk of adolescent drug use. *Journal of Primary Prevention,* 26, 529-551.

Bahr, S. J., Marcos, A. C., and Maughan, S. L. (1995). Family, educational and peer influences on the alcohol use of female and male adolescents. *Journal of Studies on Alcohol*, 56, 457-469.

Brown, P. (2002). Smoking increases among teenagers in eastern Europe. *British Medical Journal*, 324, 442.

Chen, C, Greenberger, E., Lester, J., Don, Q., and Guo, M. (1998). A cross-cultural study of peer correlates of adolescent misconduct. *Developmental Psychology*, 34, 770-781.

Chirkov, V-I., and Ryan, R. M. (2001). Parent and teacher autonomy-support in Russian and U.S. adolescents: Common effects on well-being and academic motivation. *Journal of Cross-Cultural Psychology,* 32, 618-635.

Christensen, P. (2004). The health-promoting family: A conceptual framework for future research. *Social Science and Medicine*, 59, 377-387.

Deković, M. (1999). Risk and protective factors in the development of problem behavior during adolescence. *Journal of Youth and Adolescence*, 28, 667-685.

Field, T., Diego, M., and Sanders, C. (2002). Adolescents' parent and peer relationships. *Adolescence*, 37, 121-130.

Fitzpatrick, K. M. (1997a). Aggression and environmental risk among low-income African-American youth. *Journal of Adolescent Health*, 21, 172-178.

Fitzpatrick, K. M. (1997b). Fighting among America's youth: A risk and protective factors approach. *Journal of Health and Social Behavior*, 38, 131-148.

Fitzpatrick, K. M., Piko, B. F., and Wright, D. R. (2005). A tale of two cities: Health-compromising behaviors between Hungarian and American youth. Annals of Sociology of Children. In L. E. Bass (Ed.), *Sociological Studies of Children and Youth* (Vol. 10., pp. 189-212). Amsterdam: Elsevier.

Formoso, D., Gonzales, N. A., and Aiken, L. S. (2000). Family conflict and children's internalizing and externalizing behavior: Protective factors. *American Journal of Community Psychology*, 28, 175-199.

Frey, C. U., and Röthlisberger, C. (1996). Social support in healthy adolescents. *Journal of Youth and Adolescence*, 25, 17-31.

Gilvarry, E. (2000). Substance abuse in young people. *Journal of Child Psychology and Psychiatry*, 41, 55-80.

Gray, M. R., and Steinberg, L. (1999). Unpacking authoritative parenting: reassessing a multidimensional construct. *Journal of Marriage and the Family*, 61, 574-587.

Harland, P., Reijneveld, S. A., Brugman, E., Verloove-Vanhorick, S. P., and Verhulst, F. C. (2002). Family factors and life events as risk factors for behavioural and emotional problems in children. *European Child and Adolescent Psychiatry*, 11, 176-184.

Hawkins, J. D., Catalano, R. F., and Miller, J. Y. (1992). Risk and protective factors for alcohol and other drug problems in adolescence and early adulthood: Implications for substance abuse prevention. *Psychological Bulletin*, 112, 64-105.

Jackson, C., Henriksen, L., and Foshee, V. A. (1998). The Authoritative Parenting Index: Predicting health risk behaviors among children and adolescents. *Health Education and Behavior*, 25(3), 319-337.

Jaffee, S. R., Moffitt, T. E., Caspi, A., Taylor, A., and Arseneault, L. (2002). Influence of adult domestic violence on children's internalizing and externalizing problems: an environmentally informative twin study. *Journal of the American Academy of Child and Adolescent Psychiatry*, 41, 1095-1103.

Li, X., Feigelman, S., and Stanton, B. (2000). Perceived parental monitoring and health risk behaviors among urban low-income African-American children and adolescents. *Journal of Adolescent Health*, 27, 43-48.

Li, X., Stanton, B., and Feigelman, S. (2000). Impact of perceived parental monitoring on adolescent risk behavior over 4 years. *Journal of Adolescent Health*, 27, 49-56.

Norton, D. E., Sivarajan-Froelicher, E., Waters, C. M., and Carrieri-Kohlman, V. (2003). Parental influence on models of primary prevention of cardiovascular disease on children. *European Journal of Cardiovascular Nursing*, 2, 311-322.

Paterson, J., Pryor, J., and Field, J. (1995). Adolescent attachment and friends in relation to aspects of self-esteem. *Journal of Youth and Adolescents*, 24, 365-376.

Piko B. (2000). Perceived social support from parents and peers: which is the stronger predictor of adolescent substance use? *Substance Use and Misuse*, 35, 617-630.

Piko B. (2001). Smoking in adolescence: Do attitudes matter? *Addictive Behaviors*, 26, 201-217.

Piko B., and Fitzpatrick K. (2001). Health risk behaviors in adolescence: Comparison of Hungarian and American youth. *Health Education*, 42, 249-252. (in Hungarian)

Piko B. F, Fitzpatrick, K. M., and Wright, D. R. (2005). A risk and protective factors framework for understanding youth's externalizing problem behavior in two different cultural settings. *European Child and Adolescent Psychiatry*, 14, 95-103.

Piko B., Luszczynska, A. Gibbons, F. X., and Teközel, M. (2005). A culture-based study of personal and social influences of adolescent smoking. *European Journal of Public Health*, 15, 393-398.

Poikolainen, K. (2002). Antecedens of substance use in adolescence. *Current Opinion in Psychiatry*, 15, 241-245.

Radziszewska, B., Richardson, J. L., Dent, C. W., and Flay, B. R. (1996). Parenting style and adolescent depressive symptoms, smoking, and academic achievement: Ethnic, gender, and SES differences. *Journal of Behavioral Medicine*, 19, 289-305.

Rohner, R. P., and Britner, P. A. (2002). Worldwide mental health correlates of parental acceptance – rejection: Review of cross-cultural evidence. *Cross-Cultural Research*, 36, 16-47.

Sargent, J. D., and Dalton, M. (2001). Does parental disapproval of smoking prevent adolescents from becoming established smokers? *Pediatrics*, 108, 1256-1262.

Search Institute (1998). Search Institute Profiles of Student Life Administration Manual. Search Institute, Minneapolis, MN.

Simons-Morton, B., Haynie, D. L., Crump, A. D., Eitel, P., and Saylor, K. E. (2001). Peer and parent influences on smoking and drinking among early adolescents. *Health Education and Behavior*, 28, 95-107.

Steinberg, L., Fletcher, A., and Darling, N. (1994). Parental monitoring and peer influences on adolescent substance use. *Pediatrics*, 93, 1060-1064.

Steptoe, A., and Wardle, J. (1992). Cognitive predictors of health behavior in contrasting regions of Europe. *British Journal of Clinical Psychology*, 31, 485-502.

Stronski, S. M., Ireland, M., Michaud, P.-A., Narring, F., and Resnick, M. D. (2000). Protective correlates of stages in adolescent substance use: A Swiss National Study. *Journal of Adolescent Health*, 26, 420-427.

Vazsonyi, A. T. (2003). Parent-adolescent relations and problem behaviors: Hungary, the Netherlands, Switzerland, and the United States. *Marriage and Family Review,* 35, 161-187.

Wood, M. D., Read, J. P., Mitchell, R. E., and Brand, N. H. (2004). Do parents still matter? Parent and peer influences on alcohol involvement among recent high school graduates. *Psychology of Addictive Behaviors*, 18, 19-30.

In: Substance Abuse: New Research
Editors: Ethan J. Kerr and Owen E. Gibson

ISBN 978-1-60456-834-9
© 2009 Nova Science Publishers, Inc.

Chapter 6

CHILDHOOD SEXUAL ABUSE AND SUBSTANCE USE PROBLEMS: DISENTANGLING A COMPLEX ASSOCIATION

Carolyn E. Sartor, Alexis E. Duncan,
Vivia V. McCutcheon and Arpana Agrawal
Washington University School of Medicine; Department of Psychiatry,
660 S. Euclid Ave., Box 8134, St. Louis, MO 63110, USA

ABSTRACT

Evidence for the association between childhood sexual abuse (CSA) and later misuse of substances covers a wide range of licit and illicit drugs and spans multiple stages of involvement, including increased likelihood of use, higher probability of early initiation, and elevated risk for onset of substance use disorders (SUDs). Contributions to this literature represent a variety of approaches to addressing the association of CSA to alcohol and drug-related problems, which is complicated by the fact that many of the same factors that elevate risk for CSA exposure also increase risk for substance use problems. Methods for disentangling direct effects of CSA events on substance use outcomes from the effects of risk factors that are frequently present in families in which CSA exposures occurs (e.g., parental drug or alcohol problems) include measurement and adjustment for potentially confounding factors and the use of co-twin designs. Findings across methodological approaches provide support for CSA-specific risk for substance use outcomes, despite the significant contribution of family background factors to overall risk. In combination with the critical information about treatment presentation and response provided by clinical population-based studies, these investigations represent important steps for modeling the pathways from CSA to substance use outcomes and for informing intervention efforts with this high-risk population.

INTRODUCTION

The risks for substance-related problems posed by childhood sexual abuse (CSA) are substantial and far-reaching. In addition to the impairment and psychological distress that stem from substance misuse, individuals with CSA histories who abuse substances have an increased likelihood of exposure to and engagement in other health-compromising behaviors. The high rates of sexual revictimization (Coid et al., 2001; Messman-Moore & Long, 2003) and sexual practices that increase risk for HIV infection (Bensley, Van Eenwyk, & Simmons, 2000; The NIMH Multisite HIV Prevention Trial Group, 2001) underscore the vulnerability of this population and the importance of building a foundation from which prevention and intervention efforts can evolve.

Evidence for the association between CSA and substance misuse has grown significantly in the last two decades, and, as interest in this area of research has increased, the complexity of the relationship between sexual abuse history and drug and alcohol-related problems has become increasingly apparent. As a result, a wider range of approaches for identifying factors that increase CSA-associated risk and delineating pathways from CSA to substance use problems has developed. The aim of the present chapter is to review the development of the body of research on CSA and substance use problems and to highlight the utility of two methodological approaches for disentangling the contribution of risk factors common to CSA and substance use problems in determining the risk attributable specifically to CSA events.

1. CSA AND SUBSTANCE USE OUTCOMES

1.1 What we Know from Clinical and High-risk Populations

In a review of the literature, Simpson and Miller (2002) reported that the rate of CSA among females seeking treatment for substance use problems is twice that of women in the general population (Simpson & Miller, 2002). History of CSA has been associated with earlier age at initiation of alcohol use and greater alcohol-related problems among individuals using detoxification services (Brems, Johnson, Neal, & Freemon, 2004), earlier age at onset of alcohol use disorders (AUDs) for participants in a day hospital program (Zlotnick et al., 2006), and higher quantity and frequency of alcohol consumption among individuals arrested for driving while intoxicated (McMillan, Hanson, Bedrick, & Lapham, 2005). More rapid relapse rates following treatment have been documented as well for individuals exposed to CSA (Greenfield et al., 2002; Walitzer & Dearing, 2006). Evidence for the link among adolescents with alcohol abuse or dependence is even more striking. Clark and colleagues reported that, compared with control subjects, adolescents meeting AUD criteria were 18 to 21 times more likely to have histories of CSA (Clark, Lesnick, & Hegedus, 1997). Although fewer in number than clinical studies focused on alcohol-related behaviors, treatment outcome studies for illicit drug use reveal similar patterns: CSA is correlated with younger age at entry into treatment and predicts lower likelihood of abstinence following program completion (Boles, Joshi, Grella, & Wellisch, 2005).

1.2. Evidence from Community-based Studies

The relationship between CSA and substance use problems in samples representative of the general population parallel those derived from the clinical literature and extend findings to include the association of CSA history with tobacco use outcomes. Early initiation of alcohol consumption (Edgardh & Ormstad, 2000), elevated rates of alcohol problems (Galaif, Stein, Newcomb, & Bernstein, 2001; Pedersen & Skrondal, 1996), illicit drug use and dependence (Boden, Fergusson, & Horwood, 2006; Lynskey et al., 2006; Thompson, Arias, Basile, & Desai, 2002), early age at first cigarette (Anda et al., 1999), and onset of nicotine dependence/withdrawal (al Mamun et al., 2007) have all been linked to CSA history in community-based samples. In addition, several population-based investigations simultaneously examining alcohol, illicit drug, and tobacco use behaviors have found evidence for CSA-associated risk across outcomes (Harrison, Fulkerson, & Beebe, 1997; Hussey, Chang, & Kotch, 2006; Macmillan et al., 2001; Plant, Miller, & Plant, 2004; Wilsnack, Vogeltanz, Klassen, & Harris, 1997), underscoring the global nature of its link to substance use problems. Furthermore, these studies provide critical evidence that the association of drug and alcohol problems with CSA is not unique to the subset of substance users who present for treatment and who typically represent the most severe manifestations of substance misuse.

1.3. Additional Factors Influencing the Link between CSA and Substance Use Outcomes

Gender differences in substance-related behaviors are consistent across outcomes, with males initiating use at an earlier age (e.g., Sartor, Lynskey, Heath, Jacob, & True, 2007a), more commonly engaging in heavy use (e.g., Naimi et al, 2003), and meeting criteria for substance use disorders (SUDs) in larger numbers (e.g., Compton, Thomas, Stinson, & Grant, 2007; Grant et al., 2004). By contrast, males are substantially less likely to report exposure to childhood sexual abuse (general population estimates range from 2-11 % in men versus 6-34% in women [Walker, Carey, Mohr, Stein, & Seedat, 2004]), which likely contributes to the inconsistency in findings for males. Although some studies examining the relationship between CSA and substance use outcomes separately in men and women have reported that the magnitude of association is similar across gender (Dube et al., 2005; Molnar, Buka, & Kessler, 2001), others have demonstrated stronger associations for women (Nelson et al., 2002). In addition to possible distinctions by gender, investigations have explored features of the sexual abuse events (e.g., severity) as potential sources of variance in substance use outcomes. The evidence for elevated risk in sexual abuse that involves contact (Chen, Dunne, & Han, 2006), especially attempted or completed intercourse, is robust (Bulik, Prescott, & Kendler, 2001; Fergusson, Horwood, & Lynskey, 1996a; Fleming, Mullen, Sibthorpe, & Bammer, 1999; Kendler et al., 2000; Nelson et al., 2002). Some studies have also suggested that the risk for substance use outcomes is higher among those individuals with an earlier age at CSA (Spak, Spak, & Alleback, 1998; Moncrieff & Farmer, 1998).

RISK FACTORS COMMON TO CSA
AND SUBSTANCE-RELATED PROBLEMS

CSA may be best conceptualized as part of a constellation of risk factors for psychopathology and substance use outcomes. An investigation by Dube and colleagues (2003) revealed that 78% of individuals reporting a history of sexual abuse endorsed exposure to one or more additional adverse childhood experiences, such as physical abuse, neglect, or parental separation (Dube et al., 2003). Elevated rates of other risk factors for the development of substance-related problems, such as parental substance use problems (Anda et al., 2002; Legrand, McGue, & Iacono, 1999; Hill, Shen, Lowers, & Locke, 2000), marital conflict (Fergusson, Lynskey, & Horwood, 1996), disorganization or instability in the family (Hussong & Chassin, 1997; Li, Duncan, & Hops, 2001), and low parent-child attachment (Fergusson et al., 1996b) are common in families of children who have experienced sexual abuse. In such an overall dysfunctional environment (Kendler et al., 2000), parents are less likely to provide the nurturance and support that serve as protective factors against exposure to CSA and other adverse events.

2. A Direct or Indirect Relationship?

The idea that the pathway from CSA to substance use or SUD is direct, possibly resulting from attempts at regulating negative affect associated with the abuse through alcohol consumption or drug use, is intuitively appealing and commonly discussed in clinical literatures. The temporal progression, with CSA preceding onset of substance use in the majority of cases, further promotes the notion of a direct causal pathway. However, as implied in the above review of common risk factors, there may be an indirect relationship in which both CSA and substance-related problems result from a shared risk factor, such as poor parental supervision (Walsh, MacMillan, & Jamieson, 2003) or parental psychopathology (Fergusson et al., 1996a; Vogeltanz et al., 1999; Walsh et al., 2003). Two primary methodological approaches used to tease apart indirect influences of risk factors that typically co-occur with both CSA and substance use problems from those effects specific to CSA are outlined below.

METHODOLOGICAL APPROACHES

3. Epidemiological Studies Using Measured Covariates

A number of investigations seeking to clarify the nature of the relationship between CSA and substance-related outcomes have measured and adjusted for the influences of other relevant familial risk factors. For example, Fergusson and colleagues (1996) examined CSA in relation to SUDs in a study of 1,019 18 year-olds who had reported in an earlier wave of data collection on familial risk factors such as parental psychopathology, family conflict, and parental substance abuse. Analyses adjusted for these and other potential confounders revealed that CSA remained a significant predictor of AUDs and other SUDs, and in the case of other SUDs, the association was almost unaffected by the statistical adjustment for relevant covariates (Fergusson et al., 1996a). A similar approach was used by Kilpatrick et al. (2000) in their investigation of CSA and past-year alcohol and illicit drug abuse/dependence in a national probability sample of 12 to 17 year olds. Variance associated with sexual abuse was assessed after accounting for sociodemographic factors as well as family history of alcohol problems and familial drug problems, resulting in a significant association between CSA and both past-year AUD and cannabis use disorder (Kilpatrick et al., 2000). An investigation by Miller and colleagues (1993) using an all-female adult sample that included participants recruited from both treatment settings and the community led to similar conclusions. Even after adjusting for family background factors, treatment condition, and parental alcohol problems, CSA predicted women's alcohol-related problems (Miller, Downs, & Testa, 1993), further substantiating the assertion that sexual abuse history is specifically linked to substance use problems; common risk factors do not fully account for the association.

4. Co-twin Designs

Genetically informative designs have also made critical contributions to the task of disentangling indirect from direct sources of risk in the relationship between CSA and alcohol and drug-related problems. Co-twin designs are based on the premise that twins share a known proportion of genetic variance (100% for monozygotic (MZ) twins and 50% for dizygotic (DZ) twins) as well as family and other significant environments (e.g., school, neighborhood). Incorporation of data from co-twins creates the opportunity to statistically control for genetic and environmental factors shared by members of a twin pair. In this approach, the contribution of factors such as parental history of SUDs is accounted for by design and thus ruled out as a possible source of distinction in substance use outcomes between CSA-exposed and non-exposed individuals.

Recent work from our group illustrates this strategy. Using a sample of 3,536 female twins, we examined CSA history in relation to two major transitions in the course of alcohol dependence (AD) development: onset of first alcohol use and transition time from consumption of first alcoholic drink to onset of AD. CSA status was entered into the analyses after co-twin AD status, zygosity, and an interaction term reflecting zygosity by co-twin AD status, which provided an estimate of the degree to which familial risk may be attributed to genetic versus environmental factors. Results revealed that, although CSA was associated with higher rates of both lifetime alcohol use and AD, CSA-specific risk for consumption of first alcoholic drink was evident only at ages 12 and 13 and rate of transition from first alcohol use to AD did not differ by CSA status. In short, after adjusting for potential confounders through co-twin AD status, risk conferred by CSA for rapid transitions in AD development was apparent only among the earliest initiates of alcohol use and was specific to the onset of first alcohol consumption (Sartor et al., 2007b).

The discordant twin design, similar to the above described co-twin methodology, draws on the unique twin pair relationship in which genetic and environmental factors shared by twins can be accounted for in assessing variability in outcomes. However, instead of statistically adjusting for the co-twin's status on the outcome variable, the discordant twin design utilizes twin pairs who differ on exposure to the risk factor of interest, such that the unexposed co-twin serves as a matched control for the exposed twin. For investigations of

CSA and substance use behaviors, twin pairs in which one twin was sexually abused and the other was not are selected and, given that the unexposed co-twin carries identical genetic material (in the case of MZ twins) and has had the same exposures to other relevant familial risk factors, differences in substance use outcomes can be attributed to CSA.

Findings from discordant twin studies suggest that CSA poses risk for substance-related problems above and beyond risk attributable to family background factors known to contribute both to CSA exposure and to drug and alcohol outcomes. For example, Nelson and colleagues' (2006) investigation of CSA in relation to a variety of drug use outcomes concluded that a history of sexual abuse elevates risk for regular smoking, illicit drug use, and drug abuse and dependence (Nelson et al., 2006). A study conducted by Kendler et al. (2000) using an all-female twin sample to assess the role of CSA in the development of psychiatric disorders and SUDs found that CSA was associated with AD and other drug dependence, and concluded that findings support a causal link between sexual abuse exposure and SUDs (Kendler et al., 2000). Elevated risk for AD was also reported by Dinwiddie and colleagues (2000) in their investigation of psychopathological outcomes and CSA history (Dinwiddie et al., 2000). Consistent with previously discussed literature highlighting commonality of risk factors for CSA exposure and substance use problems, the authors also reported evidence for the contribution of family background factors to psychiatric and alcohol-related outcomes, as did an earlier study by Nelson et al. (2002). In sum, conclusions from studies employing co-twin methodology coincide with those derived from general population-based studies using measured covariates: familial risk factors, such as parental SUDs and family conflict contribute to substance use outcomes, but CSA poses additional risk that is not fully accounted for by these factors.

CONCLUSION

The constellation of risk factors that characterize family environments where children are at risk for CSA exposure creates significant challenges for developing a comprehensive model for the pathway (or pathways) from CSA to the manifestation of substance-related problems. The two methodologies described above present important steps toward disentangling direct from indirect influences, although much work remains to be done in the effort to identify the underlying mechanisms that link CSA to substance use problems and to fully understand the meaning of "a direct path" from one to the other. It is also important to note that neither approach addresses completely the challenges of this line of research. The use of measured covariates in epidemiological samples, for example, requires that an extensive number of potential confounders be assessed. The consequence of omitting a critical covariate may be the misattribution of risk to CSA rather than another source, yet the inclusion of a large number of covariates can compromise statistical power. Discordant twin studies, although powerful tools for accounting for familial risk, also have their drawbacks. They require access to large twin registries and, given the high concordance rates of CSA in twin pairs (Dinwiddie et al., 2000; Kendler et al., 2000), may reflect atypical sexual abuse histories. Rather than determine a single superior strategy for modeling the complexity of the association between CSA history and substance use problems, integration of the available tools and findings derived from their use provides the most reliable foundation from which clinical applications can be developed. Not the least of these sources are the clinical population-based studies, which provide essential information about treatment response that is rarely addressed in other types of investigations and which have already led to the establishment of treatment approaches specifically tailored to individuals with sexual abuse histories who also engage in problem substance use.

REFERENCES

al Mamun, A., Alati, R., O'Callaghan, M., Hayatbakhsh, M. R., O'Callaghan, F. V., Najman, J. M., et al. (2007). Does childhood sexual abuse have an effect on young adults' nicotine disorder (dependence or withdrawal)? Evidence from a birth cohort study. *Addiction, 102,* 647-654.

Anda, R. F., Croft, J. B., Felitti, V. J., Nordenberg, D., Giles, W. H., Williamson, D. F. et al. (1999). Adverse childhood experiences and smoking during adolescence and adulthood. *Journal of the American Medical Association, 282,* 1652-1658.

Anda, R. F., Whitfield, C. L., Felitti, V. J., Chapman, D., Edwards, V. J., Dube, S. R., et al. (2002). Adverse childhood experiences, alcoholic parents, and later risk of alcoholism and depression. *Psychiatric Services, 53,* 1001-1009.

Bensley, L. S., Van Eenwyk, J., & Simmons, K. W. (2000). Self-reported childhood sexual and physical abuse and adult HIV-risk behaviors and heavy drinking. *American Journal of Preventive Medicine, 18,* 151-158.

Boden, J. M., Fergusson, D. M., & Horwood, L. J. (2006). Illicit drug use and dependence in a New Zealand birth cohort. *Australian and New Zealand Journal of Psychiatry, 40,* 156-163.

Boles, S. M., Joshi, V., Grella, C., & Wellisch, J. (2005). Childhood sexual abuse patterns, psychosocial correlates, and treatment outcomes among adults in drug abuse treatment. *Journal of Child Sexual Abuse, 14,* 39-55.

Brems, C., Johnson, M. E., Neal, D., & Freemon, M. (2007). Childhood abuse history and substance use among men and women receiving detoxification services. *The American Journal of Drug and Alcohol Abuse, 30,* 799-821.

Bulik, C. M., Prescott, C. A., & Kendler, K. S. (2001). Features of childhood sexual abuse and the development of psychiatric and substance use disorders. *British Journal of Psychiatry, 179,* 444-449.

Chen, J., Dunne, M. P., & Han, P. (2006). Child sexual abuse in Henan province, China: Associations with sadness, suicidality, and risk behaviors among adolescent girls. *Journal of Adolescent Health, 38,* 544-549.

Clark, D. B., Lesnick, L., & Hegedus, A. M. (1997). Traumas and other adverse life events in adolescents with alcohol abuse and dependence. *Journal of the American Academy of Child and Adolescent Psychiatry, 36,* 1744-1751.

Coid, J., Petruckevitch, A., Feder, G., Chung, W. -S., Richardson, J., & Moorey, S. (2001). Relation between childhood sexual and physical abuse and risk of revictimization in women: a cross-sectional survey. *The Lancet, 358,* 450-454.

Compton, W. M., Thomas, Y., Stinson, F. S., & Grant, B. F. (2007). Prevalence, correlates, disability, and comorbidity of DSM-IV drug abuse and dependence in the United States:

Results from the National Epidemiologic Survey on Alcohol and Related Conditions. *Archives of General Psychiatry, 64,* 566-576.

Dinwiddie, S. H., Heath, A. C., Dunne, M. P., Bucholz, K. K., Madden, P. A. F., Slutske, W. S., et al. (2000). Early sexual abuse and lifetime psychopathology: A co-twin-control study. *Psychological Medicine, 30,* 41-52.

Dube, S. R., Felitti, V., Dong, M., Chapman, D. P., Giles, W. H., & Anda, R. F. (2003). Childhood abuse, neglect, and household dysfunction and the risk of illicit drug use: The Adverse Childhood Experiences Study. *Pediatrics, 111,* 564-572.

Edgardh, K., & Ormstad, K. (2000). Prevalence and characteristics of sexual abuse in a national sample of Swedish seventeen-year-old boys and girls. *Acta Paediatrica, 88,* 310-319.

Fergusson, D. M., Horwood, L. J., & Lynskey, M. T. (1996a). Childhood sexual abuse and psychiatric disorder in young adulthood: II. Psychiatric outcomes of childhood sexual abuse. *Journal of the American Academy of Child and Adolescent Psychiatry, 35,* 1365-1374.

Fergusson, D. M., Lynskey, M. T., & Horwood, L. J. (1996b). Childhood sexual abuse and psychiatric disorder in young adulthood: I. Prevalence of sexual abuse and factors associated with sexual abuse. *Journal of the American Academy of Child and Adolescent Psychiatry, 35,* 1355-1364.

Fleming, J. E., Mullen, P. E., Sibthorpe, B., & Bammer, G. (1999). The long-term impact of childhood sexual abuse in Australian women. *Child Abuse & Neglect, 23,* 145-159.

Galaif, E. R., Stein, J. A., Newcomb, M. D., & Bernstein, D. P. (2001). Gender differences in the prediction of problem alcohol use in adulthood: Exploring the influence of family factors and childhood maltreatment. *Journal of Studies on Alcohol, 62,* 486-493.

Grant, B. F., Dawson, D. A., Stinson, F. S., Chou, S. P., Dufour, M. C., & Pickering, R. P. (2004). The 12-month prevalence and trends in DSM-IV alcohol abuse and dependence: United States, 1991-1992 and 2001-2002. *Drug and Alcohol Dependence, 74,* 223-234.

Greenfield, S. F., Kolodziej, M. E., Sugarman, D. E., Muenz, L. R., Vagge, L. M., He, D. Y., et al. (2002). History of abuse and drinking outcomes following inpatient alcohol treatment: A prospective study. *Drug and Alcohol Dependence, 67,* 227-234.

Harrison, P. A., Fulkerson, J. A., & Beebe, T. J. (1997). Multiple substance use among adolescent physical and sexual abuse victims. *Child Abuse & Neglect, 21,* 529-539.

Hill, S. Y., Shen, L., Lowers, L., & Locke, J. (2000). Factors predicting the onset of adolescent drinking in families at high risk for developing alcoholism. *Biological Psychiatry, 48,* 265-275.

Hussong, A. M., & Chassin, L. (1997). Substance use initiation among adolescent children of alcoholics: Testing protective factors. *Journal of Studies on Alcohol, 58,* 272-279.

Hussey, J. M., Chang, J. J., & Kotch, J. B. (2006). Child maltreatment in the United States: Prevalence, risk factors, and adolescent health consequences. *Pediatrics, 118,* 933-942.

Kendler, K. S., Bulik, C. M., Silberg, J. L., Hettema, J. M., Myers, J., & Prescott, C. A. (2000). Childhood sexual abuse and adult psychiatric and substance use disorders in women: An epidemiological and cotwin control analysis. *Archives of General Psychiatry, 57,* 953-959.

Kilpatrick, D. G., Acierno, R., Saunders, B., Resnick, H. S., Best, C. L., & Schnurr, P. P. (2000). Risk factors for adolescent substance abuse and dependence: Data from a national sample. *Journal of Consulting & Clinical Psychology, 68,* 19-30.

Legrand, L. N., McGue, M., & Iacono, W. G. (1999). Searching for interactive effects in the etiology of early-onset substance use. *Behavior Genetics, 29*, 433-444.

Li, F., Duncan, T. E., Hops, H. (2000). Examining developmental trajectories in adolescent alcohol use using piecewise growth mixture modeling analysis. *Journal of Studies on Alcohol, 62*, 199-210.

Lynskey, M. T., Agrawal, A., Bucholz, K. K., Nelson, E. C., Madden, P. A. F., Todorov, A. A., et al. (2006). Subtypes of illicit drug users: A latent class analysis of data from an Australian twin sample. *Twin Research and Human Genetics, 9*, 523-530.

MacMillan, H. L., Fleming, J. E., Streiner, D. L., Lin, E., Boyle, M. H., Jamieson, E., et al. (2001). Childhood abuse and lifetime psychopathology in a community sample. *American Journal of Psychiatry, 158*, 1878-1883.

McMillan, G. P., Hanson, T., Bedrick, E. J., & Lapham, S. C. (2005). Using the bivariate dale model to jointly estimate predictors of frequency and quantity of alcohol use. *Journal of Studies on Alcohol, 66*, 688-692.

Messman-Moore, T. L., & Long, P. J. (2003). The role of childhood sexual abuse sequelae in the sexual revictimization of women: An empirical review and theoretical reformulation. *Clinical Psychology Review, 23*, 537-571.

Miller, B. A., Downs, W. R., & Testa, M. (1993). Interrelationships between victimization experiences and women's alcohol use. *Journal of Studies on Alcohol, 11*, 109-117.

Molnar, B. E., Buka, S. L., & Kessler, R. C. (2001). Child sexual abuse and subsequent psychopathology: Results from the National Comorbidity Survey. *American Journal of Public Health, 91*, 753-760.

Moncrieff, J., & Farmer, R. (1998). Sexual abuse and the subsequent development of alcohol problems. *Alcohol & Alcoholism, 33*, 592-601.

Naimi, T. S., Brewer, R. D., Mokdad, A. H., Denny, C., Serdula, M. K., & Marks, J. S. (2003). Binge drinking among US adults. *Journal of the American Medical Association, 289*, 70-75.

Nelson, E. C., Heath, A. C., Madden, P. A. F., Cooper, M. L., Dinwiddie, S. H., Bucholz, K. K., et al. (2002). Association between self-reported childhood sexual abuse and adverse psychosocial outcomes: Results from a twin study. *Archives of General Psychiatry, 59*, 139-145.

Nelson, E. C., Heath, A. C., Lynskey, M. T., Bucholz, K. K., Madden, P. A. F., Statham, D. B., et al. (2006). Childhood sexual abuse and risks for licit and illicit drug-related outcomes: A twin study. *Psychological Medicine, 36*, 1473-1483.

Pedersen, W., & Skrondal, A. (1996). Alcohol and sexual victimization: A longitudinal study of Norwegian girls. *Addiction, 91*, 565-581.

Plant, M., Miller, P., & Plant, M. (2004). Childhood and adult sexual abuse: Relationships with alcohol and other psychoactive drug use. *Child Abuse Review, 13*, 200-214.

Sartor, C. E., Lynskey, M. T., Bucholz, K. K., McCutcheon, V. V., Nelson, E. C., Waldron, M., et al. (2007a). Childhood sexual abuse and the course of alcohol dependence development: Findings from a female twin sample, *Drug and Alcohol Dependence, 89*, 139-144.

Sartor, C. E., Lynskey, M., Heath, A. C., Jacob, T., & True, W. (2007b). The role of childhood risk factors in initiation of alcohol use and progression to alcohol dependence, *Addiction, 102*, 216-225.

Simpson, T. L., & Miller, W. R. (2002). Concomitance between childhood sexual and physical abuse and substance use problems: A review. *Clinical Psychology Review, 22,* 27-77.

Spak, L., Spak, F., & Allebeck, P. (1998). Sexual abuse and alcoholism in a female population. *Addiction, 93,* 1365-1373.

The NIMH Multisite HIV Prevention Trial Group. (2001). A test of factors mediating the relationship between unwanted sexual activity during childhood and risky sexual practices among women enrolled in the NIMH Multisite HIV Prevention Trial. *Women and Health, 33,* 163-180.

Thompson, M. P., Arias, I., Basile, K. C., & Desai, S. (2002). The association between childhood physical and sexual victimization and health problems in adulthood in a nationally representative sample of women. *Journal of Interpersonal Violence, 17,* 1115-1129.

Vogeltanz, N. D., Wilsnack, S. C., Harris, T. R., Wilsnack, R. W., Wonderlich, S. A., & Kristjanson, A. F. (1999). Prevalence and risk factors for childhood sexual abuse in women: National survey findings. *Child Abuse & Neglect, 23,* 579-592.

Walitzer, K. S., & Dearing, R. L. (2006). Gender differences in alcohol and substance use relapse. *Clinical Psychology Review, 26,* 128-148.

Walker, J. L., Carey, P. D., Mohr, N., Stein, D. J., & Seedat, S. (2004). Gender differences in the prevalence of childhood sexual abuse and in the development of pediatric PTSD. *Archives of Women's Mental Health, 7,* 111-121.

Walsh, C., MacMillan, H. L., & Jamieson, E. (2003). The relationship between parental substance abuse and child maltreatment: Findings from the Ontario Health Supplement. *Child Abuse & Neglect, 27,* 1409-1425.

Wilsnack, S. C., Vogeltanz, N. D., Klassen, A. D., & Harris, T. R. (1997). Childhood sexual abuse and women's substance abuse: National survey findings. *Journal of Studies on Alcohol, 58,* 264-271.

Zlotnick, C., Johnson, D. M., Stout, R. L., Zywiak, W. H., Johnson, J. E., & Schneider, R. J. (2006). Childhood abuse and intake severity in alcohol disorder patients. *Journal of Traumatic Stress, 19,* 949-959.

In: Substance Abuse: New Research
Editors: Ethan J. Kerr and Owen E. Gibson

ISBN 978-1-60456-834-9
© 2009 Nova Science Publishers, Inc.

Chapter 7

ALCOHOL AND SUBSTANCE ABUSE AMONG OLDER ADULTS

Susanna Nemes[1], Jennifer Weil[1], Christine Zeiler[2], Kelly Munly[2], Kristen Holtz[2], and Jeffrey Hoffman[2]*

[1]Social Solutions International Inc.,MD. USA
[2]Danya International Inc., USA

ABSTRACT

This article represents an overview of the literature on substance abuse among older adults. It begins with a review of the literature on alcohol use and abuse among older adults, which represents the greater bulk of available information, followed by a review of the literature regarding prescription and illicit drug abuse within this population. Additionally, this article details demographic variations in older adult substance abusers. Recommendations for future research are offered.

A REVIEW OF THE LITERATURE

Substance abuse is viewed as a disorder of the young. Rarely does the public connect substance abuse, including alcohol abuse, with seniors or the elderly. However, research is beginning to show that abuse of substances may be an undetected, and therefore, untreated problem of individuals over the age of 55. While it is not known what proportion of all older adults suffer from a substance abuse disorder, researchers and health care providers are discovering that there are more substance abuse problems in the older adult population than commonly thought. Some have even referred to substance abuse among older adults as an "invisible epidemic" (Levin and Kruger, 2000; Blow, 2002).

---

* Corresponding author is Susanna Nemes, Ph.D., snemes@socialsolutions.info, 301-774-0897 (phone), 301-570-4772 (fax), 18303 Wickham Road, Olney MD 20832.

A recent report based on data from the Treatment Episode Data Set (TEDS)[4] found that the number of substance abuse admissions among persons aged 55 or older increased by 32% between 1995 and 2002, while the general population admissions increased by only 12%. Adults aged 55 to 59 made up the largest group of older adults in treatment. Within the total sample of older adults, alcohol abuse was the most frequently reported primary substance of abuse at admission, however, the overall proportion of older adult alcohol admissions declined from 86.5% in 1995 to 77.5% in 2002. In contrast, the proportion of primary non-alcohol drug admissions among older adults more than doubled, with increases of 106% for men and 119% for women between 1995 and 2002 (SAMHSA, 2005). Among those with a primary drug admission, opiates were the most common drug of abuse, followed by cocaine, marijuana, and stimulants.

Some posit that the over-65 age group of current day was raised with different norms and standards about drug and alcohol use and abuse than subsequent generations (Benshoff, Harrawood and Koch, 2003). The over-65 age group was more likely to be raised when the influences of alcohol prohibition were clear (National Institute on Alcohol Abuse and Alcoholism). In addition, the over-65 age group was not raised with the societal acceptance of prescription drug use that we have today and very few had experience with illegal substances. As a result, individuals in this age group are believed to be more likely to perceive drug and alcohol misuse as a moral failing (Marks, 2002).

Conversely, baby boomers (born between the years of 1946 and 1964) were exposed to multiple forms of substance use and abuse and were raised under much different community norms and standards than their predecessors. Cited as the group responsible for the dramatic rise in substance use, experts anticipate that the retiring of the baby boomer cohort will also initiate an increase in older adult substance abuse (Blow et al., 2002; SAMHSA, 2001). As the baby boomers come of retirement age, estimates suggest that the over-65 age group will increase to 21% of the overall population by 2030 (Patterson and Jeste, 1999, Spencer, 1989). This projected expansion in the elderly population has caused experts to posit that the number of elderly substance abusers could jump dramatically. While there are currently approximately 1.7 million substance dependent and abusing adults over the age of 50, forecasts indicate that there will be 4.4 million by 2020 (Epstein, 2002; Office of National Drug Control Policy, 2001).

This article represents an overview of the literature on substance abuse among older adults. It begins with a review of the literature on alcohol use and abuse among older adults, which represents the greater bulk of available information, followed by a review of the literature regarding prescription and illicit drug abuse within this population. Additionally, this article details demographic variations in older adult substance abusers. Recommendations for future research are offered.

METHODOLOGY

A review of the literature was conducted through a search of relevant databases (e.g., EBSCO, PubMed, MEDLINE, and PsychInfo), search engines (Google), and government

---

[4] TEDS is an annual compilation of data on the demographics and substance abuse problems of substance abuse treatment admissions. The data is obtained primarily through facilities receiving some public funding.

websites (e.g., SAMHSA, CSAT, CSAP, CDC, and NIDA). General content areas of interest included substance use and abuse among older adults, with a focus on alcohol, prescription drugs and illicit drugs. Additional content areas included demographic characteristics of older adult substance abusers and issues related to addiction among this population. Search terms were used to cull information related to the defined content areas. Examples of search terms used include: substance abuse, illicit drugs, alcoholism, prescription drug misuse, prescription drug abuse, definitions, older adults, elderly, baby boomers, rates of use, correlates of abuse, gender, race/ethnicity, socioeconomic status, health outcomes, treatment issues.

FINDINGS

Alcohol Use and Abuse

Older adults with alcohol problems represent a unique and growing health care problem. Alcohol is the most frequently cited drug of abuse among older adults seeking drug treatment, and yet, the rates of elder alcohol abuse are most certainly underestimated (SAMHSA, 2005, Blow, 2002). Many studies have shown that older adults are less likely to be accurately diagnosed with an alcohol use disorder than their younger counterparts (Booth et al., 1992; Geller et al., 1989). At the same time, they are more likely than younger users to face serious physical and mental health problems as a result of their drinking.

Definitional Dilemmas

One of the challenges in investigating and understanding the prevalence of alcohol misuse is that a standard definition of overuse of alcohol has not been developed for adults aged 65 and older. While there are standards set by the National Institute on Alcohol Abuse and Alcohol (NIAAA) for the healthy use of alcohol among this population, there is little agreement about whether these standards are stiff enough given the unique health and psychological challenges faced by seniors (Blow, 2002).

The NIAAA has recommended that adult men consume no more than 14 drinks per week and adult women consume no more that seven per week[5]. However, persons older than 65 years of age are recommended to consume no more than one drink per day (Dufour, Archer and Gordis, 1992). Once this one-drink threshold is crossed, the literature varies in how to characterize drinking levels for older adults.

Most clinicians use the criteria described in the American Psychiatric Association's *Diagnostic and Statistical Manual of Mental Disorders IV – Text Revision* (American Psychiatric Association, 2000) in diagnosing substance abuse. These criteria focus heavily on the impacts of substance use on the different spheres of the individual's life, including occupation, social relationships, legal status, and educational pursuits. The problem with using these criteria for older adults, however, is that they often have seriously reduced activity in these spheres (Beecham, 1997; Prigerson, Desai and Rosenheck, 2001). Older adults are often unemployed, live alone, and no longer drive. As such, their problems often go undetected by healthcare providers and other occupants of these spheres. More appropriate

---

[5] A standard drink is one can (12 oz.) of beer or ale; a single shot (1.5 oz) of hard liquor; a glass (5 oz.) of wine; or a small glass (4 oz.) of sherry, liqueur, or aperitif.

measures of abuse among this population may be accidents, poor nutrition, and inadequate self-care. As such, health care providers and others working with older adults should pay careful attention to patient appearance, include questions on accidents and nutrition, and review patient medical charts for a history of falls or other accidents.

Some experts use the model of at-risk, heavy, and problem-drinking in place of the DSM-IV model of alcohol misuse and dependence because it allows for more flexibility in characterizing drinking patterns (CSAT, 2001). In this classification scheme, an at-risk drinker is one whose patterns of alcohol use, although not yet problematic, may bring about adverse consequences, either to the drinker or to others. An example would be someone who drinks moderately at social gatherings and then drives home. Although an accident may not have occurred, all the elements for disaster are present.

The terms *heavy* and *problem* drinking signify more hazardous levels of consumption than at-risk drinking. While the distinction between the terms *heavy* and *problem* drinking is meaningful to alcohol treatment specialists interested in differentiating severity of problems among younger alcohol abusers, it may have less relevance for older adults (Atkinson and Ganzini, 1994), who experience pervasive consequences with less consumption due to their heightened sensitivity to alcohol or the presence of such coexisting diseases as diabetes mellitus, hypertension, cirrhosis, or dementia.

To increase the confusion even further, the World Health Organization (WHO) uses a similar model of at-risk, hazardous, and harmful drinking. Individuals considered *at-risk* are those whose amount of alcohol intake does not meet the thresholds established for hazardous or harmful drinking, but who score high enough on an alcohol assessment scale to be considered a problem drinker. H*azardous drinking* is defined as consumption that will lead to decreased health outcomes, while *harmful drinking* is that in which negative health outcomes have already been realized (Moore, Morgenstern, Harawa, Fielding, Higa, and Beck, 2001).

Varying definitions of alcohol abuse result in confusion about what constitutes problem drinking within older adults. In addition, many of the criteria for measuring alcohol abuse focus on areas where older adults often have seriously reduced activity, such as occupation, social relationships, legal status, and educational pursuits. A single definition of alcohol abuse among older adults is needed that includes criteria more suitable for this population, including a history of accidents, poor nutrition, and inadequate self-care.

Binge Drinking

Binge drinking is generally defined as short periods of loss of control over drinking alternating with periods of abstinence or much lighter alcohol use (CSAT 2001). A binge itself is usually defined as any drinking occasion in which an individual consumes five or more standard drinks. For older adults, the CSAT Consensus Panel defines a binge as four or more drinks per occasion (2001). People who are alcohol-free throughout the workweek and celebrate with Friday night or holiday "benders" would be considered binge drinkers.

Identifying older binge drinkers can be difficult because many of the usual clues, including disciplinary job actions or arrests for driving while intoxicated, are infrequently seen among aging adults who no longer work or drive. Although research is needed on the natural history of binge drinkers as they age, anecdotal observations indicate that younger binge drinkers who survive to their later years often become continuous or near-daily drinkers.

Continuous versus Intermittent Drinking

Tolerance is one of the criteria presented in the DSM-IV-TR for a diagnosis of substance dependence, a criteria weighted heavily by clinicians performing an assessment for substance dependence (American Psychiatric Association, 2000). However, the thresholds of consumption often considered by clinicians as indicative of tolerance may be set too high for older adults because of their altered sensitivity to and body distribution of alcohol (Atkinson, 1990). The lack of tolerance to alcohol does not necessarily mean that an older adult does not have a drinking problem or is not experiencing serious negative effects as a result of his or her drinking. Furthermore, many late onset alcoholics have not developed physiological dependence, and they do not exhibit signs of withdrawal.

Another way of understanding the patterns of drinking over a life span is to look at the time frames in which people drink and the frequency of their drinking (CSAT, 2001). In contrast to ongoing, continuous drinking, intermittent drinking refers to regular, perhaps daily, heavy drinking that has resumed after a stable period of abstinence of 3 to 5 years or more (NIAAA, 1995).

Intermittent drinking problems are easy to overlook, but crucial to identify. Even those problem drinkers who have been sober for many years are at risk for relapse as they age. For this reason, during routine health screenings, it is important for clinicians to take a history that includes both current and lifetime use of alcohol in order to identify prior episodes of alcoholism. Caregivers can then help their older patients anticipate situations that tend to provoke relapse and plan strategies for addressing them when they occur.

Problem Drinking and Age of Onset

Alcoholism can begin at any age or stage of life, and there is tremendous inter-person variation. While some people develop abusive tendencies soon after their first drink, others can drink responsibly for their entire lives. Research has shown that the age at which alcohol abuse begins has an impact on the mental and physical health of the individual (Colleran and Jay, 2002). As such, alcohol abusers are sometimes classified by their alcohol histories into the following categories: early onset, late onset, and periodic onset.

Early Onset

Early onset alcohol abusers comprise the majority of older patients receiving treatment for alcohol abuse, and they tend to resemble younger alcohol abusers in their reasons for use (CSAT 2001). Throughout their lives, early onset alcohol abusers have turned to alcohol to cope with a range of psychosocial or medical problems. Psychiatric comorbidity is common among this group, particularly major affective disorders (e.g., major depression, bipolar disorder) and thought disorders. Early onset users also typically have a family history of alcoholism and, for the most part, continue their established abusive drinking patterns as they age (Schonfeld and Dupree, 1991; Atkinson, Tolson, and Turner, 1990; Stall, 1987; Atkinson, Turner, Kofoed, and Tolson, 1985; Atkinson, 1984). The effects of extended alcohol abuse often manifest in chronic alcohol-related medical problems (e.g., cirrhosis), depression, and family problems (Colleran and Jay, 2002).

Late Onset

In comparison, late onset drinkers appear psychologically and physically healthier. Some studies have found that late onset drinkers are more likely to have begun or to have increased drinking in response to recent losses such as death of a spouse or divorce, to a change in health status, or to such life changes as retirement (Hurt, Finlayson, Morse and Davis, 1988; Finlayson, Hurt, Davis and Morse, 1988; Rosin and Glatt, 1971). Because late onset problem drinkers have a shorter history of problem drinking and therefore fewer problems than early onset drinkers do, health care providers tend to overlook their drinking. In addition, researchers report that this groups'psychological and social pathology, family relationships, past work history, and lack of involvement with the criminal justice system contradict the familiar clinical picture of alcoholism. Late onset drinkers frequently appear too healthy or "normal" to raise suspicions about problem drinking.

However, the scholarly literature suggests that about one-third of older adults with drinking problems are late onset abusers (Liberto and Oslin, 1995). Late onset alcoholism is often milder and more amenable to treatment than early onset drinking problems (Atkinson and Ganzini, 1994), and it sometimes resolves spontaneously. When appraising their situation, late onset drinkers often view themselves as affected by developmental stages and circumstances related to growing older. Early onset drinkers are more likely to have exacerbated their adverse circumstances through their history of problem alcohol use (Atkinson, 1994).

Data from the Epidemiologic Catchment Area Project (ECA), a large-scale, community-based survey of psychiatric disorders including alcohol abuse and dependence, provide relevant information on the occurrence of late onset alcoholism, which has been defined by various researchers as occurring after ages 40, 45, 50, or 60 (Bucholtz, Sheline and Helzer, 1995). From the ECA study, 3 percent of male alcoholics between 50 and 59 reported first having a symptom of alcoholism after 49, compared with 15 percent of those between 60 and 69 and 14 percent of those between 70 and 79. For women, 16 percent between 50 and 59 reported a first symptom of alcoholism after the age of 50, with 24 percent of women between 60 and 69 and 28 percent of women between 70 and 79. These percentages suggest that, while less common than early onset alcoholism, late onset alcoholism is a significant problem, particularly among women.

Both early and late onset problem drinkers appear to use alcohol almost daily, outside social settings, and at home alone. Both are more likely to use alcohol as a palliative, self-medicating measure in response to hurts, losses, and affective changes rather than as a socializing agent.

Periodic Onset

Periodic onset alcohol abusers may share many of the characteristics of either early or late onset abusers. However, periodic onset is distinguished by a pattern wherein heavy drinking returns after long periods of abstinence. Within this group, relapse can happen at any age, although older adults are at a higher risk for relapse when they experience grief, loss, or loneliness (Colleran and Jay, 2002).

Impact of Alcohol Use on Older Adult Health

As discussed previously, the threshold for at-risk alcohol use decreases with advancing age (Moore, Seeman, Morgenstern, Beck and Ruben, 2002). While most alcohol consumers decrease their rate of intake with age, the impact of alcohol on an older adult's system is more severe, creating deleterious effects despite decreased intake (Mirand and Welte, 1996). In addition, an older adult's withdrawal may take weeks or months as compared with days or weeks in younger adults (Widlitz and Marin, 2002).

Alcohol is associated with coronary artery disease, cardiovascular disease, hypertension, diabetes, and overall mortality. It is also associated with cancers of the head, neck, liver and esophagus. Mental health problems are also common among alcohol abusers, as are nutritional deficiencies and sleep disorders (Widlitz and Marin, 2002).

Although an individual's health and functional status determine the degree of alcohol-related impact, the pharmacokinetic and pharmacodynamic effects of alcohol on aging organ systems result in higher peak blood alcohol levels (BALs). In turn, increased BALs increase responsiveness to doses that caused little impairment at a younger age. For example, body-sway increases and the capacity to think clearly decreases with age after a standard alcohol load, even when controlling for BALs (Beresford and Lucey, 1995; Vogel-Sprott and Barret, 1984; Vestal; McGuire, Tobin, Andres, Norris and Mesey, 1977).

While active problem drinking results in fewer traumatic fatalities for older adults than for younger adults (Friedman, Jin, Karrison, Nerney, Hayley, Mulliken, Walter, Miller and Chin, 1999), it is more likely to exacerbate other existing health problems. An estimated 4% to 15% of older outpatients demonstrate problem drinking (Hiffe, Haines, and Booroff, et al, 1991), as do 14% of older adult emergency room patients (Adams, Magruder-Habib, Trued, and Broome, 1992) and up to 20% of geriatric inpatients (Bristow and Clare, 1992). Joseph and her colleagues (1995a,b) found that nursing home residents had a prevalence rate of 36% problem drinking and a lifetime alcohol use disorder rate of 49%. These older adults often present with non-alcohol related maladies and their alcohol use is likely undetected by medical personnel (Benshoff, Harrawood and Koch, 2003).

Joseph, Rasmussen, Ganzini and Atkinson (1997) found that patients of a Veterans Administration hospital who exhibited active alcohol use disorders (as determined by DSM-III classification for alcohol abuse or dependence) died at a significantly younger age than did patients without alcohol use disorders. Furthermore, these results were equally likely for patients who no longer used alcohol, but had a history of alcohol use disorders.

The drinking practices of many older adults who do not meet the diagnostic criteria for abuse or dependence place themselves at risk of complicating an existing medical or psychiatric disorder. Consuming one or two drinks per day, for example, may lead to increased cognitive impairment in patients who already have Alzheimer's disease, may lead to worsening of sleep problems in patients with sleep apnea, or may interact with medications rendering them less effective or causing adverse side effects.

Overall, while alcohol abuse is lower for older adults than their younger counterparts, the impact of alcohol on an older adult's system is more severe. Aside from being linked to numerous diseases and disorders, alcohol use among this population can exacerbate existing health conditions. Additionally, older adults metabolize alcohol less efficiently than their younger counterparts and withdrawal may take weeks or months as compared with days or weeks in younger adults. These realities further highlight the need for clear guidelines on healthy alcohol consumption as well as proper identification and treatment of alcohol abuse among older adults.

Prescription Drug Misuse and Abuse

The use of prescription drugs is growing nationally, with consumption costs representing approximately 160 billion USD annually (CDC, 2004). Nearly 90% of adults over the age of 65 years use prescription medication, and annual expenditures of older adults on prescription medications is estimated at more than four times that of younger adults (Center on an Aging Society, 2002; Schmucker, 1984). According to the Center for Substance Abuse Treatment, more than one-quarter (25%-28%) of older adults used a psychoactive medication within the past year, and 20% took a tranquilizer daily (Blow, 2002).

Very little research has been done on prescription drug misuse and abuse by seniors (Simoni-Wastila, 2000). Estimates of the prevalence of prescription drug abuse range from 5% to 30% (Jinks and Raschko, 1990; Ostrom et. Al., 1985), with discrepancies likely resulting from sampling and self-report biases (Patterson, Lacro and Jeste, 1999). In a recent poll of adults aged 55 or older, nonmedical use of psychotherapeutics was the second most commonly abused illicit drug (marijuana being the most common) (SAMHSA, 2005).

The most frequently abused psychotherapeutic drugs include benzodiazepines, antidepressants and opiate/opioid analgesics (Blow, 2002). Abuse of the medication is determined when a person takes the drug longer than is necessary for the condition for which it was prescribed, or ingests more than the necessary dosage in order to gain psychotropic sensations (Patterson, Lacro and Jeste, 1999). Misuse is identified when individuals simply deviate from the prescribed or advised dosage or scheduling of the medication. Misuse has been categorized into three types: 1) excessive use; 2) deficient use; and 3) wrong use of medications (Barnea and Teichman, 1994).

Co-morbid disorders (such as arthritis and sleep disorders) and gender are among the most important predictors of both prescription drug use and abuse (Simoni-Wastila, 2000; Patterson and Jeste, 1999; Finlayson and Davis, 1994). Additional predictors of prescription drug abuse include being white, less educated, being separated or divorced, having a greater number of negative life events, and having a co-occurring mental health problem (Swartz et al., 1991).

In examining a small sample (n = 27) of older adults taking long-term (continuous use over at least one year), low potency[6] opioid analgesics, Edwards and Salib (2002) found that long-term use of even low dosages of opioids can cause tolerance and dependence in elderly patients. While the authors acknowledge the limitations presented by their small sample size, their preliminary findings indicate that 40% of older adults prescribed low potency opioids experience dependence on the drugs.

Older adults are less likely to use psychotherapeutic drugs for anything other than therapeutic reasons, but the chance of misuse is greater among adults over 65 than younger individuals (Blow, 2000). Studies have found that a significant portion, up to 40%, of elderly

---

[6] Weak opioids included dextropropoxyphene 62.5 mg with paracetamol 625 mg; codeine 8 mg with paracetamol 500 mg; dihydrodocodeine 10 mg with paracetamol 500 mg; codeine 30 mg with paracetamol 500 mg; dihydrocodeine 30 mg with paracetamol 500 mg; and tramadol.

fail to follow directions of prescribed medications (Stephens, Haney, and Underwood, 1982). Reasons for misuse of medication in this age group generally center on cognitive confusion about the physician's instructions, and scheduling of dosages. Obviously, misuse that is accidental, rather than intentional requires unique forms of detection, identification, and intervention.

Smart and Adlaf (1988) found that adults over the age of 50 were more likely to report daily use of sleeping pills than were younger adults, as well as more likely to report daily use of tranquilizers. A subsequent study by the authors (Adlaf and Smart, 1995) found that "younger" older adults (i.e., those aged 60-65) reported a higher rate of tranquilizer use than the older age groups. They speculate that this age group was undergoing the greatest set of life transitions, such as retirement and loss of role.

Physicians can inadvertently contribute to the misuse of prescription medications by the elderly (Barnea and Teichman, 1994). Because the elderly often are prescribed several medications, sometimes by different physicians, safeguarding patient health requires that each physician is aware of all the medications being taken. Often this is overlooked or the treating physicians are unaware of one another (Blow, 2000). Furthermore, while older adults are more likely to see their medical provider regularly, they are less likely to question the doctor's judgment or ask for clarification about prescriptions. Physicians, in turn, are often unaware of their patients' confusion.

Similar to alcohol, older adults have increased sensitivity to psychotherapeutics. In medically prescribed doses, the recommendation for use among older adults is typically one-third to one-half of that required for middle-aged adults (Widlitz and Marin, 2002). In addition, older adults are more at-risk for drug-drug and drug-alcohol interactions. These interactions can include things such as heavy alcohol consumption and acetaminophen, high doses of benzodiazepines and alcohol, and the combination of meperidine with an MAO inhibitor – all of which can be fatal (Korrapati and Vestal, 1995).

Illegal Drug Abuse Among Older Adults

While the prevalence of illegal drug use does decline with age, the aging of the baby boomer cohort will introduce a group of older adults with vastly different experiences with substances than any previous cohort. While illicit drug use was rare in cohorts preceeding the baby boomers, national use of illicit drugs peaked in 1979, when baby boomers were within the ages of 15 to 33 (Groerer, et al, 2002). These drug experiences may carry over into old age, placing this group at higher risk for illegal substance abuse than previous generations.

While the cost of caring for elderly substance abusers is not known, information is available on the types of health problems associated with substance abuse (Schlaerth, Splawn, Ong, and Smith, 2004). Illicit drug use is known to cause cardiovascular deficits in users, as well as short-term memory loss and reduced executive functioning (Mittleman, et al, 1999; Schwartz, 2002; Liguori, Gatto, and Robinson, 1998). Experts speculate that such effects would have an even greater impact on an aging physiology than is currently known. In fact, some researchers have raised concern about a potential connection between substance abuse and Alzheimer's type dementia.. Specifically, that substance abuse may lead to severe nerve cell damage and death to essential parts of the brain (Ramage, et al., 2005; Schlaerth, Splawn,

Ong, and Smith, 2004). Additionally, illicit drug use puts users at increased risk for HIV/AIDS, hepatitis and a variety of sexually transmitted diseases (Fingerhood, 2000).

One of the challenges of developing strategies for prevention and intervention of illegal drug abuse among the elderly is the long-standing assumption that substance abuse, particularly that of illegal substances, is a phenomenon of the young (Barnea and Teichman, 1994). In fact, the decrease in substance abuse with age has often been described as a "maturing out" process (Winick, 1962), having to do with the accomplishment of developmental maturation and the increasing ability, with age, to rely on healthier and more adaptive coping styles. Further, according to Winick, heavy drug users in early age typically either burn out or die as a result of their addictions.

However, a recent study of VA inpatient and outpatient records suggests that the maturation process may not apply quite as broadly to baby boomers (Booth and Blow, 2002). Reviewing data across 11 years, the authors found that, compared with the relative ages of other veterans with substance abuse diagnoses, baby boomer veterans continued to consume substance abuse services in similar or greater proportions over the timeframe. In other words, there appeared to be no aging out process within this group.

In a study of emergency department patients over 50 in Los Angeles, Schlaerth, Splawn, Ong, and Smith (2004) found that 3% over ten months were identified as using illegal drugs (as identified by urinalysis). While low, this finding indicates that illegal drug usage among older adults is more than an anomaly. Of those with positive toxicology tests, the majority (63%) were users of cocaine, followed by opiates (16%), and marijuana (14%).

Results from a recent national survey suggest that approximately 1.4 million older adults had used an illicit drug in the past month. Marijuana was the most commonly used illicit drug followed by non-medical use of prescription drugs and cocaine (SAMHSA, 2005). As mentioned previously, primary drug admissions among older adults more than doubled from 1995 to 2002 as measured by TEDS data (SAMHSA, 2005b).

If projections for the increase of substance usage by baby boomers are accurate, the number of older adults using illegal substances is likely to continue to rise along with the use of prescription drugs and alcohol.

Differences in Substance Abuse by Demographic Characteristics

While no one has an exact formula for predicting who will and will not have problems with substances, there are numerous known factors that impact the development of substance abuse problems among older adults. Some risk factors are consistent across substances, while other factors are substance-specific.

Studies indicate that older men are much more likely than older women to have alcohol-related problems (Myers, Weissman, Tischler, Holzer, Leaf, Orvaschel, Anthony, Boyd, Burke, Kramer and Stolzman, 1984; Atkinson, 1990; Bucholz, Sheline, and Helzer, 1995). Since the issue was first studied, most adults with alcohol problems in old age have been found to have a long history of problem drinking, and most of them have been men (D'Archangelo, 1993; Helzer, Burnam and McEvoy, 1991b). About 10 percent of men report a history of heavy drinking at some point in their lives. Being a member of this group predicts that one will have widespread physical, psychological, and social dysfunction in later life (Colsher and Wallace, 1990) and confers a greater than fivefold risk of late-life psychiatric illness despite cessation of heavy drinking (Saunders, Copeland, Dewey, Davidson, McWilliam, Sharma and Sullivan, 1991). Forty-three percent of veterans (who can be assumed to be mostly male and mostly alcohol– as opposed to drug– abusers) receiving long-term care were found to have a history of substance abuse problems (Joseph, Atkinson and Ganzini, 1995a; D'Archangelo, 1993). Men who drink have been found to be two to six times more likely to have medical problems than women who drink (Adams, Yuan, Barboriak, and Rimm, 1993), even though women are more vulnerable to the development of cirrhosis.

While older women are less likely to drink and less likely to drink heavily than older men (Bucholz, Sheline, and Helzer, 1995), the exact ratio of male-to-female alcohol abusers is not known. Bucholz and colleagues (1995) noted a "substantial excess of men over women," larger than the gap observed in younger age groups (p. 30). Other studies have found "a higher than expected number of females," (Beresford, 1995b, p. 11), and an alcohol abuse ratio of 2:1 (83 men to 42 women) (Gomberg, 1995).

Both epidemiological research, including the findings of the ECA studies of the National Institute of Mental Health (Holzer, Robins, Myers, Weissman, Tischler, Leaf, Anthony and Bednarski, 1984) and clinical research consistently report later onset of problem drinking among women (Gomberg, 1995; Hurt, Finlayson, Morse and Davis, 1988; Moos, Brennan and Moos, 1991). In one study by Gomberg (1995), for example, women reported a mean age of onset of 46.2 years, whereas men reported 27.0 years. Furthermore, 38% of older female patients but only 4% of older male patients reported onset within the last 10 years.

A number of other differences between older male and female alcohol abusers have been reported: In contrast to men, women are more likely to be widowed or divorced, to have had a problem drinking spouse, and to have experienced depression (Gomberg, 1994). Women also report more negative effects of alcohol than men, greater use of prescribed psychoactive medication, and more drinking with their spouses (Brennan, Moos and Kim, 1993; Gomberg, 1994; Graham, Carver and Brett, 1995).

Although research has not identified any definite risk factors for drinking among older women, Wilsnack and colleagues suggest that increased amounts of free time and lessening of role responsibilities may also serve as etiological factors (Wilsnack, Vogeltanz, Diers and Wilsnack, 1995). It should be noted that women generally are more vulnerable than men to social pressure, so their move into retirement communities where drinking is common probably has an impact as well.

Older men are also more likely to abuse illicit drugs and more likely to be admitted to substance abuse treatment than their female counterparts. In a national survey of past month drug use, older men were almost twice as likely to report use than older women (SAMHSA, 2005). The rate of marijuana use was over two times greater for older men than older women. For non-medical use of prescription drugs, however, this trend was reversed with older women reporting slightly higher use than older men, though the differences were not statistically significant. With regard to substance abuse treatment, in 2002, admissions for older adults were more likely to be male (80%) and those rates were even greater than the rates among younger admissions, where 70% were male (SAMHSA, 2005).

Women are more likely to be prescribed psychoactive drugs at all ages than are men, and studies have found that the concurrent statuses of being female and older predicts a higher likelihood of use and abuse of prescribed drugs (Carrerata and Myers, 1990; Simoni-Wastila, 1998; Jorgenson, Isacson and Thorslund, 1994). Socioeconomic status is also a predictor of psychoactive drug use (Hohmann, 1989; Mellinger, Balter and Uhlenhuth, 1984).

Simoni-Wastila (1998) found that drug abuse is an increasing problem among impoverished and minority older women. Additionally, women and African Americans are disproportionately represented among elderly Medicare inpatients with substance use disorders. These patients often have prior substance-related hospitalizations, psychiatric comorbidities, accidents involving poisoning and falls, and adverse drug reactions. In a study examining demographic differences among substance abusers in treatment, women with substance use disorders were more likely to have a psychiatric or accident diagnosis at the index episode than were men with substance use disorders.

Research is limited regarding differences in the actual rates of older adult illicit drug abuse by racial and ethnic categories. However, a recent national survey found that overall illicit drug use among older adults within a one-month period did not differ significantly by race/ethnicity. It did, however, show that marijuana use among older adults was greater among non-Hispanic whites (1.2%) and non-Hispanic blacks (0.9%) than among Hispanics (0.2%) (SAMHSA, 2005).

IMPLICATIONS FOR PRACTICE AND RESEARCH

If the census predictions are accurate, substance use and abuse will rise to unprecedented levels in the next 20 years. As such, the medical and mental health professions will have to alter their methods and practices in intervening with older substance abusers. Before we can get to the point that practitioners can adequately address the growing problem of elderly substance abuse, however, the science of the antecedents, consequences, and best methods of treating substance abuse in this age group must catch up. The research and information we have at our disposal with regard to the elderly of the past will no longer suffice in serving the baby boomer elderly of the future.

While the literature is explicit about the physiological impacts of substances on the aging body, particularly alcohol, the correlates and causes of substance abuse in older age are less well-defined. Additionally, continuing questions exist regarding the best ways to detect substance abuse within this age group, specifically when there are co-occurring problems in the cognitive and emotional spheres.

Beyond simple identification of substance abuse among the elderly, research is also needed to determine the best treatment approaches for this population. Very few studies have examined whether treatment modality effectiveness differs between older and younger adults, though some preliminary research suggests that older adults benefit from treatment tailored to address elder-issues. Thus there is a need for the treatment community to build an infrastructure that addresses elder substance abuse and the wide spectrum of biological, psychological, and social problems associated with abuse among this population.

According to the literature reviewed, medical and mental health practitioners must also develop more effective ways of discussing medication needs and in questioning elderly patients about their drug use. Follow-up of prescription drug use is critical in maintaining healthy medication use. In addition, we must seek to understand the prevalence of prescription and over-the-counter drug abuse, so that work can be done to prevent its overuse. As noted previously, prescription drug misuse can begin as merely a misunderstanding of physician instructions. Further research into the best practices for medical instruction compliance will go a long way toward reducing prescription drug misuse.

REFERENCES

Adams, W., Yuan, Z., Barboriak, J., and Rimm, A. (1993). Alcohol-related hospitalization of elderly people. *Journal of the American Medical Association, 270,* 1222-1225.

Adams, W.L., Magruder-Habib, K., Trued, S. and Broome, H.L. (1992). Alcohol abuse in elderly emergency department patients. *Journal of the American Geriatric Society, 40,* 1236-1240

Adlaf, E.M., and Smart, R.G. (1995). Alcohol use, drug use, and well-being in older adults in Toronto. *The International Journal of Addictions, 30,* 1985-2016.

American Psychiatric Association (2000). *Diagnostic and statistical manual of mental disorders,* (4th edition, text revised). Washington DC: American Psychiatric Association.

Atkinson, R.M. (1984). Substance use and abuse in late life. In R.M. Atkinson (Ed.), *Alcohol and drug abuse in old age* (pp.1-21). Washington DC: American Psychiatric Press.

Atkinson, R.M. (1990). Aging and alcohol use disorders: Diagnostic issues in the elderly. *International Psychogeriatrics, 2,* 55-72.

Atkinson, R.M. (1994). Late onset problem drinking in older adults. *International Journal of Geriatric Psychiatry, 9,* 321-326.

Atkinson, R.M., Turner, J.A., Kofoed, L.L., and Tolson, R.L. (1985). Early versus late onset alcoholism in older persons: Preliminary findings. *Alcoholism: Clinical and Experimental Research, 9,* 513-515.

Atkinson, R.M., Tolson, R.L., Turner, J.A. (1990). Late versus early onset problem drinking in older men. *Alcoholism: Clinical and Experimental Research, 14,* 574-579.

Atkinson, R.M. and Ganzini, L. (1994). Substance abuse. In: C.E. Coffey and J.L. Cummings (Eds.). *Textbook of geriatric neuropsychiatry.* (pp. 297-321). Washington DC: American Psychiatric Press.

Barnea, A. and Teichman, M, (1994). Substance misuse and abuse among the elderly: Implications for social work intervention. *Journal of Gerontological Social Work, 21,* 133-148.

Beecham, M. (1997). Beechem risk inventory for late-onset alcoholism. *Journal of Drug Education, 27,* 397-410.

Benshoff, J.J., Harrawood, L.K., and Koch, D.S. (2003). Substance abuse and the elderly: Unique issues and concerns. *Journal of Rehabilitation, 69,* 43-48.

Beresford, T.P. and Lucey, M.R. (1995). Ethanol metabolism and intoxication in the elderly. In T.P. Beresford and E. Gomberg (Eds.), *Alcohol and aging.* New York: Oxford University Press.

Blow, F.C. (2002). *Substance abuse among older adults* (DHHS Publication No. 02-3688). Rockville, MD: US Department of Health and Human Services.

Brennan, P.L., Moos, R.H., and Kim, J.Y. (1993). Gender differences in the individual characteristics and life contexts of late-middle-aged and older problem drinkers. *Addiction, 88,* 781-790.

Bristow, M.F. and Clare, A.W. (1992). Prevalence and characteristics of at-risk drinkers among elderly acute medical in-patients. *British Journal of Addictions, 87,* 291-294.

Bucholz, K.K., Sheline, Y., and Helzer, J.E. (1995). The epidemiology of alcohol use, problems, and dependence in elders: A review. In T.P. Beresford and E. Gomberg (Eds.), *Alcohol and aging* (pp. 19-41). New York: Oxford University Press.

Carrerata, G.L., and Myers, S.M. (1990). Pathways to psychotropic drugs. Understanding the basis of gender differences. *Medical care, 28,* 285-

Colleran, C. and Jay, D. (2002). *Aging and Addiction.* Center City, MN: Hazeldon .

Colsher, P.L. and Wallace, R.B. (1990). Elderly men with histories of heavy drinking: Correlates and consequences. *Journal of Studies on Alcohol, 51,* 528-535.

D'Archangelo, E. (1993). Substance abuse in later life. *Canadian Family Physician, 39,* 1986-1993.

Dufour, M.C. Archer, L. and Gordis, E. (1992). Alcohol and the elderly. *Clinical Geriatric Medicine, 8,* 127-141.

Edwards, I. and Salib, E. (2002). Analgesics in the elderly. *Aging and Mental Health, 6,* 88-92.

Epstein, J.F. (2002). *Substance dependence, abuse, and treatment: Findings from the 2000 National Household Survey on Drug Abuse* (DHHS Publication No. SMA02-3642, Analytic Series A-16; available at /analytic.htm). Rockville, MD: Substance Abuse and Mental Health Services Administration, Office of Applied Studies.

Fingerhood, M. (2000). Substance abuse in older people. *Journal of the American Geriatric Society 48,* 985-995.

Finlayson, R., Hurt, R., Davis, L., and Morse, R. (1988). Alcoholism in elderly persons: A study of the psychiatric and psychosocial features of 216 inpatients. *Mayo Clinic Proceedings, 63,* 761-768.

Friedman, P.D., Jin, L., Karrison, T., Nerney, M., Hayley, D.C., Mulliken, R., Walter, J., Miller, A., and Chin, M.H. (1999). The effect of alcohol abuse on the health status of older adults seen in the emergency department. *American Journal of Drug and Alcohol Abuse, 25,* 529-542.

Gomberg, E.S.L. (1994). Risk factors for drinking over a woman's life span. *Alcohol Health and Research World, 18,* 220-227.

Gomberg, E.S.L. (1995). Older women and alcohol use and abuse. In M. Galanter (Ed.), *Recent developments in alcoholism: Volume 12. Alcoholism and women* (pp.61-79). New York: Plenum Press.

Graham, K., Carver, V., and Brett, P.J. (1995). Alcohol and drug use by older women: Results of a national survey. *Canadian Journal of Aging, 14,* 769-791.

Helzer, J.E., Burnam. A., and McEvoy, L.T. (1991). Alcohol abuse and dependence. In L.N. Robins and D.A. Reigier (Eds.), *Psychiatric disorders in America: The Epidemiologic Catchment Area Study* (pp.81-115). New York: Free Press.

Hiffe, S., Haines, A., Booroff, A., et al (1991). Alcohol consumption by elderly people: a general practice survey. *Age and Aging, 20,* 120-123.

Hohmann, SS. (1989). Gender bias in psychotropic drub prescribing in primary care. *Medical Care, 27,* 478-

Holzer, III, C.E., Robins, L.N., Myers, J.K., Weissman, M.M., Tischler, G.L., Leaf, P.J., Anthony, J., and Bednarski, P.B. (1984). Antecedents and correlates of alcohol abuse and dependence in the elderly. In G.L. Maddox, Robins, L.N., and Rosenberg, N. (Eds.),

Nature and extent of alcohol problems among the elderly, (NIAAA Research Monograph Series, Number 14. DHHS Pub. No. [ADM] 84-1321, pp. 217-244). Rockville, MD: National Institute on Alcohol Abuse and Alcoholism.

Hurt, R.D., Finlayson, R.E., Morse, R.M., and Davis, L.J. (1988). Alcoholism in elderly persons: Medical aspects and prognosis of 216 patients. *Mayo Clinic Proceedings, 63,* 753-760.

Jinks, M.J. and Raschko, R.R. (1990). A profile of alcohol and prescription drug abuse in a high-risk community-based elderly population. *DICP, 24,* 971-975.

Jorgensen, T.M., Isacson, D.G.I, and Thorslund, M. (1993). Prescription drug use among ambulatory elderly in a Swedish municipality. *The Annals of Pharmacoepidemiology, 27,* 1120-

Joseph, C.L., Atkinson, R.M., and Ganzini, L. (1995a). Problem drinking among residents of a VA nursing home. *International Journal of Geriatric Psychiatry, 10,* 243-248.

Joseph, C.L., Ganzini, L., and Atkinson, R.M. (1995b). Screening for alcohol use disorders in the nursing home. *Journal of the American Geriatrics Society, 43,* 368-373.

Joseph, C.L., Rasmussen, J., Ganzani, L., and Atkinson, R.M. (1997). Outcome of nursing home care for residents with alcohol use disorders. *International Journal of Geriatric Psychiatry, 12,* 767-772.

Levin, S.M. and Kruger, J (Eds.) (2000). *Substance abuse among older adults: A guide for social service providers.* Rockville, MD: Substance Abuse and Mental Health Services Administration.

Liguori, A., Gatto, C.P., Robinson, J.H. (1998). Effects of marijuana on equilibrium, psychomotor performance, and simulated driving. *Behavioral Pharmacology, 9,* 599-609.

Marks, A. (March, 2002). Illicit drug use grows among the elderly. *Christian Science Monitor, 94,* 338-346.

Mellinger, G.D., Balter, M.B., and Uhlenhuth, E.H. (1984). Prevalence and correlates of the long-term regular use of anxiolytics. *Journal of the American Medical Association, 251,* 375-

Mirand, A.L. and Welte, J.W. (1996). Alcohol consumption among the elderly in a general population, Erie County, New York. *American Journal of Public Health, 86,* 978-984.

Mittleman, M.A., Mintzer, D., Maclure, M. et al (1999). Triggering myocardial infarction by cocaine. *Circulation, 99,* 2737-2741.

Moore, A.A., Morgenstern, H., Harawa, N.T., fielding, J.E., Higa, J., and Beck, J.C. (2001). Are older hazardous and harmful drinkers less likely to participate in health-related behaviors and practices as compared with nonhazardous drinkers? *Journal of the American Geriatric Society, 49,* 421-430.

Moore, A.A., Seeman, T., Morgenstern, H., Beck, J.C., and Reuben, D.B. (2002). Are there differences between older persons who screen positive on the CAGE Questionnaire and the Short Michigan Alcoholism Screening Test – Geriatric Version? *Journal of the American Geriatric Society, 50,* 858-862.

Moos, R.H., Brennan, P.L., and Moos, B.S. (1991). Short-term processes of remission and nonremission among late-life problem drinkers. *Alcoholism: Clinical and Experimental Research, 15,* 948-955.

Myers, J.K., Weissman, M.M, Tischler, G.L., Holzer, C.E., III, Leaf, P.J., Orvaschel, H., Anthony, J.D., Boyd, J.H., Burke, J.D., Jr., Kramer, M., and Stolzman, R. (1984). Six-month prevalence of psychiatric disorders in three communities. *Archives of General Psychiatry, 41,* 1980-1982.

Office of National Drug Control Policy (Harwood, H., Fountain, D., and Livermore, G.). (2001). *The economic costs of drug abuse in the United States, 1992-1998* (NCJ-190636 and NIH Publication No 98-4327; available at http://www.nida.nih.gov:80/ EconomicCosts/Intro.html). Washington DC: Executive Office of the President.

Ostrum, J.R., Hammarlund, E.R., and Christensen, D.B., Plein, J.B., and Kethley, A.J. (1985). Medication usage in an elderly population. *Medical Care, 23,* 375-379.

Patterson, T.L. and Jeste, D.V. (1999). The potential impact of the baby-boom generation on substance abuse among elderly persons. *Psychiatric Services, 50,* 1184-1188.

Patterson, T.L., Lacro, J.P., and Jeste, D.V. (1999). Abuse and misuse of medications in the elderly. *Psychiatric Times, 16,* XXX

Prigerson, H.G., Desai, R.A., Rosenheck, R.A. (2001). Older adult patients with both psychiatric and substance abuse disorders: Prevalence and health service use. *Psychiatric Quarterly, 72,* 1-18.

Ramage, S.N., Anthony, I.C., Carnie, F.W., Busuttil, A., Robertson, R., and Bell, J.E. (2005). Hyperphosphorylated tau and amyloid precursor protein deposition is increased in the brains of young drug abusers. *Neuropathology and Applied Neurobiology, 31*(4), 439.

Rosin, A.J., and Glatt, M.M. (1971). Alcohol excess in the elderly. *Quarterly Journal of Studies on Alcohol, 32,* 53-59.

Saunders, P.A., Copelind, J.R., Dewey, M.E., Davidson, I.A., McWilliam, C., Sharma, V., and Sullivan, C. (1991). Heavy drinking as a risk factor for depression and dementia in elderly men: Findings from the Liverpool's Longitudinal Community Study. *British Journal of Psychiatry, 159,* 213-216.

Schlaerth, K.R., Splawn, R.G., Ong, J., and Smith, S.D. (2004). Change in the pattern of illegal drug use in an inner city population over 50: An observational study. *Journal of Addictive Diseases, 23 (2),* 95-107.

Schmucker, D.L. (1984). Drug disposition in the elderly: A review of the critical factors. *Journal of the American Geriatric Society, 32,* 144-149.

Schonfeld, L., and Dupree, L.W. (1991). Antecedents of drinking for early- and late-onset elderly alcohol abusers. *Journal of Studies on Alcohol, 52,* 587-592.

Schwartz, R.H. (2002). Marijuana: A decade and a half later, still a crude drug with underappreciated toxicity. *Pediatrics, 109,* 284-289.

Simon-Wastila, L. (1998). Gender and psychotropic drug use. *Medical Care, 36,* 88-

Simon-Wastila, L. (2000). The use of abusable prescription drugs: The role of gender. *Journal of Women's Health and Gender-Based Medicine, 9,* 289-297.

Smart, R.G. and Adlaf, E.M, (1988). Alcohol and drug use among the elderly: Trends in use and characteristics of users. *Canadian Journal of Public Health, 79,* 236-242.

Spencer, G. (1989). *Projections of the population of the United States, by age, sex, and race: 1988 to 2080.* Series P-25, No. 1018. Washington DC: US Department of Commerce.

Stall, R. (1987). Research issues concerning alcohol consumption among aging populations. *Drug and Alcohol Dependence, 19,* 195-213.

Stephens, R. C., Haney, C.A., and Underwood, S. (1982). *Drug taking among the elderly.* NIDA Treatment Research Report (DHHS Publication No. 83-1229). Washington DC: NIDA.

Vestal, R.; McGuire, E; Tobin, J.; Andres, R.; Norris, M.; and Mesey, E. (1977). Aging and alcohol metabolism. *Clinical Pharmacology and Therapeutics 21.* 343-354.

Vogel-Sprott, V. and Barrett, P. (1984). Age, drinking habits and the effects of alcohol. *Journal of Studies on Alcohol 48,* 517-521.

Wilsnack, S.C., Vogeltanz, N.D., Diers, L.E., and Wilsnack, R.W. (1995). Drinking and problem drinking in older women. In T. Beresford and E. Gomberg (Eds.), *Alcohol and aging,* (pp. 263-292). New York: Oxford University Press.

Winick, C. (1962). Maturing out of narcotic addition. *Bulletin on Narcotics, 14,* 1-7.

In: Substance Abuse: New Research   ISBN 978-1-60456-834-9
Editors: Ethan J. Kerr and Owen E. Gibson   © 2009 Nova Science Publishers, Inc.

Chapter 8

ENHANCING SELF-EFFICACY IN A STRENGTHS PERSPECTIVE: WORKING WITH A HOMELESS CHINESE ADULT WITH SUBSTANCE ABUSE PROBLEMS

Yau Chui Wah[*]

The Society for the Aid and Rehabilitation of Drug Abusers, Hong Kong
(3/F, Hung Fuk House, No. 47 Fuk Wa Street, Shumshuipo, Kln. Hong Kong)

INTRODUCTION

Substance abuse is one of the greatest challenges of our society. According to the Central Registry of Drug Abuse (Hong Kong Government, 2005) 9,734 heroin abusers were reported in Hong Kong. Heroin addiction remains the most common type of substance abused. Currently, heroin encompasses about 85.4% of all common types of substance abuse in Hong Kong. Heroin dependence is inevitably a chronic drug abuse behavior. Cheung et al. (2003) found that 73% of patients who sought treatments relapsed to heroin within 12 months after completion of various drug treatments in Hong Kong. In the study, patients had undergone treatments 8 times or more on average. Hence, heroin dependence has been identified as a recurrent relapsing behavior.

Substance dependence becomes a complex social problem when it is associated with homelessness. A local comprehensive research by Wang (2001) showed problems of substance abuse and homelessness, were indeed, causally constructed in a vicious cycle. The research revealed that a quarter of homeless people had a problem of substance abuse in Hong Kong. There was also an increasing trend in young age street sleepers (under age 40) in 2001. For those street sleepers who were under 40, 40% of them indeed desired an allocation of a public housing apartment. Failing to pay initial rent and deposit, however, has been an

---
[*] Email: Gloriayau22@hotmail.com

overwhelming burden for 75% of the homeless population. Since 1999, the Social Welfare Department of Hong Kong has refused to give homeless people advanced payment for renting houses, unless they could provide a down-payment rental receipt.

The enhancement of self-efficacy is recognized as an important role in helping people to avoid a relapse episode (Marlatt, 1985; Peele, 1985; Cheung et al., 2003). In frontline practice, an emphasis on working with clients' strengths in social work is receiving increasing attention in this decade (Yip, 2005; Rapp, 2006; Saleebey, 2002.) Encouragingly, the Strengths Perspective is implemented with substance abuse (Doxley, 2001; Yip, 2003; Rapp, 2002; Wormer, 2003). The strengths perspective is recognized as a new humanistic trend in substance abuse counseling. In this paper, by means of a case illustration, the writer will integrate the concepts of self-efficacy and the strengths perspective to illustrate how a homeless adult male will build his self-efficacy in recovery from substance abuse.

Working with Substance Dependance

A Strengths Perspective

The development of a Strengths Perspective is a paradigm shift in professional practice (Rapp, 2006:3). It builds on a reflection of the prevailing disease model in social work practice (Saleebey, 2002; Yip, 2003).

For decades, the directions of case assessment and intervention in drug counseling have been largely dependent on the disease model, emphasizing a pathological presentation of substance dependence. The origin of the disease model of professional practice is deep-rooted in a western dichotomy of knowledge- a distinction of good or bad, normal or abnormal, and subjective or objective (Weick, 1989:350). The disease model of addiction originated from a medical conviction of addictive behaviors (Peele, 1985). This model asserts that substance abuse behaviors are biomedical; attributed to the properties of drugs. By regarding addictive behavior as a disease, the behavior is treated as something that can be predicted, manipulated, and controlled through a diagnosis treatment process. Persons with substance dependence, hence, are perceived as having mental health problems, deteriorated health, low self-esteem, impaired thinking practices, as well as involved in crime, unemployed, socially isolated, etc. These prevailing pathological labels are silently embedded in different treatments for persons with substance abuse. A pathological presentation becomes a common language exchanged by multi-disciplinary professionals in treatments for persons with substance abuse.

In a radical political account, the social control model further reinforces the prevalence of the disease model. The government of Hong Kong finances most substance abuse treatments under the anti-drug and anti-crime policy. The underlying aim of imposing drug treatments is to decrease the demand for drugs by helping persons with substance abuse to curb their drug addictions (Narcotics Division of HK Government, 2006). The disease model, with an emphasis of problem-based assessment, further encourages an individualistic, instead of social environmental, account of human problems (Rapp, 2006).

Peele (1985) criticizes the disease model as it fails to deal with the problem of substance dependence because it misunderstands its nature. From the writer's practical experience, the disease model is either self-defeating or incompatible with the fundamental missions of social work practice. First, the disease model is self-defeating. A good treatment for persons with substance abuse is supposed to help persons with substance dependence to be accountable for their changes. However, the disease model endorses a view in that people are weak and have no self- control in their own substance dependence. Paradoxically, how can you expect a man who has no self-control to regain the control of drugs by himself? It only induces a negative self-fulfilling prophecy for persons with substance dependence. In other words, if a man believes he is powerless, then he is likely to act in a powerless way (Schaler, 1995). Secondly, a disease orientation is ineffective. Clients usually have a negative response in the helping process when receiving negative labeling because of their defense mechanism. The clients may be unmotivated because of negative labeling in the helping process. The disease model could hardly invite collaboration between persons with substance dependence and related professionals. Thirdly, the disease model is oppressive. It only creates a win-win situation for therapists and their related service organizations and a losing situation for persons with substance dependence and their family members. The disease model asserts that persons with substance dependence and their family members are problematic and are in need of help. When people fail, however, treatment and relapse to drugs, they are labeled as problematic and unmotivated in their own recovery. Related professionals, treatment models, and service organizations may try to get rid of their own responsibilities in treatment failure. Fourthly, the disease model encourages a victimization of persons with substance abuse. It ignores the fact that problems of substance abuse are correlated with an oppressive social environment. It misses one of the important working directions in substance abuse treatment by changing the oppressive social environment for persons with substance abuse. Finally, the disease model always reduces recovery to a relapse-abstinence distinction. It creates an irresolvable gap between relapse and abstinence. Small improvement of individuals in the recovery process will likely be neglected.

In view of the deficits of the disease model in substance abuse treatment, a strengths perspective is more likely to give a reforming promise. The strengths perspective affirms the potentiality, humanity, and the basic goodness of humankind (Wormer, 2001). Some basic working principles promoted by the strengths perspective are to be considered (Saleebey, 2002; Rapp, 2006; Worme, 2001). In working with persons with substance dependence, the following principles may be applicable:

1. All persons with substance dependence, despite their problems in drug abuse, have their own strengths.
2. The difficulties (e.g. homelessness, relapse, and loss) encountered by persons with substance dependence in their recovery can be transformed as opportunities and challenges for future success.
3. For persons with substance abuse, opportunities to change are limitless. Their related social environments are full of chances and resources, as is their potential and talent.
4. Related professionals and persons with substance dependence are collaborators in the process of intervention.
5. The participation of persons with substance dependence is the key to change in the intervention process.

Working with Persons with Substance Abuse: The Concept of Self-Efficacy

Theoretically, the concept of self-efficacy is developed from the grand theory of social learning theory and cognitive theory. Bandura (1977) first introduced the concept of self-efficacy as an important mediator in the change of behaviors in cognitive therapy. Self-efficacy is defined as people's confidence to accomplish a certain level of performance in a specific situation. Maddux (2002: 277) describes self-efficacy as one of important elements for a successful treatment. It promotes a psychological mechanism that if one believes one can accomplish what one wants, one will succeed. Some premises of the concept of self-efficacy proposed by Bandura (1977) and Maddux (2002: 279) exist. They are highlighted as follows:

1. Man has potential cognitive capabilities to self-reflect and evaluate his own behaviors, thoughts, and emotions. With reference to past experience , Man is also able direct their future..
2. Man is socially embedded. Environmental events, inner personal experience and behaviors are reciprocal influences. Man will change through the interactions between individual and environments.
3. Accordingly, the concept of self-efficacy asserts that the changes of addictive behaviors are mediated by a cognitive mechanism called "efficacy expectancy." Expectancy refers to the belief that a given behavior will produce a particular outcome within an individual's self-control.

The enhancement of self-efficacy plays a powerful role in attempts to overcome substance abuse problems (Cheung et al., 2003; Marlatt & Gordon, 1985). What is "self-efficacy" to persons with substance dependence? It is one's capability to resist cravings for a drug in a high-risk situation, such as the drug supply (Marlatt, 1985). Self-efficacy also refers to one's judgment about one's ability to deal competently with challenges or high-risk situations (Marlatt, 1985). The feeling of the ability to cope effectively with high-risk situations enhances one's self-efficacy in resisting drug addiction.

According to the relapse model developed by Marlatt (1985 & 2002), low levels of self-efficacy are associated with a drug relapse. High levels of self-efficacy, however, are correlated to a successful abstinence. In a three year longitudinal study, (Cheung et al., 2003) regarding the problem of relapse among persons with chronic substance dependence, self-efficacy was found to be the most influential factor among different psychological and psycho-social factors in helping persons with heroin dependence to stay drug-free. Clinical evidence has proven that high levels of self-efficacy help chronic heroin dependents to abstain in the Hong Kong context.

In practice, the theory of self-efficacy suggests that people who are undergoing drug counseling should have the skills and sense of efficacy for coping with challenges provided to them. Both Maddux (2002) and DiClemente (1995) noted intervention strategies integrated with self-efficacy concepts should make reference to a series of sources of self-efficacy. Among the different sources of self-efficacy, performance experiences and vicarious experiences are the most important (Maddux, 2002). They not only involve a cognitive process but vivid life experiences and behaviors in interacting with surrounding environments. In addition, Cheung (et al., 2004) asserts the self-efficacy of substance dependents can be enhanced and sustained by in-depth self-knowledge, self-acceptance, development of a positive identity, emancipation of identity crisis, and establishment of a good support network.

An Integrated Practice of Strengths Perspective and Concepts of Self-Efficacy

From theory to practice, the strengths perspective and the concept of self-efficacy are in fact compatible and reciprocal. Despite the fact that the strengths perspective contributes critiques on the disease model in substance abuse practice, it has been criticized as "not yet a theory" and with insufficient clinical techniques in comparing with well-established clinical therapies (Wormer, 1999). The concept of self-efficacy provides us with refined clinical and practical guidance. It facilitates intervention for persons with substance dependence into concrete actions. In fact, both theories share some similar fundamental assertions. Firstly, both emphasize the positive side of human potentials and abilities of persons with substance abuse. They are the keys to change. Secondly, both affirm working alliance between persons with substance dependence and related professionals. Both theories criticize a negative labeling and victimization of persons with substance dependence. Thirdly, both aim to empower persons with substance dependence to change their own life. Fourthly, both address the importance of the interaction between individuals and their environments in recovery. Fifthly, both avoid the over-simplification of substance abuse treatment in terms of relapse-abstinence dichotomy. They address the small changes clients have made which are crucial in the recovery process (Wormer, 1999).

Enhancing Self- Efficacy in a Strengths Perspective: A Case Illustration

In this section, the writer narrates a homeless adult male with substance abuse. He was a client of the writer in The Society for the Aid and Rehabilitation of Drug Abusers in Hong Kong. In this case, the writer applied the concepts of self-efficacy in a Strengths Perspective to help the client in his rehabilitation and recovery. Consensus of the client and agencies was obtained to use this case for academic purposes. For the sake of confidentiality, client's identity and personal information has been disguised.

Tom: A Homeless Chinese Adult Male with Poly-Substance Abuse

Tom was a 31-year-old poly-drug user with a 16 year history of abusing different types of substances. Tom's primary substance was heroin. Occasionally, he ingested other substances such as organic solvents and barbiturates for purposes of substitution and intoxication exacerbation. He sought various voluntary and compulsory drug treatments in previous years. He either quit in the middle of treatments or relapsed to drugs soon after the completion of treatments. He said only when he was in controlled environments such as prison, was he able to keep a prolonged drug free status. Usually, Tom slipped to heroin because of emotional disturbances. His drug taking behaviors were sustained in a vicious cycle.

Due to a long history of active drug use, he had never had a job for more than two weeks in the prime of his life. He floated between unemployment and casual jobs in the previous years. He was also involved in criminal business for drug consumption. He was in and out of jail in the past years.

In the past two years, Tom had trouble finding a shelter/ home. He became a new street sleeper. He also had difficulties in money management. Persistently, he had no money for housing, food, travel, job seeking or social activities. Due to drug inhalation, Tom's health deteriorated and he developed respiratory problems.

Later, Tom was admitted to the out-patient methadone maintenance program in Hong Kong. This program was based upon a harm reduction model and was an open door drug treatment. With the help of methadone, Tom eventually stabilized at 60mg in replacement therapy. He had achieved his longest abstinent experience for more than 12 months in the past two years despite having slipped to heroin for a few unhappy events. He performed chemical urine tests with consistent negative results. Hereafter, he was recruited to methadone counseling in which the enhancement of the client's self-efficacy in a Strengths Perspective was emphasized. The writer was his responsible caseworker.

Understanding Tom's Strengths, Needs and Subjective Experiences

From a pathological orientated case assessment, Tom's presenting problems included substance abuse, homelessness, unemployment, social isolation, mental health problems, criminal involvement, low self-esteem, and avoidance in problem solving. Putting aside a pathological assessment of substance dependent behaviors as above, a non-diagnostic assessment was in order. This assessment was based on client's need and strengths by listening to subjective experiences and narrative.

According to Peele (1985), a comprehensive model for explaining the problem of substance abuse should be able to capture the subjective feelings involving the experience of drug taking behaviors within his/her social and historical backgrounds. A strengths perspective in working with persons with substance dependence is recommended to focus on searching for strengths to satisfy client's normal needs (Yip, 2003). In Tom's case, understanding his experience and related feelings should not merely confine to an objective assessment of substance abuse, but an empathic listening of his narratives and subjective experiences. Such a non-judgmental, more in-depth understanding might help the writer to explore client's latent strengths, talents, aspirations, unspoken needs, and unsmoothed pain. The writer was able to further make use of narratives to encourage a positive outlook on life. In the following narration, Tom frankly shared his need of a home and stable life.

"I am homeless"-Tom's Need for a Home and a Stable Life

Tom told the writer that he had not had a permanent home for so many years.

"In the past ten years, I was in and out of jail because of the problem of addiction and related crime involvement. I failed to keep a permanent home or any home appliances." Tom became a street sleeper while he relapsed to drugs last year. Tom recalled his hardship on the streets.

"The feeling of not being secure with a regular bed time or having privacy, makes me sad. The weather is getting cold. It is no guarantee I would have my place or my quilt on rainy nights. Even when I was invited to stay at a friend's house, I had a feeling of being under other's roofs. It was not my own place. I felt like a stray dog," he said bitterly.

He was distressed by the insecure living, "It horrified me that I was attacked by another street sleeper. My mobile phone was stolen. Another horror happened to me when I was molested by a wicked man at midnight." He said it was the shame of being a street sleeper, "It is really a shame. I come to the methadone clinic and refill clean water there everyday. I try to take a bath in a public lavatory daily. I hate to be seen as a street sleeper. Of course, I did not tell others I was homeless."

Many of the counseling sessions were mainly related to the housing issues subjected to client's concern. In order to help Tom find a shelter, the writer tried to refer him to different temporary male hostels. However, all applications were rejected because of his past drug addiction records. He also failed to rent a room in a private residence since he was unable to afford an initial rent deposit. Later, Tom had suicidal thoughts when he failed to pay the rent deposit in the first round public housing offer last year.

Through Tom's narrative, the writer began to understand Tom's frustration in dealing with the homelessness. Tom disclosed that a permanent home is extraordinarily important to him. He said, "Everyone needs his own home. I did, too. I am very tired of looking for a stable home for so many years. I don't want to be like that. Having a permanent home would be a new start for me in quitting drugs."

Tom repeatedly expresses his need for a home. Helping Tom find a home would be one of the important working directions. Tom believed that he would have positive change after he could secure a home. The writer also believed that a stable living environment would encourage Tom to reflect on his cycle of substance dependence.

"I am out of control"- A Need for a Restoration of Self-Confidence

Persons with substance dependence are commonly labeled as persons lacking self-control. Actually, the problems of lacking of self-control may be caused by low self-esteem and confidence. In Tom's case, the cause of his homelessness was partly due to his low self-esteem and confidence. Tom explained in detail how he became homeless.

Tom said, "For so many years, I have been out of control in money management and drug abuse. I used to spend all my Comprehensive Social Security Assistance (CSSA) allowance to buy heroin in a single day. Even when I quit heroin, I just bought what I wanted, such as a new mobile phone or a steak in a restaurant. People said I had a problem with compulsive shopping. After I failed to pay the rent, I was kicked out by my landlord. I hated myself. I am out of control with money management. I am hopeless because I lack the willpower to control myself. I don't want to be like that."

According to Marlatt (1985 & 2002), low levels of self-efficacy are associated with relapse to drugs; while high levels of self-efficacy is co-related to successful abstinence. In the case of Tom, he lacked self-confidence, which led to low self-efficacy in resisting drugs. Helping Tom to restore his self-confidence was essential in the intervention.

"I am a failure"-The Need for a Sense of Success

Tom failed to seize the first public housing offer due to unsolved financial difficulties. He defined himself as "a failure." He said, "I am a failure. I am useless. I am not qualified to have a house. I can never have a home."

After Tom missed the second round public housing allocation, he was frustrated and mad. "One night, I thought about jumping and ending my life. I just wanted to disappear from the world."

Frustration and feeling of uselessness drove Tom to drugs again. Eventually, Tom relapsed to heroin as a compensatory, coping method. When Tom compared himself with other persons receiving methadone treatment, he devalued himself as, "the failure among the failures."

The feeling of uselessness distressed Tom. His negative feelings and emotions helped him turn to drug use. In the intervention, the writer helped Tom to rebuild a sense of success to ease his negative emotions and restore his positive self-identity.

"I am outdated"- The Need for a Sense of Belonging and Involvement with Others

From a pathological rationality, it is easy for the helper to conclude that the client has a problem with compulsive shopping and lack of self-control. If Tom's subjective experience, however, was carefully explored, we would find another picture of his compulsive shopping behavior.

In another interview, Tom explains his feelings with shopping. "Whenever I joined the self-help group activities, I felt like I was boring and did not understand conversations about trendy fashion. The others talked about PSII and computer software that were all strange to me. I spent all my money buying a new mobile phone. I just want the others to know that I am trendy, too. I just want to be able to talk about the same thing. I worry I will be outdated and rejected by society."

In fact, substance abuse behaviors are particularly evident for those who are socially isolated and uncomfortable with low self-esteem (White, 1991). Tom also admitted that he had no friends and did not want to keep any friends. His only friend was a mentally retarded neighbor. He learned to keep away from active drug-using friends. He kept a distance from other non-drug using friends, as well.

Tom insisted that he was weaker then other people even in comparison with other people receiving methadone treatment. He said, "I am so pale and thin. Even though I have stopped taking heroin for a year, no one would believe me. Among the drug addicts, I am a failure of the failures. I am weaker than the others because I cannot detoxify from methadone. Therefore, I don't like to join social activities organized by the methadone self-help group. I don't want to see others. I would rather be alone." Tom had an outcry of "I am lonely but I want to be alone." Indeed, he was in pain because he badly wanted to be accepted by others, however, he was lacking self-confidence in meeting people.

"I am so empty"- The Thirst for Love

It is important to understand the deepest subjective experience of loneliness and emptiness of Tom in the recovery process. "A few years ago, I lost contact with my family after I went back to jail. When I think about myself, I feel extremely lonely. My mother, my sister, my wife and my baby deserted me. I am so empty. I have a daughter, but I do not know what she looks like. I guess she is 7 or 8 years old now. The feeling of emptiness filled me, especially at each traditional Chinese festival. I regret I did not cherish their care and love," Tom said with great regret.

Sense of loss, insecurity, isolation, emptiness, and frustration are staples of the substance abuse experiences. Tom's sense of loneliness and emptiness were indeed associated with the interpretation of abandonment by his family. Tom used drugs to self-medicate. Tom's drug taking behaviors symbolized his need for intimacy, love, care from/to others, and interpersonal satisfaction. They were the deepest subjective needs of Tom. An intervention in Strengths Perspective and self-efficacy was recommended to help Tom cope with the pain of loneliness and emptiness in a positive way.

"I am a shame to my family." The Need to Restore a Positive Self-Identity

"I miss my mum," Tom says quietly. "I know she loves me very much since I am the only son in my family. She has high expectations for me, but I let her down. I am an embarrassment to my family. I do not dare to contact her because I am afraid I would upset her and make her disappointed again. I never know how long I can stay away from drugs." When Tom thought about his role in his family, he encountered an identity crisis. He blamed himself, "For so many years, I did nothing good. I am not a good son, not a good husband, and not a good father. I am a failure."

Tom explained why he declined all social activities organized by the social service center. "'I don't want to go because I know all activities are organized for addicts and their family members. I do not have a family. I will not go alone. It will devastate me." He continued, "I have already lost my family. Why do I have to keep drug free? It seems that there is no difference between relapse or abstinence to me. I don't know what my life is. What should I look for?" Tom doubted bitterly. "Without drugs, my time goes so slowly. I am not like others. They have their family, therefore, they could quit heroin. I do not have my family. No one helps me."

Being alone without family support poses an identity crisis to Tom. He devalued himself. He was in a difficult place to find some self-worth because of feelings of shame and guilt towards his family. As a result, Tom had to break down his internal barrier to develop a social network and search for a positive meaning of abstinence.

Understanding Tom's Identity Crisis Under the Influence of the Chinese Culture

Justifiably Tom had low self-efficacy because of the negative self-identity. In fact, Tom had a rigorous identity crisis under the influence of the Chinese culture. In the interviews, Tom devalued himself as "a *failure among the failures*," and a person who had no self-control. With the influence of Confucian ideologies, an individual's self-image is built upon one's social relation with his/her family and significant others (Lin, 2001: 51). The build-up of self-efficacy is not only limited in the strengthening of individual self-confidence or self-worth in a narrow sense. Under the influence of traditional Chinese culture, a well-defined social role is basically derived from rectification of name (proper obligations within a well defined social position) and filial piety (being obedient and showing due respect to one's parents and elders) (Lin, 2001:50). In Tom's case, he depreciated himself as a failure because he failed to fulfill his obligations as a son, a husband, and a father to his family. For an effective intervention, a deeper understanding of Tom's subjective feelings is recommended with a critical review to the specific Chinese culture that Tom is situated and embedded. This, in turn, can help Tom to reconstruct his self image with his significant others.

Mapping Tom's Strengths and Niches

In the intervention, the writer identified Tom's strengths. He had drawing and writing talent. Furthermore, he was sensible and had a good self-understanding. He was motivated to live a simple and normal life in his recovery.

Tom was good at painting and drawing. He liked to draw thank you cards and Christmas cards to the social worker. His artwork was fantastic. When he painted, he was full of self-confidence. Tom was good at writing. He was expressive and open in his diary. He liked to write in a diary from time to time and remember some important events. Tom was kind and considerate. He was willing to offer help to others, especially the elderly and people in need. Tom was sensible. He shared his unhappiness and joyful experiences with the writer. He also had a good self-understanding.

In the issues of being rejected by the Housing Authority for a public housing apartment, Tom started to understand that he indeed badly needed a home and a family reunion. He needed a normal and simple life with a stable home and job. The clarification of his wants and aspirations helped Tom to move ahead in recovery. Fortunately, he had a second opportunity to move into a public housing apartment this year. There were available funds for meeting Tom's financial difficulties. Moreover, there were supportive employment services for persons with substance dependence. The writer encouraged Tom to join a self-help group, volunteer group, leisure group, and computer classes in the service units. These groups helped Tom to reintegrate to society.

Strengths Based Self-Efficacy Enhancement

The intervention techniques used in enhancing Tom's self efficacy were derived from related intervention models such as cognitive theory, solution focus therapy, and others intervention models. The intervention models, however, were carefully selected to avoid a blaming, negative, and fatalistic view on the client. The models were to improve Tom's behaviors, cognition, and self-motivation in interacting with his environments.

Enhancing Performance Experiences: Recognizing Small Changes

Within the Strengths Perspective, the harm reduction model aims to fill the gap of a dichotomy of relapse-abstinence ideology in treatment of substance dependence. According to Peele, the basic goal of a harm reduction practice is to move clients to a more secure point in recovery, to assist them to solve their problems, and to promote a better physical and social functioning (Peele, 2002). Therefore, any small improvement in addiction practice is welcomed in the intervention. In Tom's case, the writer tried to do so. Tom discloses that he still spent all his CSSA the first day of the month. In an interview, however, the social worker found there were small changes in Tom's money management.

S-the writer T- Tom

S: I noticed you have made some changes in managing your money recently. How is that working?

T: I spent $300.00 on cereal, rice, and canned food. Then, I spent the rest of the money in a single day. I still have no money to pay the rent.

S: It is still a great change. Why did you do that?

T: I listened to your advice. I tried to make sure I would have some food for the rest of the month. I know I could not change suddenly and totally. At least, I wouldn't be hungry. I don't want to be beggar again.

S: Yes, but it is the first step to change. At least, you are making sure you have food for a few weeks. You did a fantastic job.

T: Yes. I did it.

Despite Tom spending his CSSA in one day and failing to pay his rent again, he at least made some progress in managing his money. Similarly, the writer helped Tom explore how he kept heroin-free in any one single day. Even though Tom slipped to heroin because of an unsolved housing problem and negative emotions, the writer still helped Tom to review how to recover and avoid a full-blown relapse.

Any small changes with Tom were appreciated and discussed in the interviews. By recognizing any small change, it would enhance the self-efficacy of the individual and encourage a continuous positive change with recovery. The key point was that a client needs to be aware that small successes are a personal effort instead of an external miracle. Each small success enhances the client's self-efficacy day by day.

Enhancing Performance Experiences: Highlighting Successful and Joyful Experiences

Helping Tom to highlight his joyful successes nourished his confidence and spirit. Despite Tom's hesitation, he finally joined a computer class. In the interviews, Tom was encouraged to discuss his happy and successful experiences in computer learning. Tom delightedly found that he was interested in computer games. He was a fast learner. He completed each assignment given to him in class and he even assisted older classmates in the class.

Tom reported that, "I found learning computers interesting. I can also use computers to paint. If I have money in the future, I would like to buy my own computer, even it is a second hand model. At least, I would have something to play and learn. It helps me not to be bored."

Through a new experience with computer learning, the client was hopeful he could rebuild his life. Such a joyful experience lifted Tom's spirit because he gained a sense of achievement. Becoming more proficient with computers enhanced his self-efficacy. For a transferal of learning, the writer encouraged Tom to remember such successful experiences when he faced other challenges in recovery.

Enhancing Positive Self-Identity by Verbal Persuasion

Positive feedback about us from others can ameliorate our self-efficacy (Maddux , 1995). Positive reframing helps a client to re-conceptualize important events in a positive light (Wormer, 2001). Verbal persuasion was a significant intervention that enhanced Tom's self-identity. In the end of each counseling session, the writer gave credit and praise to what Tom had done. The praise helped him to internalize his positive expectancies and develop a sense of self-control and appreciation. Some examples of these are as follows:

The writer said to Tom: I appreciate your recent effort in preparing your home assignment. You wrote down what you thought in each session. Your effort encouraged me in the counseling process because I received positive feedback from you, as well.

The writer said to Tom: I can see you have changed positively as you have stopped taking drugs for a few months with negative opioid urine test proofs. It is not easy for you to do it on your own. You are proving that you are not only seeking a drug free life, but also self-respect and dignity.

Enhancing Self-Efficacy by Self-Appreciation

Cheung's (et al., 2003 & 2004) research showed that persons with substance abuse lacked self-confidence. The increase of self-efficacy would result from a deeper level of self-knowledge, self-acceptance, and a positive sense of identity. The writer used the flashcard technique to help Tom consolidate his beliefs and coping skills.

Tom was asked to write and rewrite statements on flashcards. This could help Tom to develop positive beliefs. The flashcards were kept in Tom's wallet for self-enlightenment from time to time. Thus, Tom was encouraged to affirm a positive self-identity and problem solving skills. Eventually, Tom wrote the following:

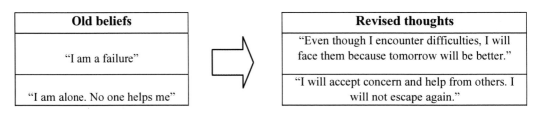

Old beliefs		Revised thoughts
"I am a failure"		"Even though I encounter difficulties, I will face them because tomorrow will be better."
"I am alone. No one helps me"		"I will accept concern and help from others. I will not escape again."

Since Tom was good at writing, the social worker designed plenty of written assignments for him. In another interview, Tom was to summarize his improvements and merits in accomplishing certain concrete tasks. Tom was encouraged to write the following points for self-affirmation.

1. I am working to solve my persisting housing problem from the past four weeks.
2. I did not avoid my problems in the last four weeks.
3. I tried hard to complete useful home assignments.
4. I did not spend money on drugs in the past few months.
5. I accepted I am indeed a patient (with many problems).

Despite Tom still regarded himself as a patient with many problems, he started to forgive himself in the interview. He not only demonstrated a self-understanding to his substance abuse behaviors, but also an ability to accept his past addictive behaviors. Dialectically, such self acceptance enhanced his self-efficacy.

Enhancing Self-Efficacy by Managing the Environment and Resources

The problem of substance dependence and homelessness is not merely an individual problem. It is also a challenge to the interaction between an individual and his/her surrounding environment (i.e. family, community, social systems, social policy etc). A Strengths Perspective and the concept of self-efficacy remain a crucial horizon. For a successful rehabilitation, persons with substance dependence have to face various challenges reintegrating in society.

For Tom, it was very important for him to find a permanent living place in Shumshuipo, the district that he lived for so many years. It was the oldest district in Hong Kong, however, with the highest rate (11%) of substance abuse reported cases in Hong Kong (Hong Kong Government, 2006). Tom received a second round public housing offer recently. It might be a calamity for Tom since he relapsed to heroin after he failed to catch the first round public housing allocation. This might be a great opportunity, however, for him to move into a new district. This could also mean a turning point for a drug free life and a chance for him to learn how to fix his own problems without the help of drugs.

The writer encouraged Tom to solve the housing problem by himself by using possible resources in the society. The first challenge was that Tom had to pay $2000.00 rent within two weeks. Tom was encouraged to discuss with the Housing Authority his difficulties paying rent. After Tom sent out a letter of petition, he successfully got a one-month deferment of the rent payment. Second, Tom started a saving plan. It was the first time Tom was able to save a few hundred dollars. Third, Tom was encouraged to apply for some grants. He finally got a grant from a local charity organization after he had undergone a series of procedures that included a home visit, written applications, and interviews. Eventually, Tom was able to obtain the key to his new home at the end of the month.

Tom learned how to make use of possible resources available to him in the community. He was able to get his own home, despite the stresses and negative emotions in the application process. His own effort greatly enhanced his self-confidence.

Building a Positive Social Identity through Voluntary Work

Having a sense of belonging is also meaningful to recovery. Therefore, assisting Tom to build up a positive social identity was essential.

Since Tom was good at painting, he was invited to help our center to repaint the activities room. He was capable of teaching other group members how to paint. Tom's social identity gradually changed to a helper and a volunteer instead of a patient or a person with substance abuse. He got a chance to contribute himself and his talent to others. By providing volunteer services, he built up a sense of belonging in the group. Tom enjoyed the work very much. It was also a chance for him to develop a good work attitude in preparing for any future employment. This new positive social identity helped Tom get involved with others and gain a sense of belonging. Hence, his self-efficacy was enhanced.

Healing Emptiness and Pains by Developing Resilience

High self-efficacy is presented as an ability to face good and bad in life, or "resilience." Saleebey (2002) described resilience as an ability to put up with difficulties or traumatic experiences in life.

In an interview, Tom said he had ups and downs in striving for recovery. One day, he started to take heroin again after he had a period of abstinence. He shared his frustrations with the writer. Toms said, "I hate being addicted to drugs. I doubt, however, whether I can stay clean. I have tried so many times, but I have failed."

In response to Tom's observation, the writer helped him to develop resilience to cope with adversity in the process of recovery. The writer said to Tom, "You have felt bad because you broke your own promise to not take drugs again. Relapse can be, however, an opportunity to reflect on how and why this slip happened. It is also the best time to learn how to cope differently and effectively in the future." The writer helped Tom to embrace the opportunity to change in a difficult situation.

Resilience involves a dialectical thinking in facing hardships. On the one hand, Tom had to acknowledge he was capable of facing difficulties in recovery. On the other hand, he had to accept things could not be changed. The only thing he could do was grieve his unpleasant experiences. Regarding Tom's feeling of emptiness and loneliness, the writer helped Tom develop a self-understanding of his needs for love and an interpersonal satisfaction. Tom was encouraged to accept the pain of loneliness and emptiness by expressing it and sharing it with others. Finally, he was supported for feeling pain and yett doing something achievable and new for himself in relation to others, such as being a volunteer in the center. When Tom's self-efficacy was developed, he started to have hope to reconnect with his family one day. Tom said he would like to stay drug-free for another year before he would contact his mother. He regarded this as an achievable goal. It was an indicator of an enhancement of self-efficacy.

As Tom understood his strengths and weaknesses in facing the challenges of recovery, he had a deeper level of self-knowledge. He was able to build up a high level of self-efficacy in order to resist the craving for drugs.

The Recent Development of Tom

Tom aspires *"to be a normal person"* with a home, a job, a family, and some good friends around.

Eventually, Tom successfully moved into a subsidized public housing apartment. He was able to move away from the old high-risk living district and entered a new district to start a new life. After he got a home, he started job hunting. With the help of supportive employment services, he got a job in a transportation company. It was a great change since he had not worked for 16 years. He praised himself that it was the first time he worked continuously for more than three months. He worked hard on his job. He planned to re-connect with his family when he successfully completed detoxification in methadone treatment. A reunion with his family is significant to Tom in the scope of traditional Chinese culture. Making improvements in his own abstinence and employment helped Tom feel free from familial shamefulness. Although Tom was still on methadone treatment, he was able to reduce the dosage steadily. He shifted from replacement therapy to a detoxification program in methadone treatment.

In this case, Tom's changes were not easy, but remarkable. The writer believes that even though Tom might relapse in the future, he would remember the successful experiences he had in a Strengths Perspective intervention. He would be able to integrate his learning experiences to meet recovery challenges.

CONCLUSION

This paper demonstrates that an integration of a Strengths Perspective with the concept of self-efficacy is effective in helping a person with substance dependence to restore a degree of dignity and a sense of achievement. The specific Chinese culture should also be considered in the case management of Chinese persons with substance abuse. In the case of Tom, the writer re-examined the ideologies of substance abuse recovery. Absolute abstinence may be preferable, but not always achievable. Relapse is normal on the way to recovery. Helping persons with substance dependence to increase their positive self-efficacy step by step would be meaningful in the process of recovery. A harm reduction model is integrated into practice and the well-being of the client is considered in the intervention. Substance abuse counseling is no longer a mere control on substance abuse behaviors. In the process of recovery, the goal of a Strengths Perspective is not shaping a perfect person. Instead, the Strengths Perspective overcomes the perfectionism of recovery and the dichotomy of relapse-abstinence.

REFERENCES

Bandura, A. (1977) *Social Learning Theory*. Englewood Cliffs, N.J. : Prentice Hall.

Bedford, O. & Hwang, K.K. (2003) "Guilt and Shame in Chinese Culture: A Cross-Cultural Framework from the Perspective of Morality and Identity." *Journal for the Theory of Social Behaviour*, 33(2):127-144

Cheung, Y.W., Ch'ien, J. M.N., Tang,C., Pi,P.,Cheung, N.W.T., Choi, J.,Wong, A.M.L., &Ho, S.C.C. (2003). *A Longitudinal Study of Chronic Drug Abusers in Hong Kong. Action Committee Against Narcotics* Hong Kong.

Cheung, Y.W., Cheung N.W.T., Choi,J., & Tang, C. (2004) "The Importance of Developing a Positive Identity to Enhance Self-Efficacy in Relapse Prevention of Chronic Drug Abusers in Hong Kong.' *Paper presented at the Conference on Chronic Drug Abuse in Hong Kong*: Latest Finding and Service Relevance in Hong Kong, May, 2004.

DiClement, C. C., Scoot, K.. (1995) Fairhurst, and Nancy A. Piotrowski., "Self-efficacy and Addictive Behaviors." In Maddux J. E.. (ed.) *Self-efficacy, Adaptation, and Adjustment: Theory, Research and Application*, New York: Plenum Press

Hong Kong Government (2006) *Report of Central Registry of Drug Abuse of Hong Kong*, HK Government.

Lin, Y.N. (2001) 'The Application of Cognitive-Behavioral Therapy to Counseling Chinese.' *American Journal of Psychotherapy*, 55(4):46-58.

Maddux, J. E.. (2001) "Self-Efficacy: The Power of Believing You Can." 277-278.In Snyder C.R. & Lopez S. J.. (ed) *Handbook of Positive Psychology*, Oxford University Press,USA.

Marlatt G. A. (1985). *Relapse Prevention: Maintenance Strategies in the Treatment of Addictive Behaviors*. New York: Guilford Press.

In: Substance Abuse: New Research   ISBN 978-1-60456-834-9
Editors: Ethan J. Kerr and Owen E. Gibson   © 2009 Nova Science Publishers, Inc.

Chapter 9

SUICIDE RISK IN SUBSTANCE ABUSERS WITH SCHIZOPHRENIA

Maurizio Pompili, Caterina Tatarelli, Giorgio D. Kotzalidis and Roberto Tatarelli
Department of Psychiatry, Sapienza University of Rome, Italy

ABSTRACT

Substance use/abuse/dependence is often comorbid with schizophrenia; psychosis and substance use were found to increase suicide risk. However, the interaction of factors involved in increased suicide risk in patients with comorbid schizophrenia and substance use disorder are quite complex and not explained by simple potentiation between psychosis and substance use. The factor that is almost always present is depression; it gives way to hopelessness, which was found to be the most powerful predictor of suicide in this comorbid population. Insight unto one's own illness may both increase and decrease suicide risk; increased awareness of having e debilitating disease may lead to depression and suicide, whereas realizing the need to comply with treatment to stay well may decrease it. Genetic, ethnic and social factors seem also to play a role. Western culture favors isolation of the mentally ill, thus paving the way to illicit drug use, hence loneliness and depression; homelessness and unemployment may also play a role, although new social bonds are likely to be established among the homeless and be protective to a certain extent, while unemployment may be worse for men than women and has a culture-dependent effect. Treatment should aim to manage both schizophrenic symptoms and substance use simultaneously, as improvement in one aspect may help the other. Integrated treatment approaches, such as treating the symptoms of the disease and the effects of the abused substance while rebuilding the patient's social network, are likely to yield the best results.

INTRODUCTION

Substance use and abuse is an alarming phenomenon worldwide; data from various sources indicate that substance use disorders are particularly prevalent among individuals with psychiatric disorders (Gold and Brady, 2003). Recently, comorbidity of schizophrenia with substance misuse became the focus of special interest (Mueser et al., 1992; Smith and Hucker, 1994; Soyka, 2000). Around the early nineties, lifetime prevalence estimates of misuse and/or dependence emerging from a review of 32 studies dealing with schizophrenia and substance abuse (Mueser et al., 1990) were 12.3–50% for alcohol, 12.5–35.8% for cannabis, 11.3–31% for stimulants, 5.7–15.2% for hallucinogens, 3.5–11.3% for sedatives, and 2–9% for opioids (Soyka, 2000). As comorbidity is higher than expected, there must be some kind of interaction and mechanisms shared. The changing patterns of illicit drug abuse has affected also the expression of psychopathology of mental illness; a much debated issue is whether it is drug abuse that triggers mental illness or there is a special predisposition or vulnerability in the subpopulation of mental illness patients that choose to abuse drugs, for pleasure or for self-medication, and there is limited evidence allowing to reject any of the above, at least for some comorbidity cases (Bersani et al., 2002; Chakroun et al., 2004). How do the coexistence of substance use and mental illness affect suicide risk is an important issue, raised by the fact that both mental illness and substance use elevate this risk with respect to the general population. Early cannabis use may precede the onset of major depression and predispose to suicide (Lynskey et al., 2004), but this has not been investigated in patients with schizophrenia.

EPIDEMIOLOGICAL FEATURES AND FACTORS INVOLVED

Substance use (Suominen et al., 2004) and psychosis (Warman et al., 2004) are *per se* risk factors for suicidal behavior. The question is, when they are present together in one patient, do they collaborate in producing an even higher risk or do higher risks derive from interaction with other factors? In bipolar patients, it appears that substance abuse disorder doubles suicide risks and the presence of substance-related symptoms triples it (Comtois et al., 2004). Epidemiological data gathered so far are unlikely to respond to this question, since they vary in the rates they detect, which in turn depend on sampling, cultural and ethnic differences, and differences in gender, clinical conditions, socioeconomic differences, which all load on one another. However, a recent meta-analysis of prospective and case-control studies yielded a higher suicide risk in the presence of drug, but not alcohol abuse (Hawton et al., 2005).

For example, *culture* and *ethnicity* may influence the lifestyle of patients with schizophrenia, protecting them from or exposing them to substance use. This may in turn influence suicide rate. Substance use may increase suicide behavior in Western countries, whereas in Eastern countries, where people with schizophrenia usually live in their family of origin (thus being less socially isolated) and show low rates of illicit substance use, the latter does not appear to play a role in completed suicide (Kuo et al., 2005).

Immigration is another condition that increases suicide ideation (Aubert et al., 2004; Kennedy et al., 2005) (although actual suicide rates among immigrants tend to be more like those in their countries of origin [Malenfant, 2004]) and is also associated with increased prevalence of psychosis (Zolkowska et al., 2001; Mortensen et al., 1997), particularly schizophrenia (Selten et al., 2002; Cooper, 2005), although other factors than migration itself might be responsible for the data obtained in these studies (Zolkowska et al., 2001; Selten et al., 2002). However, when psychotic immigrants were compared with autochthonous psychotics, they displayed less alcohol misuse and suicide attempts, but higher unemployment, which was a contributing factor to psychosis (Fossion et al., 2004). Again, *unemployment* was found to be related to suicide in the US (Stack and Haas, 1984; Kposowa, 2001), New Zealand (Blakely et al., 2003), Italy (Preti and Miotto, 1999), but in Japan (Yamasaki et al., 2005), England and Wales (Lester, 2000; Gunnell et al., 1999) controversial results were obtained. Summarizing, the picture is by no means clear, with social factors certainly involved in determining both abuse, mental illness and suicidality, but these again are related to ethnic, hence cultural, and occupational, hence economic factors, the role of which may be protective in a context and exposing to vulnerability in another. Ethnic and cultural factors, however, may also lead to underreporting of suicide among immigrants in specific immigration contexts (Pavlović and Marušić, 2001).

A factor increasing suicide risk may be *impulsiveness*, although not all suicides share such trait (Turecki, 2005); substance abusing schizophrenic patients were found to have higher impulsiveness scores on the Barratt Impulsivity Scale with respect to nonabusers (Gut-Fayand et al., 2001).

In a study of 333 patients with schizophrenia, *hopelessness*, substance abuse, better performance on neurocognitive tests, and increased insight into their condition were all associated with current and lifetime suicidal ideation and attempted suicide, with hopelessness being the most accurate predictor (Kim et al., 2003). In a review of risk factors for suicide in schizophrenia, depression turned out to be one of the most important factors underlying perceived hopelessness and associated with suicide (Caldwell and Gottesman, 1990).

Insight into illness was found to correlate with treatment compliance in schizophrenic patients in an American (Smith et al., 1997), but not in an Irish sample (Garavan et al., 1998). In the former, the use of marijuana, but not other substances was related with noncompliance (Smith et al., 1997). Poor compliance with medication was significantly associated with substance (Owen et al., 1996) and alcohol (Pristach and Smith, 1990) abuse in schizophrenia in other two American samples. Substance nonusers from an Irish cohort scored significantly higher on the Birchwood Self-report Questionnaire, a measure of insight, in a study of patients with schizophrenia or schizoaffective disorder who were on oral antipsychotic medication; all but one regularly compliant patients were nonusers (Kamali et al., 2001). Data from the InterSePT study show that clozapine treatment both reduces suicidal risk and enhances insight and compliance (Meltzer, 2002). At a first glance, this might appear to be at odds with the fact that people with schizophrenia and enhanced insight (Kim et al., 2003; Crumlish et al., 2005) or symptom awareness (Amador et al., 1996) have higher risk for suicide, but this is likely to be accounted for by increased depression with insight unto one's awareness of having schizophrenia (Kim et al., 2003; Crumlish et al., 2005). At any rate, controversial results have been heretofore obtained as regards insight and suicide risk, with one study finding no relationship (Yen et al., 2002); others propose a more complex view, that envisages insight as able to both increase and decrease suicide risk according to context (Lewis, 2004; Pompili et al., 2004). The InterSePT results may be framed as showing increased insight and adherence to treatment as causally related; in turn, this would enhance the therapeutic effects of clozapine and these effects would encourage patients to stay on treatment. This would decrease suicide risk, as clozapine appears to protect from suicide while the patient is taking it (Modestin et al., 2005). Furthermore, clozapine treatment is effective in schizophrenia comorbid with substance abuse (Marcus and Snyder, 1995); generally, comorbidity decreases treatment response (Hättenschwiler et al., 2005), but clozapine improved psychopathology and social functioning in patients with schizophrenia or schizoaffective disorder independently from whether they abused substances or not (Buckley et al., 1994).

Symptomatology as a contributing factor. Schizophrenic patients who use substances have more positive symptoms, especially hallucinations (Soyka et al., 2001), and more suicide attempts than patients with the same diagnosis and no substance use (Soyka et al., 2001; 1993). Interestingly, hallucinations (Harkavy-Friedman et al., 2003), but not delusions (Grunebaum et al., 2001), were found to increase suicide attempts in patients with schizophrenia, independently from alcohol/drug abuse/dependence (Harkavy-Friedman et al., 2003).

Loas et al. (2005) investigated suicidality in addictive disorders. These authors examined a population composed of drug and alcohol abusers, anorectic and bulimic patients, and controls; they administered the Interpersonal Dependency Inventory (IDI) and correlated the scores obtained with suicidal ideation and actual attempts. They found that excessive dependency and DSM-IV diagnosis of *dependent personality* disorder were associated with higher suicide risk; addiction increased further such risk, and male addicts and female alcoholics with excessive dependency or dependent personality disorders had a higher suicide risk than their counterparts without dependency. Moreover, male drug abusers had significantly increased both suicidal ideation and actual attempts than the other groups.

Social problems. There is growing evidence that substance misuse has deleterious effects on the course and outcome of schizophrenia (Martinez-Arevalo et al., 1994; Swofford et al, 1996; 2000). Substance misuse is in most cases associated with non-compliance (Owen et al., 1996; Kampman and Lehtinen, 1999) and relapse of psychotic symptoms requiring hospitalization (Linszen et al., 1994; Haywood et al., 1995). Kamali et al. (2000) found more suicidal ideation in their sample of patients with schizophrenia in the subset reporting current substance misuse, as compared to the subsets with only past or no substance misuse. Their findings are consistent with some (Landmark et al., 1987; Allebeck et al., 1987; Verdoux et al., 1999) but not all (Roy et al., 1984) studies. Drake et al. (1984) also found a relationship between comorbid substance misuse and completed suicide in patients with schizophrenia. A possible link between increased suicide risk in substance abusers with schizophrenia may be related to social problems; for example, the *emotional warmth* of relatives towards patients with schizophrenia, as assessed with the Camberwell Family Interview, is associated with no substance abuse, (Bentsen et al., 1998). *Homelessness* is another factor associated with both suicide and drug abuse in youths (Sibthorpe et al., 1995; Greene and Ringwalt, 1996) and in the mentally ill (Drake et al., 1989b; Prigerson et al., 2003; Desai et al., 2003); homelessness is more frequent than expected in schizophrenia, and is associated with heavy substance use, and suicidality (Susser et al., 1989; Folsom and Jeste, 2002). However, suicide rate among homeless people with schizophrenic is not higher than that of those without schizophrenia (Babidge et al., 2001); furthermore, in a sample of Australian patients with schizophrenia, those patients who currently abused drugs did not attempt suicide more often than patients with no or past drug abuse or dependence, despite the former were more symptomatic (Ian L. Fowler et al., 1998). Homelessness is a serious post-hospitalization problem of patients with mental illness; more than one out of three patients will become homeless within six months after discharge from a state mental hospital; those with concurrent substance abuse are at increased risk of homelessness, due to their increased disruptiveness and consequent loss of social support (Belcher, 1989); the latter constitutes a protective factor against suicide (Suppapitiporn et al., 2004; Compton et al., 2005). However, to account for the negative results, new social bond formation, as the one that occurs among homeless people, thus creating a sort of companionship, is likely to protect also the drug-abusing homeless individual with schizophrenia from suicide.

According to various self-medication hypotheses, the psychotropic effects of abused substances are used to wipe out psychotic symptoms (Test et al., 1989; Verdoux et al, 1999). Krausz et al. (1995), analyzing suicidality among patients with schizophrenia, reported more suicide among men, although women made more attempts. They also observed that many adolescents suffering from schizophrenia belong to socially marginalized groups; furthermore, a large proportion of their parents are separated from their partners; moreover, there is an increased occurrence of mental disorders, such as addiction related problems (Krausz et al., 1996). There results a decrease in stability of primary relationships, disruption of family bonds and disturbance of familial interactions, which are consistently interpreted as risk factors for suicidal behavior. P.McC. Miller et al. (2000) support that there is a strong relationship between lifetime positive schizophrenic symptoms and alcohol abuse/illicit drug use; such behavior may exacerbate symptoms which in turn may lead to violence or suicidal behavior. Alcoholism increases the likelihood that a person with schizophrenia will engage in violent behavior (Rasanen et al., 1998). There is recent evidence that poor family functioning predicts gender-independent physical violence by intimate partner in the last year; in turn, this is related to suicidal intent in acutely ill psychiatric patients, even after controlling for alcohol use (Heru et al., 2006). However, causation could also be the other way round.

Past or current alcohol or substance use, along with other ten variables, predicted suicide risk in a two-year follow-up study of schizophrenic or schizoaffective patients (Potkin et al., 2003). This matched the results of a retrospective study carried-out in patients with schizophrenia during the years 1983 to 1987, that showed suicidal patients to display higher substance abuse than the nonsuicidal ones (Dassori et al., 1990). However, Axelsson and Lagerkvist-Briggs (1992) failed to find substance use among factors predicting suicide in Swedish psychotic men.

All these factors are combined to yield an increased risk for suicide in patients with schizophrenia and drug abuse. The strongest predictor of suicide in schizophrenia is *depression* (Kreyenbuhl et al., 2002; Hawton et al., 2005), and all these factors may act through increasing depression. Hence, attention must focus on lessening the effect of all depressogenic stimuli on the patient, so that suicide be avoided.

SUICIDE RISK AND SUBSTANCE ABUSE

Rich et al., in a series of studies of two American cohorts, found significantly more comorbid substance abuse among people with schizophrenia who were suicidal in the eighties, particularly among the younger ones (Rich et al., 1988a; 1988b; Richard C. Fowler et al., 1986). They stated that it is important, in view of the changing patterns in epidemiology of schizophrenia comorbid with substance use/abuse, that clinicians obtain accurate drug use history to detect and treat promptly drug use/abuse. Youths who abuse drugs are at increased risk for committing suicide; drug or alcohol abuse is found in about 70% of children and adolescents who commit suicide (Shafii et al., 1985).

Harris and Barraclough's (1997) meta-analysis on suicide as outcome in mental disorders reported on the standardized mortality ratio (SMR) for various psychoactive substance use disorders. After combining the studies included, they compared suicide risks of drug users and nonusers. They found the ratios of users to be higher than those of nonusers in all groups; in subjects with alcohol dependence and abuse it was 6-fold, in opioid dependence and abuse 14-fold, and in cannabis users 4-fold. In this meta-analysis, suicide risk among schizophrenic patients was 8.5 times than among nonschizophrenics. Subsequently, Wilcox et al. (2004) located twenty studies not included in the Harris and Barraclough review and identified another 22 studies published after 1997; by combining data of all these studies, they found more robust associations between suicide on one hand, and opioid use disorder overall, alcohol use disorders among women, as well as mixed intravenous drug use.

SUBSTANCE ABUSE AND SCHIZOPHRENIA

Substantially higher rates of substance abuse are consistently reported among schizophrenic and schizoaffective patients (Drake and Wallach, 1989; Galanter et al., 1988; Kivlahan et al., 1991; Lehman et al., 1989; Safer, 1987; Schneier and Siris, 1987; Siris, 1990; Test et al., 1989). The pattern of drug use differs between comorbid schizophrenic/substance abusers and abusers with no mental health problems, with the latter using more cocaine than patients with schizophrenia, perhaps due to the fact that social marginalization in people with schizophrenia renders cocaine unavailable (Lammertink et al., 2005). Some studies suggest that substance abuse is associated with an increased number of hospital admissions (Safer, 1987; Drake et al., 1989a; 1990; Brady et al., 1990; Duke et al., 1994) which is a risk factor for suicide, but other studies did not confirm such association (Mueser et al., 1990; Ian L. Fowler et al., 1998). Prognosis is usually poor among patients with schizophrenia and substance use/abuse/dependence comorbidity (Cuffel et al., 1994; DeQuardo et al., 1994, Linszen et al, 1994). Patients with such comorbidity have better premorbid functioning and less severe negative symptoms compared with patients with the same diagnosis but no abuse (Arndt et al., 1992; Serper et al., 1995; Kirkpatrick et al., 1996; Sevy et al., 2001), but show more tardive dyskinesia than the latter (Dixon et al., 1992); this high incidence of tardive dyskinesia is particularly prominent in patients abusing alcohol alone or in combination with cannabinoids (Olivera et al., 1990). The "dual diagnosis" patient usually displays the following features: male, younger, high incidence of homelessness, more positive and less negative symptoms, more affective disturbance, increased suicide rate, treatment refractoriness, noncompliant with medication, higher rates of tardive dyskinesia, higher doses of neuroleptic, higher rates of hospital admission, higher rates of violence, younger age at time of first hospitalization (Scheller-Gilkey et al., 1999). Soyka (2000) reported that substance abuse is a major risk factor for violence in patients with a major mental disorder, especially schizophrenia.

Table 1. Possible reasons for drug abuse in
schizophrenia (from Ian L. Fowler et al., 1998)

- Drug intoxication effects: "to feel good", "enhance things", etc.
- To reduce dysphoria: "to relax", "feel happier", "stop the depression";
- Social effects: "be sociable", "be part of a group", "something to do with friends", "to face people better";
- Illness and medication-related effects: "to get away from the thought", "help forget positive and negative symptoms"

A large epidemiologic study established that patients with schizophrenia have 7.6 times higher risk for the development of drug abuse and 10.5 times higher risk for the development of alcohol abuse than nonschizophrenics (Boyd, 1984). There is evidence to support the notion that patients with schizophrenia and substance abuse suffer from severe psychiatric symptoms (Barbee et al., 1989; Cleghorn et al., 1991; Osher et al., 1991). In such patients aggression and self-aggression is an easily traceable feature compared with schizophrenics without substance abuse (Yesavage and Zarcone, 1983; Safer, 1987; Drake et al., 1989b). Schizophrenic patients often abuse substances to reduce anxiety. DeVito et al., (1970) support that chronic alcohol consumption helps patients with schizophrenia to maintain ego integrity whereas other authors stressed that alcohol helps to reduce discomfort in the presence of hallucinations (Alpert and Silvers, 1970). Still other scholars hold that drug or alcohol abuse is used to abate negative effects, while the productive psychotic symptoms are only experienced following substance abuse. Kesselman et al. (1982) found in their sample of schizophrenic patients that 75% of subjects with alcohol abuse suffered from psychotic symptom worsening. Krausz et al. (1996) studied a sample of patients suffering from both schizophrenia and substance abuse. They found that "dual diagnosis" patients showed more severe psychopathology. Similar findings were also reported by other investigators (Barbee et al., 1989; Osher et al, 1991; Drake and Wallach, 1989). It should be remarked that substance abusing schizophrenic patients manifest more paranoia and depression (Alterman et al., 1981). Krausz et al. (1996) and Dixon et al. (1990) reported that the consumption of mood-altering substances reduce anxiety, depression and tension, i.e., some affective symptoms characterizing schizophrenia. Noncompliance with antipsychotic treatment may often lead patients to seek drugs for their pharmacological effects, but also the reverse could occur, i.e., schizophrenic patients wishing to overcome neuroleptic drug-induced dysphoria, depression or negative symptoms might seek drugs, that in turn prompts them to stop taking medication. At this point, it should be underlined that most schizophrenic patients committing suicide are off-medication.

The increased suicide risk of substance abusing schizophrenic patients (Barbee et al, 1989; Osher et al, 1991; Lorenzen, 1990; Yesavage and Zarcone, 1983; Safer, 1987; Drake et al., 1989b; Lindqvist and Allebeck, 1989) could be the result of a cumulative effect of many factors or events, such as the loss of remaining social control through the consumption of psychotropic substances, noncompliance with antipsychotic medication, presence of paranoia and depression (Krausz et al., 1996).

In Allebeck and Allgulander's (1990) sample of young male substance abusers, the diagnostic category associated with the highest suicide risk was schizophrenic psychosis. Abuse substances worsen both symptoms and prognosis of the illness and are related to higher relapse rates.

SUICIDE, SCHIZOPHRENIA AND SUBSTANCE USE

Suicide may become the ultimate remedy to reduce suffering caused by hopelessness and social isolation. Various studies recognized the importance of substance abuse in suicide of patients with schizophrenia (Bowers et al., 1990; Duke et al., 1994; F.T. Miller and Tanenbaum, 1989; Rich et al., 1988b; Satel et al., 1991). Drug and alcohol abuse increase the risk of suicide in the general population (Allgulander et al., 1987; Berglund, 1984; Murphy and Robins, 1967; Murphy et al., 1979; Rich et al., 1988a), and when this behavior is associated with a diagnosis of schizophrenia, the risk is much higher. Also, it is important to take into consideration the difficulties in reaching marginalized individuals. A comparison of patients who began drug abuse before their first admission with those who began abusing drugs after their first admission showed that the use of specific drugs was associated with significant differences in age, age at first hospitalization, premorbid functioning and subtype of schizophrenia. The differences were not uniform across the different drugs (Silver and Abboud, 1994).

However, when it comes to compare suicide attempter patients with schizophrenia *versus* nonattempters as to drug or alcohol abuse/dependence, abuse is not found to differ between the two groups (Harkavy-Friedman et al., 1999).

It does not appear that the use of *specific substances* affects suicide risk differentially. However, data on this subject are scanty. In one study, self-harm did not differ between stimulant abusers compared with alcohol and/or cannabis abusers, but the former showed more lifetime history of violence (Miles et al., 2003). *Cannabis* abusers had more often attempted suicide than stimulant abusers in a French sample (Dervaux et al., 2003).

In a study of patients seeking help at a psychiatric emergency room in Dallas, Texas, there was a trend among substance users to be more suicidal than users; however, psychotic users were significantly more suicidal than nonpsychotic users and differed also for type of substance used (mostly cannabis among psychotics) (Gilfillan et al., 1998).

Conversely, Siris et al. (1993) found no association between suicidal ideation and lifetime history of drug abuse of patients with schizophrenia, but rather an association with lifetime history of panic attacks. An increase in suicidal behavior of patients with schizophrenia and panic attacks has also been found by Goodwin et al. (2002). However, since cannabinoid dependence is related with increased rate of panic episodes (Zvolensky et al., 2005) and more than half of patients with cannabinoid use and panic disorder had their onset of panic disorder within two days after cannabis consumption (Dannon et al., 2004), the results of Siris et al. (1993) should be interpreted with caution.

*Alcohol*ic patients with schizophrenia could be at higher risk for suicide than nonalcoholic schizophrenic patients due to the development of depression in the former; depression was found to explain more than 80% of variance in suicidal behavior in two independent samples of schizophrenic patients, while correlation between depression and alcohol use added little to the amount of variance (Bartels et al., 1992).

In a sample of Swedish youths hospitalized between 1982 and 1993 for first episode psychotic disorder, subjects with schizophrenia and at least one suicide attempt were more likely to have tried an illegal drug (Jarbin and von Knorring, 2004). Thirty-two Swedish patients suffering from schizophrenia who committed suicide within an eleven-year follow-up period were compared with 64 patients with the same diagnosis who did not commit suicide during the same follow-up period; the stronger predictor of suicide was past suicide attempts, while alcohol abuse was associated with higher suicide risk in men only (Allebeck et al., 1987).

WHEN DO PATIENTS WITH SCHIZOPHRENIA AND ILLICIT DRUG USE KILL THEMSELVES?

It is important to know whether there is a period of increased probability to commit suicide so that timely treatment plans are enforced.

The first period after onset and hospitalization is the most vulnerable for committing suicide; about 65% of patients with schizophrenia display aggressive behavior, with about 17% of men and about 26% of women who attempt suicide; alcohol abuse accounts only for other than self-directed aggression (Steinert et al., 1999). First-episode psychotic patients with drug misuse show increased rates of parasuicide (Verdoux et al., 1999).

CONCLUSION

We stress the need to implement protocols for the early identification of individuals who are substance abusers, manifest a vulnerability to develop schizophrenia and are at risk for suicide as a result of comorbidity. Goldberg et al. (2001) provided data regarding alcohol or other substance abuse and suicidality from several perspectives in affective disorders. These authors identified and analyzed a number of factors, among which impulsivity, aggression, family history and neurobiology. Future research should clarify the role of specific risk factors for suicide among schizophrenic patients who are substance abusers.

It is probable that effectively treating both psychosis and depression, both associated with higher substance use rates, will reduce suicide risk in schizophrenic patients (Tandon, 2005). It has been recommended to treat psychosis effectively, since its timely management is associated with decreased substance use during the course of illness (Lambert et al., 2005); alternatively, since drug-induced psychotic episodes have a benign outcome, it has been suggested to treat aggressively the dependence (Rich et al., 1998b). We believe it is essential to treat both conditions simultaneously, using both drugs and psychotherapy: dual diagnoses need dual treatment approaches. We agree with Harkavy-Friedman and Nelson (1997) that "treatment focused on the reduction of symptomatology and maintenance of an effective social environment may attenuate the risk for suicidal behavior in schizophrenia" and also that treatment should focus on the management of psychosis, depression, and substance abuse, which are all factors increasing suicide risk. To this end, it is essential that the patient's social network be redesigned and reconstructed; psychoeducation, involving the comorbid patient's parents may also prove to be useful in achieving a reduction of suicide risk in a patient with schizophrenia and comorbid substance abuse.

REFERENCES

Allebeck P, Allgulander C. Suicide among young men: psychiatric illness, deviant behaviour and substance abuse. *Acta Psychiatr Scand* 1990;81:565-70.

Allebeck P, Varla A, Kristjansson E, Wistedt B. Risk factors for suicide among patients with schizophrenia. *Acta Psychiatr Scand* 1987;76:414-9.

Allgulander C, Ljungberg L, Fisher LD. Long-term prognosis in addiction on sedative and hypnotic drug analyzed with the Cox regression model. *Acta Psychiatr Scand* 1987;75:521-31.

Alpert M, Silvers KN. Perceptual characteristics distinguishing auditory hallucinations in schizophrenia and acute alcoholic psychoses. *Am J Psychiatry* 1970;127:298-302.

Alterman AI, Erdlen FR, Murphy E. Alcohol abuse in the psychiatric hospital population. *Addict Behav* 1981;1:69-73.

Amador XF, Friedman JH, Kasapis C, Yale SA, Flaum M, Gorman JM. Suicidal behavior in schizophrenia and its relationship to awareness of illness. *Am J Psychiatry* 1996;153:1185-8.

Arndt S, Tyrrell G, Flaum M, Andreasen NC. Comorbidity of substance abuse and schizophrenia: the role of pre-morbid adjustment. *Psychol Med* 1992;22:379-88.

Aubert P, Daigle MS, Daigle JG. Cultural traits and immigration: hostility and suicidality in Chinese Canadian students. *Transcult Psychiatry* 2004;41:514-32.

Axelsson R, Lagerkvist-Briggs M. Factors predicting suicide in psychotic patients. *Eur Arch Psychiatry Clin Neurosci* 1992;241:259-66.

Babidge NC, Buhrich N, Butler T. Mortality among homeless people with schizophrenia in Sydney, Australia: a 10-year follow-up. *Acta Psychiatr Scand* 2001;103:105-10.

Barbee JC, Clarck PD, Crapanzaro MS, Heintz GC, Kehoe CE. Alcohol and substance abuse among schizophrenic patients presenting to an emergency psychiatric service. *J Nerv Ment Dis* 1989;171:400-7.

Bartels SJ, Drake RE, McHugo GJ. Alcohol abuse, depression, and suicidal behavior in schizophrenia. *Am J Psychiatry*. 1992;149:394-5.

Belcher JR. On becoming homeless: a study of chronically mentally ill persons. *J Community Psychol* 1989;17:173-85.

Bentsen H, Munkvold OG, Notland TH, Boye B, Oskarsson KH, Uren G, Lersbryggen AB, Bjorge H, Berg-Larsen R, Lingjaerde O, Malt UF. Relatives' emotional warmth towards patients with schizophrenia or related psychoses: demographic and clinical predictors. *Acta Psychiatr Scand* 1998;97:86-92.

Berglund M. Suicide in alcoholism. A prospective study of 81 suicides. I. The multidimensional diagnosis at first admission. *Arch Gen Psychiatry* 1984;41:888-91.

Bersani G, Orlandi V, Kotzalidis GD, Pancheri P. Cannabis and schizophrenia: impact on onset, course, psychopathology an outcomes. *Eur Arch Psychiatry Clin Neurosci* 2002;252:86-92.

Blakely TA, Collings SC, Atkinson J. Unemployment and suicide. Evidence for a causal association? *J Epidemiol Community Health* 2003;57:594-600.

Bowers MB Jr, Mazure CM, Nelson JC, Jatlow PI. Psychotogenic drug use and neuroleptic response. *Schizophr Bull* 1990;16:81-5.

Boyd JH. Exclusion criteria of DSM III: a study of co-occurence of hierarchy-free syndromes. *Arch Gen Psychiatry* 1984;41:983-9.

Brady K, Anton R, Ballanger JC, Lydiard B, Adinoff B, Selander J. Cocaine abuse among schizophrenic patients. *Am J Psychiatry* 1990;147:1164-7.

Buckley P, Thompson PA, Way L, Meltzer HY. Substance abuse and clozapine treatment. *J Clin Psychiatry* 1994;55[9 suppl B]:s114-6.

Caldwell CB, Gottesman II. Schizophrenic kill themselves too: a review of risk factors for suicide. *Schizophr. Bull* 1990;16:571-89.

Chakroun N, Doron J, Swendsen J. Consommation de substances psychoactives, problèmes affectifs et traits de personnalité : test de deux modèles d'association. *Encéphale* 2004;30:564-9.

Cleghorn JM, Kaplan RD, Szechtman B. Substance abuse and schizophrenia: effect on symptoms but not on neurocognitive function. *J Clin Psychiatry* 1991;51:26-30.

Comtois KA, Russo JE, Roy-Byrne P, Ries RK. Clinicians' assessments of bipolar disorder and substance abuse as predictors of suicidal behavior in acutely hospitalized psychiatric inpatients. *Biol Psychiatry* 2004;56:757-63.

Compton MT, Thompson NJ, Kaslow NJ. Social environment factors associated with suicide attempt among low-income African Americans: the protective role of family relationships and social support. *Soc Psychiatry Psychiatr Epidemiol* 2005;40:175-85.

Cooper B. Schizophrenia, social class and immigrant status: the epidemiological evidence. *Epidemiol Psichiatr Soc* 2005;14:137-44.

Crumlish N, Whitty P, Kamali M, Clarke M, Browne S, McTigue O, Lane A, Kinsella A, Larkin C, O'Callaghan E. Early insight predicts depression and attempted suicide after 4 years in first-episode schizophrenia and schizophreniform disorder. *Acta Psychiatr Scand* 2005;112:449-55.

Cuffel BJ, Chase P. Remission and relapse of substance use disorder in schizophrenia. Result from a one year prospective study. *J Nerv Ment Dis* 1994;182:342-8.

Dannon PN, Lowengrub K, Amiaz R, Grunhaus L, Kotler M. Comorbid cannabis use and panic disorder: short term and long term follow-up study. *Hum Psychopharmacol.* 2004;19:97-101.

Dassori AM, Mezzich JE, Keshavan M. Suicidal indicators in schizophrenia. *Acta Psychiatr Scand* 1990;81:409-13.

DeQuardo JR, Carpenter CF, Tandon R. Patterns of substance abuse in schizophrenia: nature and significance. *J Psychiatr Res* 1994;28:265-75.

Dervaux A, Laqueille X, Bourdel MC, Leborgne MH, Olié J-P, Lôo H, Krebs MO. Cannabis et schizophrénie : données cliniques et socio-démographiques. *Encéphale* 2003;29:11-7.

Desai RA, Liu-Mares W, Dausey DJ, Rosenheck RA. Suicidal ideation and suicide attempts in a sample of homeless people with mental illness. *J Nerv Ment Dis* 2003;191:365-71.

DeVito RA, Flaherty LA, Mozdzierz GJ. Toward a psychodynamic theory of alcoholism. *Dis Nerv Syst* 1970;31:43-9.

Dixon L, Haas G, Weiden P , Sweeney J, Frances A. Acute effects of drug abuse in schizophrenic patients: clinical observation and patients' self-report. *Schizophr Bull* 1990;11:60-79.

Dixon L, Weiden PJ, Haas G, Sweeney J, Frances AJ. Increased tardive dyskinesia in alcohol-abusing schizophrenic patients. *Compr Psychiatry* 1992;33:121-2.

Drake RE, Wallach MA. Substance abuse among the chronic mentally ill. *Hosp Community Psychiatry* 1989;40:1041-5.

Drake RE, Gates C, Cotton PG, Whitaker A. Suicide among schizophrenics. Who is at risk? *J Nerv Ment Dis* 1984;172:613-7.

Drake RE, Osher FC, Wallach MA. Alcohol use and abuse in schizophrenia: a prospective community study. *J Nerv Ment Dis* 1989a;177:409-14.

Drake RE, Wallach MA, Hoffman JS. Housing instability and homelessness among after care patients of an urban state hospital. *Hosp Community Psychiatry* 1989b;40:46-51.

Drake RE, Osher FC, Noordsy DL, Hurlbut SC, Teague GB, Beaudett MS. Diagnosis of alcohol use disorders in schizophrenia. *Schizophr Bull* 1990;16:57-67.

Duke PJ, Pantelis C, Barnes TRE. South Westminster schizophrenia survey. Alcohol use and its relationship to symptoms, tardive dyskinesia and illness onset. *Br J Psychiatry* 1994;164:630-6.

Folsom D, Jeste DV. Schizophrenia in homeless persons: a systematic review of the literature. *Acta Psychiatr Scand* 2002;105:404-13.

Fossion P, Servais L, Rejas MC, Ledoux Y, Pelc I, Minner P. Psychosis, migration and social environment: an age–and–gender controlled study. *Eur Psychiatry* 2004;19(6):338-43.

Fowler IL, Carr VJ, Carter NT, Lewin TJ. Patterns of current and lifetime substance use in schizophrenia. *Schizophr Bull* 1998;24:443-55.

Fowler RC, Rich CL, Young D. San Diego suicide study. II. Substance abuse in young cases. *Arch Gen Psychiatry* 1986;43:962-5.

Galanter M, Dermatis H, Egelko S, De Leon G. Homelessness and mental illness in a professional- and peer-led cocaina treatment clinic. *Psychiatr Serv* 1998;49:533-5.

Garavan J, Browne S, Gervin M, Lane A, Larkin C, O'Callaghan E. Compliance with neuroleptic medication in outpatients with schizophrenia; relationship to subjective response to neuroleptics; attitudes to medication and insight. *Compr Psychiatry* 1998;39:215-9.

Gilfillan S, Claassen CA, Orsulak P, Carmody TJ, Sweeney JB, Battaglia J, Rush AJ. A comparison of psychotic and nonpsychotic substance users in the psychiatric emergency room. *Psychiatr Serv* 1998;49:825-8.

Gold PB, Brady KT. Evidence-based treatment for substance use disorders. *Focus* 2003;1:115-22.

Goldberg JF, Singer TM, Garno JL. Suicidality and substance abuse in affective disorders. *J Clin Psychiatry* 2001;62 (Suppl 25):35-43.

Goodwin R, Lyons JS, McNally RJ. Panic attacks in schizophrenia. *Schizophr Res* 2002;58:213-20.

Greene JM, Ringwalt CL. Youth and familial substance use's association with suicide attempts among runaway and homeless youth. *Subst Use Misuse* 1996;31:1041-58.

Grunebaum MF, Oquendo MA, Harkavy-Friedman JM, Ellis SP, Li S, Haas GL, Malone KM, Mann JJ. Delusions and suicidality. *Am J Psychiatry* 2001;158:742-7.

Gunnell D, Lopatatzidis A, Dorling D, Wehner H, Southall H, Frankel S. Suicide and unemployment in young people. Analysis of trends in England and Wales, 1921-1995. *Br J Psychiatry* 1999;175:263-70.

Gut-Fayand A, Dervaux A, Oliè JP, Loo H, Poirier MF, Krebs MO. Substance abuse and suicidality in schizophrenia: a common risk factor linked to impulsivity. *Psychiatry Res* 2001;102:65-72.

Hättenschwiler J, Ruesch P, Modestin J. Comparison of four groups of substance-abusing in-patients with different psychiatric comorbidity. *Acta Psychiatr Scand* 2001;104:59-65.

Harkavy-Friedman JM, Nelson EA. Assessment and intervention for the suicidal patient with schizophrenia. *Psychiatr Q* 1997;68:361-75.

Harkavy-Friedman JM, Restifo K, Malaspina D, Kaufmann CA, Amador XF, Yale SA, Gorman JM. Suicidal behavior in schizophrenia: characteristics of individuals who had and had not attempted suicide. *Am J Psychiatry* 1999;156:1276-8.

Harkavy-Friedman JM, Kimhy D, Nelson EA, Venarde DF, Malaspina D, Mann JJ. Suicide attempts in schizophrenia: the role of command auditory hallucinations for suicide. *J Clin Psychiatry* 2003;64:871-4.

Harris EC, Barraclough B. Excess mortality of mental disorder. *Br J Psychiatry* 1998;173:11-53.

Hawton K, Sutton L, Haw C, Sinclair J, Deeks JJ. Schizophrenia and suicide: systematic review of risk factors. *Br J Psychiatry* 2005;187:9-20.

Haywood TW, Kravitz HM, Grossman LS, Cavanaugh JL Jr, Davis JM, Lewis DA. Predicting the "revolving door" phenomenon among patients with schizophrenic, schizoaffective, and affective disorders. *Am J Psychiatry* 1995;152:856-61.

Heru AM, Stuart GL, Rainey S, Eyre J, Recupero PR. Prevalence and severity of intimate partner violence and associations with family functioning and alcohol abuse in psychiatric inpatients with suicidal intent. *J Clin Psychiatry* 2006;67:23-9.

Jarbin H, Von Knorring AL. Suicide and suicide attempts in adolescent-onset psychotic disorders. *Nord J Psychiatry* 2004;58:115-23.

Kamali M, Kelli L, Gervin M, Browne S, Larkin C, O'Callaghan E. The prevalence of comorbid substance misuse and its influence on suicidal ideation among in-patients with schizophrenia. *Acta Psychiatr Scand* 2000;101:452-6.

Kamali M, Kelly L, Gervin M, Browne S, Larkin C, O'Callaghan E. Psychopharmacology: insight and comorbid substance misuse and medication compliance among patients with schizophrenia. *Psychiatr Serv* 2001;52:161-3, 166.

Kampman O, Lehtinen K. Compliance in psychoses. *Acta Psychiatr Scand* 1999;100:167-75.

Kennedy MA, Parhar KK, Samra J, Gorzalka B. Suicide ideation in different generations of immigrants. *Can J Psychiatry* 2005;50:353-6.

Kesselman MS, Solomon J, Beaudett M, Thornton B. Alcoholism and schizophrenia. In: Solomon J (ed.): *Alcoholism and Clinical Psychiatry*. New York, Plenum Press, 1982, pp. 69-80.

Kim CH, Jayathilake K, Meltzer HY. Hopelessness, neurocognitive function, and insight in schizophrenia: relationship to suicidal behavior. *Schizophr Res.* 2003;60:71-80.

Kirkpatrick B, Amador XF, Flaum M, Yale SA, Gorman JM, Carpenter WT Jr, Tohen M, McGlashan T. The deficit syndrome in the DSM-IV Field Trial: I. Alcohol and other drug abuse. *Schizophr Res* 1996;20:69-77.

Kivlahan DR, Heiman JR, Wright RC, Mundt JW, Shupe JA. Treatment cost and rehospitalization rate in schizophrenic outpatients with a history of substance abuse. *Hosp Community Psychiatry* 1991;42:609-14.

Kposowa AJ. Unemployment and suicide: a cohort analysis of social factors predicting suicide in the US National Longitudinal Mortality Study. *Psychol Med* 2001;31:127-38.

Krausz M, Müller-Thomsen T, Haasen C. Suicide among schizophrenic adolescents in the long-term course of illness. *Psychopathology* 1995;28:95–103.

Krausz M, Mass R, Haasen C, Gross J. Psychopathology in patients with schizophrenia and substance abuse. *Psychopathology* 1996;29:95-103.

Kreyenbuhl JA, Kelly DL, Conley RR. Circumstances of suicide among individuals with schizophrenia. *Schizophr Res* 2002;58:253-61.

Kuo CJ, Tsai SY, Lo CH, Wang YP, Chen CC. Risk factors for completed suicide in schizophrenia. *J Clin Psychiatry*. 2005;66:579-85.

Lambert M, Conus P, Lubman DI, Wade D, Yuen H, Moritz S, Naber D, McGorry PD, Schimmelmann BG. The impact of substance use disorders on clinical outcome in 643 patients with first-episode psychosis. *Acta Psychiatr Scand* 2005;112:141-8.

Lammertink M, Löhrer F, Kaiser R, Hambrecht M, Pukrop R. Differences in substance abuse patterns: multiple drug abuse alone versus schizophrenia with multiple drug abuse. *Acta Psychiatr Scand* 2001;104:361-6.

Landmark J, Cernovsky ZZ, Merskey H. Correlates of suicide attempts and ideation in schizophrenia. *Br J Psychiatry* 1987;151:18-20.

Lehman AF, Myers CP, Corty E. Assessment and classification of patients with psychiatric and substance abuse syndromes. *Hosp Community Psychiatry* 1989;40:1019-25.

Lester D. Unemployment and suicide over nine regions in England and Wales. *Percept Mot Skills* 2000;91:782.

Lewis L. Mourning, insight, and reduction of suicide risk in schizophrenia. *Bull Menninger Clin* 2004;68:231-44.

Lindqvist P, Allebeck P. Schizophrenia and assaultive behaviour: the role of alcohol and drug abuse. *Acta Psychiatr Scand* 1990;82:191-5.

Linszen DH, Dingemans PM, Lentor ME. Cannabis abuse and the course of recent-onset schizophrenic disorders. *Arch Gen Psychiatry* 1994;51:273-9.

Loas G, Guilbaud O, Perez-Diaz F, Verrier A, Stephan P, Lang F, Bizouard P, Venisse JL, Corcos M, Flament MF, Jeammet P; Reseau Inserm no. 494013. Dependency and suicidality in addictive disorders. *Psychiatry Res* 2005;137:103-11.

Lorenzen U. Problematik psychiatrischer Patienten mit doppel Diagnose „*Schizophrenie und Suchtmittelmissbrauch*" am Beispiel der Lebenslaufanalyse ehemaliger Bewohnerinnen eines psychiatrischen Übergans Wohnheimes. Hamburg, Diss. Universität, 1990.

Lynskey MT, Glowinski AL, Todorov AA, Bucholz KK, Madden PA, Nelson EC, Statham DJ, Martin NG, Heath AC. Major depressive disorder, suicidal ideation, and suicide attempt in twins discordant for cannabis dependence and early-onset cannabis use. *Arch Gen Psychiatry* 2004;61:1026-32.

Malenfant EC. Suicide in Canada's immigrant population. *Health Rep* 2004;15(2):9-17.

Marcus P, Snyder R. Reduction of comorbid substance abuse with clozapine [letter]. *Am J Psychiatry* 1995;152:959.

Martinez-Arevalo MJ, Calcedo-Ordonez A, Varo-Prieto JR. Cannabis consumption as a prognostic factor in schizophrenia. *Br J Psychiatry* 1994;164:679-81.

Meltzer HY. Suicide in schizophrenia: risk factors and clozapine treatment. *J Clin Psychiatry* 1998;59 [suppl 3]:15-20.

Meltzer HY. Suicidality in schizophrenia: a review of the evidence for risk factors and treatment options. *Curr Psychiatry Rep.* 2002;4:279-83.

Miles H, Johnson S, Amponsah-Afuwape S, Finch E, Leese M, Thornicroft G. Characteristics of subgroups of individuals with psychotic illness and a comorbid substance use disorder. *Psychiatr Serv* 2003;54:554-61.

Miller FT, Tanenbaum JH. Drug abuse in schizophrenia. Hosp Community Psychiatry 1989;40:847-9.

Miller PMcC, Johnstone EC, Lang FH, Thomson LDG. Differences between patients with schizophrenia within and a high security psychiatric hospital. *Acta Psychiatr Scand* 2000;102:12-8.

Modestin J, Dal Pian D, Agarwalla P. Clozapine diminishes suicidal behavior: a retrospective evaluation of clinical records. *J Clin Psychiatry* 2005;66:534-8.

Mortensen PB, Cantor-Graae E, McNeil TF. Increased rates of schizophrenia among immigrants: some methodological concerns raised by Danish findings. *Psychol Med* 1997;27:813-20.

Mueser KT, Yarnold PR, Levinson DF, Singh H, Bellack AS, Kee K, Morrison RL, Yadalam KG. Prevalence of substance abuse in schizophrenia: demographic and clinical correlates. *Schizophr Bull* 1990;16:31-56.

Mueser KT, Bellack AS, Blanchard JJ. Comorbidity of schizophrenia and substance abuse: implication for treatment. *J Consult Clin Psychol* 1992;60:845-56.

Murphy GE, Robins E. Social factors in suicide. *JAMA* 1967;199:303-8.

Murphy GE, Amstrong JW, Herlene SL, Fischer JR, Clendenin WW. Suicide and alcoholism: interpersonal loss confirmed as a predictor. *Arch Gen Psychiatry* 1979;36:65-9.

Olivera AA, Kiefer MW, Manley NK. Tardive dyskinesia in psychiatric patients with substance use disorders. *Am J Drug Alcohol Abuse* 1990;16:57-66.

Osher FC, Drake RE, Teague GB, Hurlbut SC, Beaudett MS, Paskus TS. Correlates of alcohol abuse among rural schizophrenic patients. New Hampshire-Dartmouth *Psychiatric Research Center*, 1991, pp. 30-8.

Owen RR, Fischer EP, Booth BM, Cuffel BJ. Medication noncompliance and substance abuse among patients with schizophrenia. *Psychiatr Serv* 1996;47:853-8.

Pavlović E, Marušić A. Suicide in Croatia and in Croatian immigrant groups in Australia and Slovenia. *Croat Med J* 2001;42:669-72.

Pompili M, Ruberto A, Kotzalidis GD, Girardi P, Tatarelli R. Suicide and awareness of illness in schizophrenia: an overview. *Bull Menninger Clin* 2004;68:297-318.

Potkin SG, Alphs L, Hsu C, Krishnan KR, Anand R, Young FK, Meltzer H, Green A; InterSePT Study Group. Predicting suicidal risk in schizophrenic and schizoaffective patients in a prospective two-year trial. *Biol Psychiatry* 2003;54:444-52.

Preti A, Miotto P. Suicide and unemployment in Italy, 1982-1994. *J Epidemiol Community Health* 1999;53:694-701.

Prigerson HG, Desai RA, Liu-Mares W, Rosenheck RA. Suicidal ideation and suicide attempts in homeless mentally ill persons: age-specific risks of substance abuse. *Soc Psychiatry Psychiatr Epidemiol* 2003;38:213-9.

Pristach CA, Smith CM. Medication compliance and substance abuse among schizophrenic patients. *Hosp Comm Psychiatry* 1990;41:1345-8.

Rasanen P, Tiihonen J, Isohanni M, Rantakallio P, Lehtonen J, Moring J. Schizophrenia, alcohol abuse, and violent behavior: a 26-year follow-up study of an unselected birth cohort. *Schizophr Bull* 1998;24:437-41.

Rich CL, Fowler RC, Fogarty LA, Young D. San Diego suicide study. III. Relationship between diagnosis and stressors. *Arch Gen Psychiatry* 1988a;45:589-92.

Rich CL, Motooka MS, Fowler RC, Young D. Suicide by psychotics. *Biol Psychiatry* 1988b;24:595-601.

Roy A, Mazonson A, Pickar D. Attempted suicide in chronic schizophrenia. Br J Psychiatry 1984;144:303-6.

Safer DJ. Substance abuse by young adult chronic patients. *Hosp Community Psychiatry* 1987;38:511-4.

Satel SL, Seibyl JP, Charney DS. Prolonged cocaine psychosis implies underlying major psychopathology. *J Clin Psychiatry* 1991;52:349-50.

Scheller-Gilkey G, Lewine RR, Caudle J, Brown FW. Schizophrenia, substance use, and brain morphology. *Schizophr Res* 1999;35:113-20.

Schneier FR, Siris SG. A review of psychoactive substance use and abuse in schizophrenia. Patterns of drug choice. *J Nerv Ment Dis* 1987;175:641-52.

Selten JP, Cantor-Graae E, Slaets J, Kahn RS. Odegaard's selection hypothesis revisited: schizophrenia in Surinamese immigrants to The Netherlands. *Am J Psychiatry* 2002;159:669-71.

Serper MR, Alpert M, Richardson NA, Dickson S, Allen MH, Werner A. Clinical effects of recent cocaine use on patients with acute schizophrenia. *Am J Psychiatry* 1995;152:1464-9.

Sevy S, Robinson DG, Holloway S, Alvir JM, Woerner MG, Bilder R, Goldman R, Lieberman J, Kane J. Correlates of substance misuse in patients with first-episode schizophrenia and schizoaffective disorder. *Acta Psychiatr Scand* 2001;104:367-74.

Shafii M, Carrigan S, Whittinghill JR, Derrick A. Psychological autopsy of completed suicide in children and adolescents. *Am J Psychiatry* 1985;142:1061-4.

Sibthorpe B, Drinkwater J, Gardner K, Bammer G. Drug use, binge drinking and attempted suicide among homeless and potentially homeless youth. *Aust N Z J Psychiatry* 1995;29:248-56.

Silver H, Abboud E. Drug abuse in schizophrenia: comparison of patients who began drug abuse before their first admission with those who began abusing drugs after their first admission. *Schizophr Res* 1994;13:57-63.

Siris SG. Pharmacological treatment of substance-abusing schizophrenic patients. *Schizophr Bull* 1990;16:111-22.

Siris SG, Mason SE, Shuwall MA. Histories of substance abuse, panic and suicidal ideation in schizophrenic patients with histories of post-psychotic depressions. *Prog Neuropsychopharmacol Biol Psychiatry* 1993;17:609-17.

Smith CM, Barzman D, Pristach CA. Effect of patient and family insight on compliance of schizophrenic patients. *J Clin Pharmacol* 1997;37:147-54.

Smith J, Hucker S. Schizophrenia and substance abuse. *Acta Psychiatr Scand* 1994;165:13-21.

Soyka M. Substance abuse, psychiatric disorders and violent and disturbed behaviour. *Br J Psychiatry* 2000;176;345-50.

Soyka M, Albus M, Kathmann N, Finelli A, Hofstetter S, Holzbach R, Immler B, Sand P. Prevalence of alcohol and drug abuse in schizophrenic inpatients. *Eur Arch Psychiatry Clin Neurosci* 1993;242:362-72.

Soyka M, Albus M, Immler B, Kathmann N, Hippius H. Psychopathology in dual diagnosis and non-addicted schizophrenics–are there differences? *Eur Arch Psychiatry Clin Neurosci* 2001;251:232-8.

Stack S, Haas A. The effect of unemployment duration on national suicide rates: a time series analysis, 1948-1982. *Sociol Focus* 1984;17:17-29.

Steinert T, Wiebe C, Gebhardt RP. Aggressive behavior against self and others among first-admission patients with schizophrenia. *Psychiatr Serv* 1999;50:85-90.

Suominen K, Isometsä E, Haukka J, Lonnqvist J. Substance use and male gender as risk factors for deaths and suicide–a 5-year follow-up study after deliberate self-harm. *Soc Psychiatry Psychiatr Epidemiol* 2004;39:720-4.

Suppapitiporn S, Thavichachart N, Suppapitiporn S. Social support in depressed patients who attempted suicide. *J Med Assoc Thai* 2004;87 (Suppl 2):S266-71.

Susser E, Struening EL, Conover S. Psychiatric problems in homeless men. Lifetime psychosis, substance use, and current distress in new arrivals at New York City shelters. *Arch Gen Psychiatry* 1989;46:845-50.

Swofford CD, Kasckow JW, Scheller-Gilkey G, Inderbitzin LB. Substance use: a powerful predictor of relapse in schizophrenia. *Schizophr Res* 1996;20:145-151.

Swofford CD, Scheller-Gilkey G, Miller AH, Woolwine B, Mance R. Double jeopardy: schizophrenia and substance use. *Am J Drug Alcohol Abuse* 2000;26:343-53.

Tandon R. Suicidal behavior in schizophrenia. *Expert Rev Neurother.* 2005;5:95-9.

Test MA, Wallisch LS, Allness DJ, Ripp K. Substance use in young adults with schizophrenic disorders. *Schizophr Bull* 1989;15:465-76.

Turecki G. Dissecting the suicide phenotype: the role of impulsive-aggressive behaviours. *J Psychiatry Neurosci* 2005;30:398-408.

Verdoux H, Liraud F, Gonzales B, Assens F, Abalan F, van Os J. Suicidality and substance misuse in first-admitted subjects with psychotic disorder. *Acta Psychiatr Scand* 1999;100:389-95.

Warman DM, Forman EM, Henriques GR, Brown GK, Beck AT. Suicidality and psychosis: beyond depression and hopelessness. *Suicide Life Threat Behav* 2004;34:77-86.

Wilcox HC, Conner KR, Caine ED. Association of alcohol and drug use disorders and completed suicide: an empirical review of cohort studies. *Drug Alcohol Depend* 2004;76(Suppl. 1):S11-9.

Yamasaki A, Sakai R, Shirakawa T. Low income, unemployment, and suicide mortality rates for middle-age persons in Japan. *Psychol Rep* 2005;96:337-48.

Yen CF, Yeh ML, Chen CS, Chung HH. Predictive value of insight for suicide, violence, hospitalization, and social adjustment for outpatients with schizophrenia: a prospective study. *Compr Psychiatry* 2002;43:443-7.

Yesavage JA, Zarcone V. History of drug abuse and dangerous behavior in inpatient schizophrenics. *J Clin Psychiatry* 1983;41:259-61.

Zolkowska K, Cantor-Graae E, McNeil TF. Increased rates of psychosis among immigrants to Sweden: is migration a risk factor for psychosis? *Psychol Med* 2001;31:669-78.

Zvolensky MJ, Bernstein A, Sachs-Ericsson N, Schmidt NB, Smith JD, Bonn-Miller MO. Lifetime associations between cannabis, use, abuse, and dependence and panic attacks in a representative sample. *J Psychiatr Res*. 2005; doi:10.1016/j.psychires.2005.09.005.

INDEX

B

C

H

I

J

K

L

M

Q

R

S

T